W9-BVC-926

Women Warriors

Women Warriors
A History

by
David E. Jones

BRASSEY'S
Washington • London

Library of Congress Cataloging-in-Publication Data

Jones, David E., 1942–
    Women warriors : a history / David E. Jones.
       p.   cm.
    Includes bibliographical references and index.
    ISBN 1-57488-106-X
    1. Women and the military—History.   I. Title.
    U21.75.J66   1997
    355'.0082—dc20   96-35003
                                                                  CIP

First Edition

10 9 8 7 6 5 4 3 2 1
Printed in the United States of America

Contents

Illustrations

Preface

Two experiences, one academic and one personal, brought me to the study of the female martial heritage. For the past several years, while pursuing research on warrior elites and their role in the rise of states, I occasionally encountered references to women sword fighters, archers, and cavalry officers. The first, as I recall, was the account of the death of Cyrus the Great of Persia and the destruction of his vast army by a tribe of Asian steppe horsemen commanded by their queen, Tomyris. Days later, when researching Celtic military customs in ancient Britain, I read of the two major martial arts schools of the time, both run by women warriors.

It occurred to me, as I thought of Queen Tomyris and the Celtic women martial arts masters—and adding Joan of Arc, Molly Pitcher, and the Amazons from my own meager store of knowledge on the subject—that most of the cultures I have investigated in my twenty-five years as a cultural anthropologist boast tales of women war goddesses, heroes, and myth figures. But, like most of my colleagues, I either dismissed these faint references or channeled them into some psychoanalytic/symbolic/Jungian "sense." They were projections; they were archetypes. They were symbols of social/sexual conflict. A true product of my cultural conditioning, I never considered that the women warrior goddesses and Amazons might have been reflections of something quite real.

I was also motivated to engage in the study of the women warriors by my experiences as an instructor of a Japanese martial art. Year after year, I observed in my classes women who seemed in some mysterious way to have been robbed of their natural right to a sense of bodily dignity and strength. Whereas males could relate to my martial demonstrations, gradually assuming the correct posture and understanding force and "command presence," the women often seemed to move through a maze of conflicting factors that the men did not face to achieve the fighting technique I was teaching. In some way, they had to "become male" to perform the technique. I often sensed a female student's body communicating loudly, "Not me," as she executed a fighting maneuver. I wondered about that barrier and how the women in the class could execute the techniques of hand-to-hand combat as women, as themselves, not as women acting like men.

As a fighting arts instructor,* I was drawn to address and remedy this "structural weakness," which was neither a universal female condition nor a lack of physical strength. Some people with a slight build are stronger than larger people. I have taught women who have a very powerful sense of their psychophysical selves, but they are the exception. In the same vein, some males do not have this sense of martial self, but considerably more males than females, in my martial arts teaching experience, possess this "command presence" of mind and body or can be taught to access it.

I concluded that one of the reasons for these variations, perhaps THE reason, relates to male conditioning for generations to their warrior heritage. To think warrior in the Western tradition is to think male. For example, *Webster's New Collegiate Dictionary* defines *warrior* as "a **man** [author's emphasis] engaged or experienced in warfare," and *army* as "a large, organized body of **men** [author's emphasis] armed and trained for war." When I asked speakers of various Western languages for a term in their language for women warriors, few could precisely translate the phrase before considering for a time or consulting a relative or colleague.

The ideals of a culture, a people's deepest sense of what is right and true, are expressed in traditional verbal formulae (morals, proverbs, myths, etc.). Embedded in a society's institutions, they are represented by historical heroes revered by the culture. Historical reality renders the hero model compelling, obviously more so than a fictional hero.

Little boys are told, when in need of some inner bolstering, to "act like a soldier," or they are praised by being compared to soldiers. If the culture had a stronger image to offer male children during such experiences, it would. To similarly praise or motivate girls would be considered by most as inappropriate and even possibly confusing to a young girl's still-forming sense of female. Males, therefore, have the warrior built in to strengthen them, while females have been misled into believing that the warrior's power historically and biologically belongs only to men.

As a martial arts teacher, I can elicit a male student's martial response by connecting his self-image to that of a warrior. In aikido, the Japanese martial art I teach, the samurai provides the warrior image for this psychophysical modeling. The student can internalize this male historical reference, identify with it, and use it to enhance his endurance, courage, fortitude, dignity, sensitivity, and strength, not only in the *dojo* (practice

---

*The author holds a fourth-degree black belt in Ueshiba Ryu Aikido; a second-degree black belt in Shorinji-Ryu Karatedo; and first-degree black-belt ranks in Shinto Muso Ryu Jyodo (staff fighting) and Kyudo (traditional archery), both earned in Japan.

place of Japanese martial arts) but also, and most importantly, in everyday life. But how many examples of real, historically verified women warriors can be elicited as models for young women?

The strength of women, we are assured, is of a different kind: it is the ability to bear up under childbirth; it is nurturant depth; it is simple endurance of hardship. These qualities are admirable, no doubt, but the story of women's strength must not end there.

To be denied the warrior legacy undermines the grandeur of virtue. Gentleness is a virtue to the degree that it comes from strength; otherwise, the act may simply be a reflection of timidity. This is true of all virtue. Because virtue is not labeled male- or female-only, its validity lies in direct relationship to the strength of the individual who displays it. To be robbed of any element that comprises the strength of mind, body, and spirit cripples the engines of personal freedom, and anyone or anything that attacks one's freedom obviously becomes one's adversary.

Women might consider adding to the complex strands woven into the making of the self, the historically based model of the warriors that constitutes their history. Particularly in today's dangerous environment, women should employ every power source available, not only the political, legal, and economic spheres, but also the rights and responsibilities for the enduring warrior foundations of modern civilization. Women, as well as men, hold a military history and a chivalrous tradition. Women, as well as men, own the images of Galahad, Charlemagne, Robin Hood, Arthur the Lionhearted, El Cid, and Sir Lancelot. As you will read in *Women Warriors*, Countess Jane of Montfort, Ma Ying Taphan of Siam, the Visigoth Queen Brunehaut, the Rani of Jhansi, and Queen Bat Zabbai of Syria equal them in every way.

For women to deny their martial tradition results in the loss of a power that males freely employ—the certainty based on historical record that males are by nature warriors, commanders, protectors of the weak, and fighters for justice. Men can call up great reserves of strength by tapping their male martial legacy by calling on this truth; their nature as men, as warriors, entitles them to do so. Women who do not understand that they have equal claim on this warrior tradition might doubt their place in the subtle and not so subtle power grid of the modern state society, a substructure explicitly and implicitly based on ancient warrior codes and the assumption that these are innately the prerogative of men.

Consider the implications in our cultural tradition of viewing the warrior as an exclusive male role: women are disconnected from the foundation of state citzenship and become merely a part of the male warriors' charge. When females are not seen as warriors, their aspirations—the warrior prerogatives of power, choice, and control—become suspect as unnatural or unwomanlike. Indeed, women who exemplify the warrior are often viewed as sexually suspect or neurotic.

In all the state-level societies I have studied, the codes of the male military elites have formed the basis of modern etiquette, gentlemanly behavior, and diplomacy. *Chivalry* references the ideal behavior patterns of European knights, and the modern Japanese still view the samurai as models of male behavior. Without these rules, this substructure of agreement, the superstructure of the state could not stand. Warrior codes flowered early in the formation of states, and the historical records reveal active women warriors not only reflecting male martial codes but also forming them.

In modern states, women are barred from the game at its most basic level. They are often believed to have no biological connection and therefore no deep understanding of the warrior tradition, the baseline of the rules played by state leaders. Men and women will never reach a common consciousness of their equality as humans until both accept that women have a claim on the title "Warrior." Modern women leaders of states are relatively rare and therefore insufficient to alter the public assumption that politicomilitary leadership is not normal for women.

Women who violate the role assigned to them by warriors, to be owned and protected, are usually perceived as sexually unconventional. A man acting in a similar fashion would be regarded as a rogue perhaps, or even an outlaw, but his sexual identity would not be called into question because of the deep-seated notion that males are warriors by nature and females are not. But history denies this conclusion, no matter how compatible it may be to modern Western ideas about the innate natures of males and females. Some women will no doubt be repulsed by a treatise that exposes members of their sex engaged in carnage and bloodshed, and I certainly do not present this material as encouragement for women to enter combat. No sane person would wish involvement in war on anyone—male or female.

I approach the study of war and warriors as a philosopher of alchemy, the ancient wellspring of modern chemistry, which sought to extract gold from lead. As much metaphor as science, the physical desire of the alchemist reflected a human desire to believe that there is good in bad, there is gold in lead, there is always hope. The base metal for us becomes "war," and the gold, those human traits, pounded to purity in the fire of warfare, which all civilizations come to venerate—courage, honor, steadfastness, justice, toughness, loyalty, and, strange as it may seem, love. The warrior plays a featured part in all state origin myths and national sagas.

Because the number of warriors, both male and female, throughout history can never be counted, the degree of military activity by women cannot be known, although most observers, myself included, would agree that many more men than women have died in warfare, and generally more civilians die in warfare than the soldiers who fight the wars. The issue is one of degrees. Modern state society, operating on its largely male warrior foundations, tends to greatly diminish historical awareness of women warriors. Hence, Joan of Arc is typically the only woman warrior from western Europe most can name, although in fact, as the following materials will corroborate, many "Joans" rode through European history.

The primal power of the warrior ideal is fueled by tradition and myth. History, as you will read, demonstrates that the warrior's mantle is a woman's birthright as surely as it is a man's and that the hand that rocks the cradle can also wield the sword.

A major difficulty in research that spans the globe and all of recorded (or archaeologically revealed) history is that the sources testifying to worldwide phenomena are expressed in many different cultural and historical styles, ones that Western scholars might perhaps interpret as myth, national saga or legend, or self-serving accounts of ancient nobility. Of course, the Western notion of linear and referenced history stands as merely one cultural expression of history. The Chinese often wrote history as a summation of a dynastic period, with emphasis on the behavior of earlier rulers that would benefit the moral instruction of rulers of a later period. Nonlinear languages such as that of the Trobriand islanders of Melanesia prohibited the development of a linear history in the Western sense. But does this mean that they lack history or have no way of storing information learned from past events?

In my research for *Women Warriors*, I have sought references that purport to be historical as opposed to mythological texts. Sometimes the differences are barely discernible, and, of course, for those and other errors I must accept responsibility. I include at the same level of reliability such texts as the war chronicles of Japan, the *Primary Chronicles* of Russia, the accounts of the ancient Greek travelers Herodotus and Strabo, and the descriptions of the Roman historian Tacitus, along with the accounts of modern-day historians, ethnologists, and archaeologists. The majority of cases cited in *Women Warriors* are, in fact, derived from sources considered legitimate by modern Western historians.

I have confidence in this method for the pattern of evidence it reveals. All accounts, whether derived from a Greek traveler in India two thousand years ago or a twentieth-century anthropologist working in Africa among the Dahomey or a World War II military historian, paint the same picture of the woman warrior. From the beginning women shared the qualitative experience of the warrior; everything men have ever done in warfare, women have also done, and, in many instances, they have done it better.

The literature on the subject of martial women has a long history. Boccaccio's *Concerning Famous Women* and Christine De Pisan's *The Book of the City of Women* reach back half a millennium; before that, ancient chroniclers such as Tacitus, Strabo, Herodotus, Diodorus, and Saxo Grammaticus had much to say on the female martial traditions of their times. Works like Sarah Hale's *Woman's Record* (1855), Elizabeth Starling's *Noble Deeds of Women* (1857), Francis Gribble's *Women in War* (1917), Magnus Hirschfeld's *The Sexual History of the World War* (1934), and, in more recent times, Mary Beard's *Women as Force in History* (1967), Kathryn Taylor's *Generations of Denial* (1971), Jessica Salmonson's *The Encyclopedia of Amazons* (1991), John Laffin's *Women in Battle* (1967), and Rosalind Miles's *The Women's History of the World* (1988) include some of the major entry-level resources for an appreciation of female martial history worldwide.

In some cases, certain writers are key resources for various specific cultural and historical periods. Antonia Fraser's *The Weaker Vessel* (1984) and *The Warrior Queens* (1987) and Robert Scott Fittis's *Heroines of Scotland* (1889) are necessary reads for an understanding of the female martial tradition in the British Isles. Arlene Bergman's *Women of Viet Nam* (1974), Joseph and Frances Gies's *Women in the Middle Ages* (1978), Elizabeth Stone's *Women and the Cuban Revolution* (1981), Shirlene Soto's *The Mexican Woman: A Study of Her Participation in the Revolution, 1910–1940* (1979), Linda Grant DePauw's *Seafaring Women* (1982), and David Mitchell's *Monstrous Regiment* (1965) are a few key examples of specialized sources.

Given the number of works on the subject of martial women, the reader might ask, Why is yet another such treatise, *Women Warriors*, advisable? My answers to that question spring from my training as a cultural anthropologist. As a scientist, I wished to compile a record of real cases, as opposed to literary or mythological examples of women warriors. I am presenting in *Women Warriors* the most up-to-date, inclusive, and complete account of the female martial heritage in a pan-historical and global perspective. By surveying the available literature in history and adding the ethnographic findings of anthropology to the general discussion, I have sought to demonstrate the ancient and continuing place of the woman warrior in world culture. By including recent cases from United States military involvement in Desert Storm, Panama, Libya, and Grenada as well as acknowledgment of women in modern wars for independence in Africa, Southeast Asia, and the World Wars, I have endeavored to show the female martial heritage not as a curiosity of antiquity but as a living reality because of its intrinsic presence in world history and the human condition. *Women Warriors* is, therefore, the most comprehensive, detailed, and current account of the female martial heritage available.

*   *   *

Women Warriors was a labor of love, and, fittingly, my wife, Jane Morris Jones, provided the support, editorial expertise, and encouragement without which I would have never finished and perhaps never begun to research female martial history. Many others provided invaluable aid as readers and critics of early drafts of the manuscript and as expert commentators on various cultural/historical sequences covered in the research.

I would like to thank Dr. Sheila Baksi, Dr. Robert Bledsoe, Dr. Ida Cook, Dr. Michael Davis, Dr. David Fabianic, Dr. Linda Glennon, Sheila Graves, Joanne Harrison, Nancy Hirst, Dr. Joyce Lillie, Dr. John Lynxwiler, Claudia Mackey, Tim and Patrice Ryan, Dr. Kathryn Seidel, Tracy St. Benoit, Dr. Allyn Stearman, Daniel Vaccaro Sensei, Dr. Wayne Van Horne, and Dr. Ronald Wallace for their support and assistance. My gratitude also extends to editors Don McKeon and Kathleen Graham at Brassey's, Inc. for their skill, patience, and wise counsel, and to Brassey's president, Dr. Frank Margiotta, for his faith and encouragement.

Women Warriors

The legendary Amazons and women warrior goddesses, often dismissed as myth, have been reflections of something quite real. Anthropological evidence has shown they likely did exist and lived in Northern Europe. Moreover, history shows the female warrior in a variety of functions across the globe.

From Women: A Pictorial Archive from Nineteenth Century Sources

CHAPTER 1

Sugar and Spice and Everything Nice?

In the summer of 1677, coastal settlements in New England were harassed by a confederacy of Indian tribes led by the war chief of the Sokokis to capture boats for a marine assault on Boston. By midsummer he had taken twenty vessels, most of them manned by crews from Marblehead, Massachusetts; the crewmen were either murdered or taken hostage.

On July 15, 1677, a ketch sailed into Marblehead carrying two Indians en route to Boston to be tried for piracy and murder. When the news spread, a crowd intent on revenge gathered at the dock demanding the immediate execution of the prisoners. The constable refused to release the Indians, announcing that they would answer to the proper authorities in Boston. Robert Roules, one of the crewmen of the ketch, later described in a sworn deposition what happened next.

> Being on shore, the whole town flocked around them, beginning at first to insult them, and soon after, the women surrounded them, drove us by force from them, (we escaping at no little peril), and laid violent hands upon the captives, some stoning us in the meantime, because we would protect them, others seizing them by the hair, got full possession of them, nor was there any way left by which we could rescue them. Then with stones, billets of wood, and what else they might, they made an end of these Indians. We were kept at a distance that we could not see them until they were dead, and then we found them with their heads off and gone, and their flesh . . . pulled from their bones.[1]

Mr. Roules commented in his deposition, wisely it appears after noting what the Marblehead women were capable of, ". . . for my life I could not tell who these women were, or the names of any of them."[2]

3

One seventeenth-century New England sister of Marblehead, the subject of the first memorial statue honoring an American woman, is known. Hannah Duston, her teenage son, and a nurse were captured by marauding Indians after an attack that left her husband and eleven of her twelve children dead. Several nights later, on River Islet near Boscawen, New Hampshire, Hannah escaped and led her small party against their captors, killing the two men, their wives, and six children. Then she scalped them.

One does not have to pursue esoteric historical research to discover that women, in groups and alone, are capable of horrendous violence, of acting out the antipodes of "everything nice"; a look at a police blotter will tell the same story. According to the "Uniform Crime Reports for 1992" (Department of Justice, Federal Bureau of Investigation), 1,899 women were arrested for murder, 420 for rape, 13,082 for robbery, and 64,539 for aggravated assault—the "violent crimes" category in police parlance. In 1992, women accounted for 12.5 percent of all arrests for violent crimes.

But what of the role of women in the most complex and deadly act of violence thus far evolved by humans—warfare? Can women act effectively as shock troops and battlefield commanders? Can women fulfill the ancient function of the warrior?

The language of martial activities is notoriously vague, analogous perhaps at the linguistic level with the "fog of war," a condition clearly understood by the participants in warfare. It also may be that the lack of specificity in the language of warfare is deliberate, permitting the political entities that engage in this type of behavior room to maneuver on the diplomatic fronts that often precede warfare.

Words such as *soldier, martial, war, warrior, army*, and *military* are obscure and circular; each depends on the other for delineation. *Webster's Ninth New Collegiate Dictionary* offers the primary definition of *warrior* as "a man engaged or experienced in warfare," and *warfare* as "military operations between enemies." *Military* is defined as "of, or relating to soldiers, arms, or war." *Soldier* is rendered "one engaged in military service . . . a skilled warrior; a militant leader, follower, or worker." *Martial* is defined as "of, relating to, or suited for war or a warrior," and *army* is "a large, organized body of men armed and trained for war." A sifting of these related terms derives a definition of *warrior* in its most inclusive sense as anyone who engages in organized armed conflict. The "engages in" phrasing allows for a broad range of activities to be logically included in the warrior category. According to Webster, the word *engage* suggests involvement with or commitment toward some objective, as well as, significantly, "a hostile encounter between military forces." Therefore, warrior behavior includes all those behaviors that support or augment an organized armed conflict—commanders in chief or the commander of commanders, shock troops, demolitions specialists, fighter pilots, military assassins, spies, etc. To enlarge the context of the specific definition somewhat, I include in the following accounts various martial behaviors of women such as dueling, in that these quasi-military behaviors demonstrate the use of weaponry and combat. To reveal women as leaders of men, I also present accounts of female ship captains. Further, these female duelists and ship captains often became legitimate war leaders when they applied their solo skills to an organized armed conflict.

*   *   *

Because scientists often look to the behavior of the chimpanzee, the animal most like modern humans, for insights into the origins of human behavior, a window into the primal roots of this subject might be revealed in a famous experiment in central Africa on chimpanzee behavior engineered by the zoologist Dr. Adriaan Kortlandt of Amsterdam.

On August 3, 1965, Kortlandt and his colleagues staged a leopard attack on a band of chimpanzees. A stuffed leopard crouching in an attack posture, complete with a chimpanzee doll between its paws and a twitching tail made possible by a windshield wiper motor, was hidden in a blind next to an often used chimpanzee trail. A wire snaked from the wheeled cart upon which the leopard was mounted to a hidden platform forty feet up in a tree, where Kortlandt and his cameraman waited.

When a band of chimps approached the site, Kortlandt triggered the attack. The chimpanzees frantically climbed nearby trees and, safely in the branches, hooted at the leopard at top volume. Some of the more adventuresome chimps descended to the ground, gesturing to the young to stay back. Vitus Droscher, author of *The Friendly Beast*, noted that ". . . they made precisely the same sort of hand signals that men would use in similar circumstances."[3]

Several of the chimps picked up three- to four-foot branches, reared up on their hind legs, and one by one attacked the leopard while waving the clubs threateningly, barking, and screaming. Others ran at the leopard and hurled their clubs from a distance. Several threw fruit and dirt clods, and others pounded on tree trunks and hooted shrilly. A few tore saplings out of the ground and wielded them like whips against the leopard. Significantly, this ferocious chimpanzee band was composed almost entirely of females, implying that weapon-using, aggressive, martial behavior is obviously part of the repertoire of the female chimpanzee and presumably also of the human female.

On the other hand, recent congressional testimony from retired Marine Corps Commandant General Robert H. Barrow revealed a very different perspective.

> Exposure to danger is not combat. Being shot at, even being killed, is not combat. Combat is finding . . . closing with . . . and killing or capturing the enemy. It's killing. And it's done in an environment that is often as difficult as you can possibly imagine. Extremes of climate. Brutality. Death. Dying. It's . . . uncivilized! And women can't do it! Nor should they even be thought of as doing it. The requirements for strength and endurance render them unable to do it. And I may be old-fashioned, but I think the very nature of women disqualifies them from doing it. Women give life. Sustain life. Nurture life. They don't take it.[4]

The ancient Greeks, one of the major wellsprings of Western civilization, firmly believed in the effectiveness of women warriors. When Herodotus, the renowned ancient Greek historian, began one of his travel accounts with a casual reference to war between the Greeks and the Amazons, he could assume that his audience would accept the reality of the allusion, only wondering perhaps to which of the many such wars he might be referring. Herodotus, his fellow scholars, and the Greek population were quite sure of the existence of a society of women warriors pressing on their northern borders, women who fought both from horseback and on foot—the double-headed battle-ax their signature weapon.

Amazons were described as wearing long trousers, midthigh-length coats, leather boots, and Phrygian hats, the outfit still worn by nomadic pastoral groups in the area. They sometimes carried a small crescent shield, a light battle-ax, and a short sword. The bow was included in their arsenal, as was the war spear, which they adopted after observing the Greeks fight with it.

The Amazons reputedly possessed a society in which a young girl's right breast was removed to facilitate strength on the right side of the body and more efficiency in drawing a bow. It was said that they mated randomly and reared only the healthy female children. Boys were crippled to use as slaves or killed at birth. Supposedly they fought battles with magical beasts and scattered gold and silver sands from the hooves of their horses as they galloped to war against the Greek demigods Heracles and Theseus.

The idea that the classical Amazons removed their right breasts to facilitate their warrior roles—the drawing of the bow, for example—leads many to dismiss the whole issue as myth. No proof exists that any group performed such an operation, but the anthropological record is so replete with societies that have altered the human body to adhere to culturally defined ideas that to dismiss the Amazons on these grounds is not advisable. The Chinese bound the feet of women and crippled thousands in so doing in the name of beauty. From American Indian history, examples abound of cranial deformation techniques to lengthen the head or flatten the forehead or back of the head. Into the 1960s in New Guinea, the Dugum Dani removed the finger joints of young girls as part of funeral rituals. Sexual operations such as clitorectomy, circumcision, subincision, and techniques in which small objects are inserted into the skin of the penis are widely recorded. Some peoples distend the lips to the size of saucers by systematically inserting lip plugs and elongate the neck by adding copper coils over time. Most societies pierce ears, and many sharpen teeth, blacken teeth, or remove certain teeth to be in tune with their culture's norms of beauty. Modern Western society has surpassed them all with plastic surgery and cosmetic orthodontia. Surgically altering breasts, eyes, noses, buttocks, hips, joints, lips, and even skin color is routine today. The putative breast removal of the Amazons seems tame in comparison.

Plutarch, referring to a lost earlier text, described the Amazon hordes streaming out of their homeland on the Bosphorus and pillaging across Thrace as they moved on Greece. In their gleaming armor, mounted on sleek war horses and led by women chieftains, they descended on Athens in the fifth century B.C.

After an arduous siege, the Amazons were rebuffed, according to the ancient histories, and returned to their own country. However, the memory of that event proved so powerful that fourteen hundred years later a second-century Greek named Pausanius compiled a tour guide of Athens for his friends in which he indicated the sites of Amazonian graves lining the road from Athens to Piraeus.

Helen Diner, in *Mothers and Amazons: The First Feminine History of Culture*, affirmed, concerning the Amazons, "The entire Ionian tradition refers to them as the founders of cities and sanctuaries."[5] She listed Smyrna, Sinope, Cyme, Gryne, Pitania, Magnesia, Clete, Mytilene, and Amastris as cities making that claim.

Kleinbaum, however, does not agree. The first sentence of *The War against the Amazons* reads, "The Amazon is a dream that men created, an image of a superlative female that men constructed to flatter themselves."[6] Writers like Kleinbaum view the stories of the Amazons as convenient mythic devices to delineate the roles of women in Athenian society. The Amazonian image, according to such theories, represents for the Athenians the opposite of all that is good and right in women—at least from the point of view of Greek men. Good Athenian women married, bore their husband's children, and lived safely and demurely within the ordered world of the patriarchal community, a model of "normalcy" the Greeks passed to the Romans who, in turn, impressed it into the lifeways of the tribes of Europe.

The Amazons, on the other hand, were denizens of the fringes of the known world. Wild women. They did not marry. They often used men and then killed them. They wore male clothing, defied male attempts to control them, and lived under the rules of a matriarchy. They were, in short, the worst nightmare of the Athenian male.

Herodotus referred to a tribe called the Sarmatians who lived north of the Greeks and west of the Amazons and who the Greeks thought resulted from a union between Amazons and Scythians. That theory explained the customs of Sauromation women: riding with the men in hunting and warfare, wearing the same type of clothing as males, and ritually killing an enemy warrior as a precondition to marriageable status.

Recent burial finds in the Don River area, identified as Sarmatian by Russian archaeologists, offer a striking affirmation of the accounts of Herodotus. Twenty percent of the female Sauromation burials dating to the sixth and fifth centuries B.C., the time when the Amazons were said to have attacked Athens, feature armor and weapons, "grave goods" universally associated with the burial of warriors.[7]

So, what are we to make of the ancient women warriors of the North who fascinated and terrorized the Greeks in ancient times? Were they fantasy? Fact? The result of cultural misunderstandings? Or, as Kleinbaum suggests, "a kind of alphabet soup summation of centuries of Greek historical experience"?[8]

The classical Amazons of the Greek reports are lost to us beneath layers of time and the fog of endless and ofttimes hysterical debates by a wide range of advocates and debunkers. Feminist historians vie with classical archaeologists who pit their sherds and bones against the mythologists and linguists and art historians. Still, the image continues to intrigue. Did women warriors ever exist? Were there ever women wielders of military weapons, leaders of armies, planners of strategy, directors of generals, commanders in chief, military empire builders? Have they existed in historical times? Do they exist now? Do women have a martial heritage?

This book approaches the subject of female martial history from a cultural and historical perspective. Each geocultural area is observed from the beginning of recorded time to the present era to suggest the density of women warriors in space and time and to reveal recurring patterns that transcend cultural and historical boundaries. Without the context of cultural history, a specific episode of female valor in battle could seem like a strange and isolated incident, as in the case of Joan of Arc. With the organization of the historical cases structured in terms of cultural areas and historical sequence, the seemingly isolated incident is seen as part of an ancient global pattern.

The accounts will be allowed to stand on their own as cases collected and organized to reveal a particular truth of female historical experience and as tales of warriors, derring-do, and battles won and lost.

Queen Bat Zabbai of Palmyra (modern Syria) rode through the deserts with the nomads, wore armor, and hunted with zeal. She also conquered Egypt and extended her domain from the Mediterranean to India—for a time making her the de facto ruler of the eastern part of the Roman Empire. After the Romans defeated her, they brought Septima Zenobia, as Bat Zabbai was known to them, to Rome, where she became a leader of the cultural elite.

From the Lives of Illustrious Women of All Ages

CHAPTER 2

Arabia: Land of the Battle Queens

From ancient times, the austere vastness of the Arabian peninsula has been home to the *Badawi-yin*, "dwellers in the desert." Called bedouin in the West, these nomadic Arabs, goat and camel herders, wander the Empty Quarter and the eastern Sahara. On the backs of the one-humped camels domesticated by their ancestors almost four thousand years ago, they carry their "houses of hair" (tents), families, and belongings on traditionally prescribed routes of migration from oasis to oasis in an ancient and endless cycle.

The northern Arabs speak the Arabic of the Koran. The southerners, situated mainly around port cities and coastal towns in Africa, speak a more ancient Semitic tongue closely related to the contemporary languages of Ethiopia. The southerners pride themselves on the priority of their strides toward civilization vis-à-vis the northern Arabs.

The trade routes that tracked from the southern ports of Arabia through the peninsula to the coast of the Mediterranean were some of the richest of the ancient world. Meandering north on plodding camel caravans, traders brought myrrh and frankincense, aromatics much in demand in the religious rituals of the high civilizations that edged the Mediterranean; gold and ivory from Africa; and trade goods of all kinds from Siam, India, and China.

For centuries the tribes of southern Arabia controlled this immense wealth by functioning as caravanners, camel salesmen, guides, armed guards, sellers of protection, businessmen, and traders. Their wealth and power opened doors to the courts of Persia and Constantinople.

Between 750 and 115 B.C., Saba in southeast Arabia, one of the homes of the famous Queen of Sheba, developed its lush cities and opulent court life. By the first century A.D., Petra, the kingdom of the Nabataeans and a large bedouin confederacy, controlled desert trade and had extended its influence from Akaba in the south to Damascus in the north.

Not to be outdone by their rich relatives to the south, the northern Arabs, under the banner of Islam, strode onto the stage of history in the early seventh century A.D. and quickly spread across North Africa to Spain and east to Iran, India, and Southeast Asia. At their peak, the Arab Muslims managed an empire larger than that ever achieved by Rome.

Two related themes interweave the complex tapestry of Arabian history—warfare and the associated "cult of the battle queen." The maintenance of trade safety along caravan routes, port and market security, and protection of essential camel herds against the ubiquitous raiders necessitated military control.

Raiding and fighting were considered a bedouin man's prime occupation, favored sport, most lucrative business, and unabashed passion. From the beginning, the camel held the key to wealth and usually became the raiding target of a competitor neighbor. It produced milk and meat, which, along with dates and flour, composed the staple foods of the desert nomads; its hide provided the material of tents; it furnished the means to move freely over the desert; it supplied the vehicle of desert warfare par excellence; and it proved a man's status and power. The great Arab armies that swarmed over the ancient world through the centuries were essentially camel-mounted bedouin desert tribesmen.

Arabian women in pre-Islamic times often possessed considerable power. As was noted, the aforementioned city of Sheba in southern Arabia had been ruled by a famous queen. In addition, the presence of women in martial encounters was not uncommon. The British soldier of fortune Sir Richard Francis Burton, traveling in southern Arabia in the nineteenth century, noted that among the Homerite tribes customary law stated that wives should avenge in battle the deaths of their husbands and mothers their sons. In particular, he singled out the Sulliote women who "rivaled the men in defending their homes against Osmanli invaders."[1]

The emotional center of traditional Arab tribal warfare, the cult of the battle queen, derived from the earliest roots of Arabic culture, evolved through time, and still exists in the twentieth century. It expressed in myth, ritual, song, and action the bedouin concept of the sacred and profane roles of women in warfare.

The battle queen typically emerged from the higher levels of nomad society, a custom that was possibly a vestige of the earlier historical reality of warrior queens in ancient Arab history. She formed the center of the cult, the members of which included ranking women of the tribe, who functioned to incite fiery patriotism, iron resolve, and battle fervor in male warriors. Prior to a raid or battle, the women of the battle queen's court gathered before a shrine, which had been erected on ground considered sacred to the spirits of their tribe, and sang songs that celebrated valor and the warrior spirit. When the warriors were stirred to a frenzy, the battle queen mounted her camel and led them into battle.

Sometimes this woman functioned merely as a ritual figure with little direct military purpose: a combination cheerleader, symbolic commander in chief, goddess, and living pinup. At other times, however, when not a weapon-wielding combatant, she served as field general. The center of the battle was always occupied by the battle queen in her litter with her accompanying retinue. She acted as a visual and spiritual rallying point for her soldiers.

The battle queen Hind al-Hunud met her enemy, the prophet Mohammed, in a battle in the seventh century A.D. Far more than a symbol of the warrior spirit in this encounter, the Hind is described by the chroniclers of the fight as "brandishing a broadsword with great gusto."[2] After victories, she stood atop heaped enemy corpses and rhapsodized about her martial prowess. When her husband surrendered Mecca to Mohammed against her wishes, she argued for his death as a just reward for his cowardice and treason.

In all historical periods, ancient and modern, allowing the battle queen to be taken by the enemy brought terrible shame to an Arab warrior. Her fighting spirit was sacred, as was the camel litter, the *hoodah*, that bore her in battle. The Rwala, a major tribe of the bedouin, treasured a battle queen ark called *Abu Duhur*. They believed that their seers could predict the outcome of battles from the movement of the feathers decorating it.

The women warriors of Arab antiquity burst into history about the second millennium B.C. at the time the Arab desert cultures confronted the high cultures of the Fertile Crescent and the Mediterranean. The highly literate enemies of the Arabian battle queens often recorded the queens' names, nations, and battles on monuments, tombs, statues, and buildings.

Spanning the centuries from 1700 to 1500 B.C., a number of women warriors, including Queen Iati'e, Queen Te'Elhunu, and Queen Tabua, ranged out of territories in northern Arabia, leading their troops against Assyria and Egypt and successfully defending their independence. At least two dozen such women warriors commanded Arabian armies between 1000 and 400 B.C.

Around 840 B.C. Queen Athaliah, daughter of Queen Jezebel, controlled Jerusalem. Many times Athaliah directed her soldiers in defense of Jerusalem until the day her only son fell in battle to the sword of a warrior of the house of David. This event turned the queen from her efforts to enhance Jerusalem's prestige to obsession with vengeance for her deceased son. Athaliah swore that she would destroy all the descendants of the house of David. She nearly succeeded in her war. Before the daughter of Jezebel was finished, she had killed most members of the Jerusalem branch of the family she held accountable for her son's death.

A hundred years later, in the vicinity of modern-day southern Iraq, the redoubtable Assyrian warrior prince, Tiglath Pileser IV, seeking to expand his domain in Arabia, encountered two Arabian warrior queens, Zabibi and Samsi. In an attempt to achieve a victory without committing his army, he sought to intimidate the queens into submission by a show of his armies. Each queen, in her turn, proved unimpressed. Neither was willing to accede to Pileser's demands for tribute, and the Assyrians were compelled to fight both women, who, according to Assyrian historians, rode at the head of their troops.

To appreciate the enormous skill and courage of the resistance offered by Queen Zabibi and Queen Samsi to their enemy, it must be remembered that the Assyrians possessed the greatest military machine to date. They could transport and support tens of thousands of troops and provide them with fine metal armor and excellent bladed weapons. Their army comprised engineers, catapults, battering rams, a variety of missile weapons, and some of the finest generals in the world. Queen Zabibi arranged a tribute relationship with them; however, the Assyrians found that they could not force the obedience of Queen Samsi.

A thousand years later, another Arabian woman warrior, Bat Zabbai, stood up to an empire greater than that of the Assyrians and for a time won. The Romans called her Septima Zenobia.[3] Her Syrian name suggests her father's membership in the rich Arab merchant class that flourished in Palmyra (central Syria) in the third century A.D.

When Bat Zabbai was born, Palmyra was considered a prize colony of the Roman Empire, because of its key position in trade between East and West. In recognition of this status, the Emperor Septimus Severus allowed the Palmyrans to elect their own officials.

In A.D. 227 the Parthian regime of Persia fell, throwing that nation into turmoil and disrupting the trade routes from the East. In the West, Rome was also diverted with problems, none more dangerous than the continuing attacks of barbarian Europeans on its northern frontiers. The husband of Bat Zabbai, Odainat, a Syrian noble who had been named the Roman consul of Palmyra in A.D. 258, took advantage of the opportunity.

He was a man for the times. Odainat had been reared, as was customary, not by his urban kin but by the desert bedouin to instill in him the pure Arabic tongue as well as the toughness and discipline of the desert nomads. He was celebrated as an intrepid hunter of lions and panthers, a man who would endure all hardship to fight the beasts and test himself against their fury.

Bat Zabbai hunted, rode, and camped in the wilds with him. During those years, as well as during her time of notoriety, Bat Zabbai eschewed the accoutrements of the court when she was hunting or making war. She slept on the ground with the men and rode with them astride her stallion. Present in the thick of a fight, she delighted in wearing armor and accompanying her husband on forays against their enemies. Her skill with the hunting bow enabled her to participate in her husband's wild animal hunts, and she could hold her own in drinking bouts with her soldiers and generals.

Zabbai should not be seen as an unsophisticated bedouin desert princess. She spoke five languages, was literate during a time when writing was unknown to most people, and wrote a history of Palmyra. She kept a Greek tutor, Longinius, as a permanent part of her court to serve both as a teacher and as a conversationalist.

Odainat and the formidable Bat Zabbai, sensing the weakness of the tottering empires on their eastern and western borders, struck first at Persia. The Roman Emperor Valerian had been murdered by Sapor I of Persia, thus providing the diplomatic excuse for the Palmyrans to invade Persia. Odainat combined the famous archers and spearmen of Palmyra, the cavalry of the bedouin, and the remnants of the Roman legions garrisoned in the area and overcame the Persians. Bat Zabbai commanded the army that laid siege to Sapor. Odainat then turned to his western borders and won several victories that added sizable domains to the rapidly expanding Palmyran city-state.

In A.D. 266 Odainat and his heir died under suspicious circumstances, and Queen Bat Zabbai assumed control of the Palmyran Empire, acting as regent for her son Vaballathus Athenodorus. She immediately launched her armies on a campaign of further conquest. First Egypt fell to her in A.D. 269; then she annexed what remained of Syria. In a few years, sometimes leading her men and sometimes delegating leadership to her general Zabdas, Bat Zabbai extended her domain from Egypt to the Bosphorus and from the Mediterranean to India. After her troops took Antioch and eastern Anatolia, she made military alliances with Persia, Arabia, and Armenia. She was, in effect, ruler of the eastern Roman Empire. She acknowledged that fait accompli by declaring herself independent of Rome, the new owner of half of their empire, and new controller of the Roman trade routes through the Arabian peninsula and the Near East.

She struck coins with her likeness, a particular snub to Rome, and spent millions to escalate her court to the fabled opulence of her hero, Cleopatra of Egypt. She claimed descent from the ancient queen and even used gold plates and vessels at state banquets, which she bragged were bequeathed from Cleopatra through her line. Bat Zabbai's interest in education established her court as a center for intellectuals, philosophers, scholars, and artists of all kinds.

Her driving ambition to control the entire Roman Empire (she even had a golden chariot made for her triumphal entry into Rome) proved her downfall. Assured that cutting off Rome's agricultural imports from Egypt would impress Rome with her power, she succeeded only in drawing the military attention of the new Roman Emperor Aurelian.

He quickly retook Egypt and moved on Ankara. Bat Zabbai staged her first direct engagement with the Romans in the Taurusian wilds outside Ankara. In a rearguard action, she hoped to cover the retreat of the main body of her forces north to Emesa, and she faced Aurelian with a line of Palmyran archers, the most feared in the East, flanked with infantry and heavy cavalry. The Romans were pushed back by Bat Zabbai, who was regularly seen riding among her troops and communicating her commands through General Zabdas.

The Palmyran cavalry charged the Roman lines, which broke before them. Losing discipline in what they thought was a rout, the cavalry pursued only to be drawn into a trap in which their support from the archers and infantry in the rear was severed. Aurelian regrouped his soldiers and slaughtered the Palmyran forces.

Queen Zabbai fell back to Emesa and prepared to defend the town, urging her men to stand strong as she rode among them in her battle armor, but Aurelian's legions once more outfoxed the Palmyran cavalry. The queen, in typical fashion, wrote a letter to Aurelian after this battle in which she boasted, "I have suffered no great loss, for almost all who have fallen were Romans." She referred to the fragments of the Roman legions, once garrisoned in Palmyra who had earlier joined Odainat's army.

Within days of the battle at Emesa, Bat Zabbai led a retreat through several hundred miles of desert as her armies withdrew to the stronghold of Palmyra for their last effort against the Romans. Aurelian's war on the Palmyran queen was proving costly in time and lives. As he maneuvered through the unfamiliar desert, she sent her mounted archers, Parthian fashion, to pick away at the advancing legions. Thus impeded, he could not catch Zabbai before she attained her stronghold and prepared for the siege she knew was coming. She stripped the mausoleums outside the city of marble and granite to augment the walls of Palmyra and sent her ambassadors to neighboring kingdoms to request assistance.

On Aurelian's first charge against the walls of Palmyra, he was wounded by a Palmyran arrow. The wound, coupled with the news that the senators in Rome were questioning why the great Emperor Aurelian was having such difficulty fighting a woman, stirred him to write a famous letter, a testimony in effect to the martial reality of Bat Zabbai. He addressed the Senate:

> The Roman people speak with contempt of the war I am waging against a woman. They are ignorant both of the character and the power of Zenobia [the Roman name for Bat Zabbai]. It is impossible to enumerate her warlike preparations of stones, of arrows, and every species of missile weapons. Every part of the walls is protected with two or three balistae, and artificial fires are thrown from their military engines. The fear of punishment has armed her with a desperate courage.

Aurelian had understood the military competence of Bat Zabbai and brought with him the best of his legions and commanders. Still, the price she was forcing him to pay was seriously impacting his campaign. Rather than face her for many more months, he offered her generous surrender terms. Using her famed literacy once more, she wrote this letter in reply.

> It is not by writing, but by arms, that the submission you require from me can be obtained. You have dared to propose my surrender to your prowess. You forget that Cleopatra preferred death to servitude. The Saracens, the Persians, and the Armenians are marching to my aid; and how are you to resist our united forces, you who have been more than once scared by the plundering Arabs of the desert? When you shall see me march at the head of my allies, you will not repeat an insolent proposition, as though, you were already my conqueror and master.

Finally, Bat Zabbai, realizing that Palmyra was lost, mounted her fastest camel and with a small retinue retreated sixty miles across the desert to the Euphrates, where she hoped to find a boat that could take her eastward into the lands of her allies. She was captured on the river bank and returned to Aurelian, who transported her to Rome to march in his triumphal procession.

The parade in A.D. 273 presented to the Roman people twenty elephants, four Bengal tigers, several hundred exotic animals, ambassadors in their native costumes, thousands of war captives (including a group of Gothic women identified as Amazons), sixteen hundred gladiators who would later take part in celebratorial combats, and kings, queens, generals, and warrior elites whom Aurelian bettered in his reconquest of the Eastern Empire. Each captive bore a plaque around his neck identifying him for the populace. Bat Zabbai, however, was spared that indignity; it was assumed that everyone would know her. She was so heavily weighed down with her famous jewels and gold chains that a slave assisted her to walk. As a final mockery, her golden chariot, the one she had planned to ride when she conquered Rome, followed her, riderless.

Queen Bat Zabbai lived the remainder of her life in grand style. Her fame and wit gained her the sympathy of a number of Roman senators, including one who married her and gave her a villa near the present-day city of Tivoli. Her salons, with the literati of the day in attendance, became a principal feature of Roman cultural life.

If the Romans thought that Queen Bat Zabbai was an aberration, they were reinstructed in the power of Arabian women warriors in A.D. 375 by the Saracen queen, Mavia. She led her troops into Palestine, Phoenicia, and Egypt in rebellion against Rome. The general of the Roman legions in Phoenicia, after confronting Mavia in battle, applied for assistance to the supreme commander of the eastern Roman army. Mavia responded to this threat by smashing the Romans in battle after battle until they sued for a safe retreat from her domains. Remembering the effectiveness of her forces, the Romans later requested assistance from her against the invading Goths. She dispatched a fleet of Arab cavalry.

In the seventh century, the prophet Mohammed united the desert nomads into a nation driven by the effectiveness of Arab warfare and ordered by the tenets of Islam. Many women's names appear in the military history of these times. Salaym Bint Malhand fought among Mohammed's soldiers with an armory of swords and daggers strapped round her pregnant belly. Umm Omara fought side by side with her husband and sons, her garments wrapped around her waist. She lost a hand in one fight and received wounds in several others.

In the time of Mohammed, women taking part in battles was not unusual, both in the traditional role of the battle queen encouraging and directing her troops from her *hoodah* and as a blade fighter in the midst of the fray. The battle queens were in action in A.D. 657 when the forces of Khalif Ali met his enemy Khalif Mo'awiya. In another battle of the early Islamic era, the Arab women turned the tide of battle by tying their veils to pikes in the manner of battle flags and appearing behind their troops, thus convincing the enemy that reinforcements had arrived. Generally, in the early days of Islam, women of noble status had the same rights as their husbands, which included the right to wage war, to raid, and to fight in battles.

The most famous woman warrior of the early Islamic era was Ayesha, the youngest wife of the prophet Mohammed.[4] In the struggles for succession after his death, the eighteen-year-old Ayesha clashed with Khalif Ali and mounted a revolt against what she considered his usurpation of her husband's authority. Joined by the generals Telha and Zobier at Mecca, she assembled an army and rode at its head in a camel litter to Ali's city of Basra.

In October A.D. 656 she captured Basra and took Ali's governor into custody. When Ali tried to negotiate with her, her generals urged acceptance of his terms, but she would not be bought. Infuriated that her officers would even consider dealing with Ali, she led them into a bloody battle along the city walls.

After the initial impact of the two forces, Ayesha's troops yielded, leaving the battle queen in a dangerous situation. When she refused to retreat, her soldiers rallied around her, and the fighting reignited.

Khalif Ali, recognizing Ayesha's camel as the symbolic heart of the battle, ordered it attacked. Seventy of her soldiers died protecting her, some losing their hands as they tried to maintain control of the camel's reins. One of Ali's men cut the hamstrings of the camel, tumbling Ayesha from her *hoodah* unhurt, but arrows so covered her litter that the scribes at the scene likened it to a hedgehog.

Telha and Zobier were dead and her army was defeated, but Ayesha was treated with great respect by Khalif Ali and safely returned to Medina after she swore never to war again. She kept her promise to Ali and spent the remaining years of her life tending her husband's grave. She died in A.D. 678 at the age of sixty-four, the honored "Mother of the Faithful." Her martial apogee, "the Battle of the Camel" as it came to be called, has taken its place in the history of Islam. Khalif Ali's experience with Ayesha could not have been far from his mind when he later married the woman warrior Khawlah Bint al-Kindiyyah.

Khawlah and her female captains, riding in the front ranks of an Arab army, confronted a large and highly organized Greek invasion force at Yermonks. The discipline of the Greek system quickly proved itself against the melee fighting style of the Arabs, and the latter retreated in panic.

Khawlah Bint al-Kindiyyah and several other women captains assumed control of the army and turned back on the pursuing Greeks. Khawlah, surrounded by her women captains, Alfra'Bint Ghifar al-Humayriah, Oserrah, and Wafeira, led the charge on the Greeks. In true battle queen fashion, she urged the men to follow her into the center of the battle.

When a Greek soldier knocked Khawlah to the ground with a stunning blow and advanced for the kill, the gallant Wafeira severed his head with a sword and displayed it to inspire the Arab soldiers. The Arabs rallied and drove the Greeks from the battlefield.

A historian who saw Khawlah Bint al-Kindiyyah in action described her as a "tall knight muffled in black and fighting with ferocious courage."[5] She and her women captains were eventually captured by the Greeks in a battle near Damascus, where their weapons were confiscated, and they were confined. The proud Khawlah perceived that her treatment was rude and stirred her captains to escape, and the Arab women took on their Greek guards with tent poles, forcing them to flee.

The improbability of a woman wielding a tent pole matching a Greek knight armed with a sword can be addressed by appealing to the training methods of the fighting systems of the Orient (kung fu, Kempo, karate, etc.). The staff (tent pole in this case) is generally the first and the last weapon taught. A Chinese kung fu master once remarked to the author, only half in jest, that in China one should most fear having to fight "some old person with a stick." Khawlah and her retinue were experienced warriors with the strength and know-how to control a camel in battle, fight with the sword and lance, and render a simple tent pole into a very effective weapon.

In the seventh century, the Arab armies under the Rightly Guided Caliphs, the first four caliphs or "successors" of the prophet Mohammed, sought to expand Islam. They selected targets that would provide trade and agricultural wealth to support the rapidly growing Islamic population. The Byzantine and Persian empires, already weakened in the wars they had been waging against each other for decades, were prime targets of the Arab forces. During an attack against Damascus, which at the time was under the leadership of the Greek governor Thomas, a daughter of the Arab Himar tribe took up her war bow when her husband was mortally wounded by a poisoned arrow. She moved directly into the midst of the battle and shot Thomas the Greek in the eye. As she insisted on fighting in the most dangerous positions near the walls of Damascus, she was captured during the battle but subsequently rescued. Again and again, in the true tradition of the battle queen, she rallied the Arab forces against the Greeks. Rothery reminds us that these female heroics occurred on both sides and caused little surprise because these women had been "accustomed from their youth to mount the horse, play the bow, and launch the javelin."[6]

The accounts of Arab women warriors grow scarce as Islam ascends in importance as the proper guide to Arab life, the decline due in part to the evolution of the professional Arab military class during Islam's rise to empire. Still, in A.D. 800, warrior Queen Zobeida, referred to as "the

Whipper," founded the city of Tauris,[7] and as late as 1915 in a battle between Ibn Saud and Ibn Rashid, a Saudi woman, breasts bared and hair flying loose, rode along the front lines in true battle queen fashion exhorting her warriors to victory.

Women fought on all sides during the Indochina wars of the twentieth century. Here, two Cambodian women soldiers walk toward the front in August 1972 in an effort to clear North Vietnamese forces from the only highway to Cambodia's rice supply.

CHAPTER 3

Asia: The Sword Is My Child

In 1927 about forty miles southwest of Peking, China, limestone deposits were being quarried near a site called Chou Kou Tien, or Dragon Hill. Rich in fossils, the area had for years been a local source of "dragon bones," the general term for any fossil bone used in the preparation of folk medicines.

A human-looking tooth found in the dragon bones was sent to Dr. Davidson Black, anatomist at the Union Medical College in Peking. He recognized it as a tooth from an ancient form of human and dubbed his discovery *Sinanthropus pekinensis*, "Chinese Man of Peking." Now referred to as *Homo erectus pekinensis*, or, colloquially, Peking Man, the identification led to archaeological research in the area of Chou Kou Tien, which ultimately unearthed the remains of forty humans who had lived in Asia over five hundred thousand years ago.

The ancient humans at Chou Kou Tien were accomplished hunters, succeeding in killing ninety species of mammals, including their own kind; however, specialists assume that the bulk of their diet was vegetable. The great quantities of hackberry seeds found at the site indicate that they were a dietary staple. The foods eaten by the *Homo erectus* at Chou Kou Tien were rendered more palatable by fire, which these ancient humans were some of the first to domesticate.

Several hundred thousand years after the time of Peking Man, about 6000 B.C., farmers living in what is now northern China were building permanent villages and using sickles to harvest millet and grinding stones to process it. In the south of China, similar transformations from hunting and gathering to farming, although based around rice horticulture, were taking place. These vast expanses of time, only recently revealed by archaeologists, are found described in Chinese myths concerning the primordial epochs of the three sovereigns and the five emperors.

China

The ancient civilization of China moved from myth into history during the Shang Dynasty (1850–1100 B.C.), a time of cultural florescence that in a few centuries produced writing, a highly organized society with a ruling class, industries, bronze production, glazed pottery, and walled cities with imposing ceremonial centers and documented women warriors. Those first glimmers of Chinese history tell of Queen B'iug-Xog of Miwo-Tieng, who dispatched an army of ten thousand soldiers against hostile northern tribes, and of Shih Hu's all-woman army in the state of Chao, who dressed in sable furs and carried war bows painted yellow.[1]

About 100 B.C. Empress Nee Lu, widow of the first Han Dynasty emperor, ruled China in her own name; when her son came of age, she continued as the de facto leader and resumed formal control after his death. She not only maintained a strong grip on her own country but also sent an army against Yueh (Vietnam) to prevent its involvement in the iron trade.

China's most renowned woman warrior, Hua Mu-Lan, went into battle in the fifth century A.D., replacing a conscripted father too ill to fight. When she first suggested taking her father's place, he adamantly refused. She proposed a sparring match with swords, the outcome of which would determine her fate. Hua Mu-Lan won.

She cut her hair short, buckled on her father's armor, and entered the forces of the emperor. She fought as a knight on the front lines for over ten years, her sex never being discovered. Her extraordinary fighting skill prompted her general to offer her his daughter's hand in marriage.

Hua Mu-Lan lived to return home and "throw off the link-iron clothing." The traditional "Mu-Lan Play," which honors her memory, concludes with these lines: "She had much fighting ability, and could act the leader. Her body passed through one hundred battles, always at the front, and compared to the fiercest soldiers, she was still better."

Women warriors as castle defenders emerge early in Chinese history. In A.D. 503 the prince of Wei challenged the emperor for control of China. Ginching, an ally of the prince of Wei, fought out of the walled fortress city of Changyang, and in his absence his wife, Lady Mongchi, assumed command of the fortress. On the date in question, imperial troops marched on Changyang when General Ginching was fighting in a neighboring province. Mongchi saved the town and routed the emperor's soldiers. Such women warriors were not rare in old China. Female household servants were also instructed in the martial arts in order to better defend their masters.

An exploit comparable to that of Mongchi's transpired twelve years later. A woman general, Lieouchi, successfully defended the stronghold of Tsetong against the assaults of the Imperial Army. In the same year, A.D.

515, Queen Honchi wrested the rule of Wei from her ineffective husband and waged war against the emperor as general and commander in chief of, her armies.

The Imperial Army was assisted by a woman in 590 in wars against invading non-Chinese tribes. The widow of Feng Pao, lady of the Hsi clan of Kwangtung province, organized and with her son Feng Ang led an army in the recapture of a town taken by the tribesmen. Wearing armor, she accompanied her army during the assault.

The Tang Dynasty (A.D. 618–906), the most brilliant epoch in early Chinese history, was a time of peace, great achievements in art and poetry, the invention of printing, and the zenith of the flowering of Buddhism. The Empress Wu Chao of Whang Ho created the foundations of this cultural and artistic apex of Chinese civilization. She was believed to be the daughter of a powerful general during the time of the first Tang emperor. Prince Kung-ti, Wu Chao's real father, stood in the line of succession to the throne of China and, fearful of attacks against his child, had entrusted her to the general to rear as his own child.

Wu Chao grew up traveling with the army and learning martial arts. At age fourteen, she was told of her real father, Prince Kung-ti, when he was assassinated and his rightful throne was taken by the murderer. His daughter swore revenge.

She heard that the emperor, her father's killer, was staging an archery competition at the palace. Wu Chao, who had shot a bow and arrow for years under the watchful eye of her foster father, entered the competition to gain admittance to the palace. She trounced her closest challenger, the emperor's son, who in his humiliation set his bodyguards on her. Wu Chao held her own against the attackers and in the excitement proclaimed the emperor a murderer and herself the true empress of China.

When she became empress in 666, she turned her attention to the lingering war with Korea, devised an efficient attack plan involving sea invasion, and quickly took the country. Though much turmoil beset her reign, the army remained loyal through many battles. In addition to her military exploits, she is remembered for lowering taxes, building a number of great monuments and cities, and placing justice ministers in public office. Her rule was one of the longest and most prosperous of any Chinese monarch.

Another daughter of a Tang Dynasty general, Nie Yin-Niang, took a different route to fame by becoming the Chinese "Robin Hood." Using fighting skills learned at age ten from a nun, Nie Yin-Niang haunted the wild country of China helping the weak and poor and punishing the unjust.

During the succeeding Sung Dynasty (A.D. 960–1126), a young Tartar woman, Liu Chin Ting, learned fighting arts as a child with her brothers and planned for the day when her people could be free of the tyrannical hold of the Sung emperor. At age sixteen she led the defense of her clan's mountain territory, striking such fear in rival clans that they believed her to be the reincarnation of a war goddess.

When the Tartars of the North finally defied the emperor, Sung General Chun Pao was sent with the Imperial Army to crush the rebellion. He was particularly eager to neutralize Liu Chin Ting's tribal army, but his attacks were easily repelled by the young woman and he was taken prisoner.

Sometime shortly after she sentenced him to death, she fell in love with the courageous general, and he with her, and they married. When the emperor heard of the defection, he ordered Chun Pao's execution, but Liu Chin Ting protected him and offered the Emperor a deal for her husband's amnesty. She promised to capture the city of Yangchow for the emperor if he would release her husband from his wrath. She succeeded, and the emperor made peace with her and offered her a general's commission as well as the freedom of her husband. For the next thirty years, with her husband as second in command, Liu Chin Ting, once the implacable enemy of the Sung emperor, led his troops in battle and captured new territories for his empire.

The chronicles of the Sung Dynasty describe a number of women warriors fighting along the northern frontiers of China. Yang Yanshao, commander of the Sung armies active in the north, heard that two of his generals, his sisters, were surrounded by enemy soldiers in a mountain pass. He sent word to his commander in chief and requested her assistance. The aging general, who had been a famous warrior in her youth, suggested that a young woman named Yang Paifeng could effect the rescue of the cornered generals.

Yanshao was ready to agree until he discovered that Yang Paifeng was not of the aristocratic class. He haughtily communicated to his general that such a woman was suited only for leading housemaids in battle; however, as conditions worsened, Yanshao bowed to the choice of his general. Yang Paifeng led a surprise assault with a small group through the enemy lines and safely withdrew the embattled generals.

What Yanshao did not know was that Yang Paifeng's grandmother and great-grandmother had been Sung army commanders. Yang Paifeng's maternal grandmother, Mu Guiying, even held the position of commander in chief of the Sung armies.

The turbulent times of the Ming Dynasty (A.D. 1368–1644) revealed a number of valiant Chinese martial women. Famous writer and fighter Chin Liang-Yu rode in battle at the side of her husband, General Ma Siancheng, as an archer. She rose to the rank of division commander and, after her husband's death, took full command of the army. She is credited with many victories during the civil wars in which she took part as a combatant. Even when the Ming government collapsed, she preserved her personal power base in Szechwan until she died in 1668. One of Chin Liang-Yu's most famous battle captains, woman warrior Ma Feng-I, commanded Ming troops toward the end of the dynasty.

During the Ming times, both rebels and loyalists in the civil war boasted units of martial nuns and women soldiers. The prevalence of women in the violent and secret White Lotus Society, a Nationalist group that served as inspirations for the Boxer rebellion of 1900, has also been chronicled. The era also witnessed Shen Yun-Ying as she led her murdered father's troops in battle. She successfully defended her capital several times and took territory from her father's enemies.

* * *

The latter part of the Ming Dynasty saw a rise in Japanese pirates preying on the coastal towns and sea trade of eastern China, and from time to time Chinese pirates cruised the coastal waters of Japan. Such Chinese privateers provided the means by which the first Europeans, soldiers of fortune, set foot in Japan.

The magnitude of the Chinese pirate bands dwarfs comparable maritime criminal enterprises in the West. Rather than a single pirate vessel waylaying a hapless merchant ship as in the heyday of Captain Kidd, fleets of highly organized and hostile Chinese ships numbered into the hundreds. An entire seagoing pirate community of tens of thousands of men, women, and children roamed the Chinese coast from north to south and defeated all who challenged them.[2]

In 1804 Captain Ching Yih commanded a Chinese pirate fleet of six hundred ships and precipitated such damage that Peking sent a fleet of forty warships after him. Ching Yih captured twenty-eight of the emperor's ships and sank most of the rest. He was so powerful that he even threatened to depose the emperor and take the throne for himself.

Flushed with success, Ching Yih desired a wife. Twenty beautiful women captured in raids were bound and brought before him. Hsi Kai, an exceptionally statuesque and powerful young woman, caught his attention. Ching Yih ordered her unbound so that he might better inspect her, a decision that almost cost his eyesight, for she leapt on him and tried to gouge his eyes out. She was dragged to the ground by his guards, but Captain Ching Yih was charmed by her ferocity and beauty and asked her to marry him of her own free will. She refused, and Ching Yih responded by offering her gold, silks, slaves, and property. Ignoring his offers, she agreed to marry him for joint command of his fleet with the right to all booty she captured. Ching's fleet was divided into six squadrons—red, blue, yellow, green, black, and white—with Hsi Kai Ching in command of the white and red fleets.

A typhoon took the life of Ching Yih in 1807, and a council was called for the captains of his fleet to determine the future of the vast pirate armada. Hsi Kai came clothed in her husband's captain's uniform, a robe of purple embroidered with golden dragons, his helmet planted firmly on her head. In her sash she tucked several of his swords. The message was clear, but she drove the point home with words.

> Look at me, Captains. Your departed chief sat in council with me. Your most powerful fleet, the White, under my command, took more prizes than any other. Do you think I will bow to any other chief?[3]

In the succeeding three years, Hsi Kai Ching expanded the operation to two thousand vessels and over seventy thousand pirates, including entire families. Queen of a floating pirate empire, Hsi Kai Ching dominated the ocean lanes of China and made a fortune for herself and her stalwarts by charging Chinese sea merchants "protection money" for safe passage over her briny domain. Showing no mercy, however, to the ships of Portugal, England, and the Chinese emperor, she assailed them on sight.

Captain Hsi Kai Ching's expertise at navy tactics intimidated the Mandarin Navy, which sometimes simply withdrew when she raised her battle standard. In 1808, she drew them into an ambush and captured almost thirty of their war junks. In desperation, the Chinese government forbade all shipping in the waters controlled by Hsi Kai's pirates, hoping to starve them out, and offered a generous bounty to foreign pirate hunters for her capture. When those measures failed, a joint Portuguese and Chinese offensive was designed. Not one of Captain Ching's ships was lost.

In total capitulation, the Chinese government pledged the pirates amnesty and even paid them to surrender. In 1810 Madame Ching was pardoned. She retired, with a rich government pension, to a coastal town with her second husband, bore three sons and a daughter, and embarked on a new career—smuggling. In terms of the sheer magnitude of her operation, Hsi Kai Ching may have been the greatest pirate in history.

One of the reasons that the Chinese government was willing to placate Madame Ching with what were in effect lavish bribes was the far greater difficulties they were experiencing with the masses of discontented peasant farmers on the mainland. In the Taiping rebellion of the mid-1800s, Chinese peasants rose against the government and formed an independent state, which extended over what is now Hupeh, Anhwei, Kiangsi,

Kaingsu, and Chekiang. Women were enlisted at all levels of the revolution, including the army. The Tien-Wang, or "Heavenly King of the Tae-Pings," had a one-thousand-soldier female army.

Ch'iu Chin was one of the first modern Chinese revolutionaries.[4] In 1900, when she was twenty-five, her family moved to Peking, where she was horrified by what she saw as the corruption and decadence of the Manchu court that ruled China. She became a passionate Nationalist and one of the first women to join Sun Yat-sen's party at its inception in 1904.

She traveled China, lecturing against foot binding and involuntary concubinage, and secretly organizing a rebellion against the Empress Tzu Hsi. Married and the mother of two children, Ch'iu Chin dressed like a man, wore a sword, wrote poetry, drank like a trooper, and excelled in horsemanship, fencing, and unarmed fighting arts. Her physical skills, plus her intelligence and education, led to her appointment as the principal for the Ta-t'ung School of Physical Culture in Shao-hsing. She secretly trained her one thousand students as soldiers for the rebellion she was planning.

Word of her plans leaked to the government, and a raid by imperial troops found weapons at Ch'iu Chin's school. At the age of thirty-two, she was arrested, tried, and beheaded within a few days. Though tortured extensively, her confession consisted of but seven Chinese characters: "Autumn rain and autumn wind sadden us." But what Ch'iu Chin had set in motion could not be denied, and within four years the Manchu Dynasty was defeated. Ch'iu Chin was disinterred and reburied with state honors.

* * *

In the early twentieth century, Macao was home to a Chinese woman pirate, Lai Cho San ("Mountain of Fortune"), second only to Madame Ching Yih. At an early age, she inherited her father's criminal domain, consisting of gambling houses and twelve junks that he had used in a small-scale shakedown racket that he perpetrated on local fishermen.

Lai Cho San upgraded her business ventures by expanding her gambling halls with profits she gained by directing her pirate fleet toward targets more lucrative than poor fishermen. She turned the profits of her pirate ventures into backing for other pirates and was soon known all along the Chinese coast.

An American journalist named Aleko Lilius spent some time as her guest on board one of her war junks. He wrote that her usual costume was a white silk gown decorated with jade buttons. In battle, however, she dressed in shirt and trousers and carried a sidearm. Lilius observed that she did not fight but was always armed and on deck during an action.

In December of 1937 several modern Japanese destroyers of the Fubuki class attacked the fleet of pirate junks operating under Lai Cho San's personal command. The Japanese armored ships, carrying six five-inch guns and moving at over thirty knots, easily overpowered Lai Cho San's antique fleet, and within several hours the pirate fleet was exterminated with all hands, including Lai Cho San, assumed lost in battle.

Six months later, however, officials recognized a familiar pattern of pirate activity on the south China coast and, in 1939 in Shanghai, a court passed a sentence of life imprisonment on a woman witnesses identified as Lai Cho San. The woman denied it vigorously. Before the claim could be verified, however, the woman escaped and was never seen again.[5]

As Lai Cho San followed Hsi Kai, Huang Pemei, also known as "Madame Two Revolvers," followed Lai Cho San. She personally commanded seventy vessels that plundered fishing and merchant shipping. She is thought to have worked for the U.S. intelligence community and at one time offered her services to General Chiang Kai-shek in any bid he might make for the reconquest of China.

Early twentieth-century Chinese history was dominated by the revolution led by Mao Tse-tung. Kang Ke-Ching joined the peasant revolt in 1928 at the age of sixteen and survived the twelve-month, six-thousand-mile "Long Walk" of Mao's revolutionaries. She came to be known as "the Red Amazon" and fought in military engagements with Nationalist armies, bandits, and war lords. Several times she carried wounded comrades in addition to her own pack and weapons. She was given command of a military unit in 1934.

Mongolia

The steppes, upland prairies and deserts, which span a fifth of the globe, roll westward from China to the gates of Russia. This is the ancient home of the horse-riding Mongol tribesmen who over centuries impacted the history of East and West.

The chief of the Mongol tribes was called a khan, and his territory was a khanate. In this aristocratically ranked society, his wife usually came from the noble warrior class. Such women often held great power. Even after marriage they kept their own tents and herds, and many supported their own courts, complete with advisers, guards, diplomats, and a variety of other retainers.

When a khan died, the khatun, his widow, ruled as regent until a council of tribal leaders could gather to select a new khan, which sometimes required years because of the scattered pastoral Mongol society. Throughout that time, the khatun ruled with complete authority over all aspects of the government, including the military.

Sorghaqtani Khatun is perhaps the greatest of all the khatuns. Genghis Khan, her father, took her counsel regularly, and, through many of her ideas, his realm was territorially expanded.

Living at the same time, Toragana Khatun ruled for four years after the death of her husband. In another khanate, Organa Khatun was in the midst of a nine-year rule, while the head of a neighboring khanate, Koquz Khatun, led an army into battle conjointly with her husband.

Some of the khatuns fared well in war, and some did not. Mandughai Khatun in 1470 took the field to defend the khanate for her five-year-old son from would-be usurpers. For twenty-one years, she held it for him against all comers. Goldan Khatun, however, died beside her husband in battle in 1696.[6]

Siam

The Southeast Asian peninsula was home to a number of nations by the early 1800s. Vietnam dominated the east; Burma and Malaya, the west; and Laos, Cambodia, and Siam were situated in the central regions. During the nineteenth century the area was hotly contested by the British and the French. The British took Burma from India, while the French captured Vietnam, Cambodia, and Laos. Siam, now called Thailand, was pressed between the two European powers; in 1893, the French invaded the Thai capital, Bangkok. Thirty years earlier, a French journalist first revealed to the West the presence of a Siamese women's elite military corps.

The four-hundred-woman army, composed of four companies each under the direction of a female captain, was drawn from the strongest and most beautiful women in the country and was highly paid. Each female soldier was given five servants to enable her to devote her time to martial arts practice and military duties. The corps was created to guard the king and his family as well as the royal palaces and crown lands, and they accompanied the king on all his travels.

Their uniform consisted of a knee-length white tunic, embroidered with gold; on state occasions, they wore gilt armor and carried spears. In battle, however, they were all business, abandoning their spears and carrying muskets and swords.

Their skills with a variety of weapons were polished during a mandatory practice every two days at a parade ground near the capital, which served as the major training facility for lance, pistol, musket, rifle, sword, and hand-to-hand combat. Once a month, the king would judge martial arts competitions among the women and reward the winners with expensive jewelry.

The Siamese elite female guard sanctioned dueling among its members. These battles, over real or imagined slights and offenses, were fought with swords in the presence of the entire female guard and must have been sanctioned by the commanding officer, who at the time of the first report was Ma Ying Taphan, "the Great Mother of War." The loser in these dramatic duels was given a state funeral, and the winner was required to go on pilgrimage to religious sites to purify herself and pray for the soul of her victim.[7]

Vietnam

To the east of Siam in the first century B.C., the Chinese invaded Vietnam and maintained control of the small country intermittently until A.D. 981. Naturally, the people rose in rebellion when the conditions were favorable. Of the five revolutions fomented against Chinese control in Vietnam, the first two were led by women.[8]

In A.D. 40, the Chinese governor of Vietnam, General Dinh, executed the noble husband of Lady Trung Trac for his revolutionary behavior, moving Trung Trac and her sister Trung Nhi to action. Realizing the difficulty of drawing people to their revolution, the sisters decided on a bold gesture. For years a rogue tiger had been killing and maiming people and livestock, and, because no one could kill him, the people had come to believe he was supernatural and invincible. Trung Nhi, always the strategist, suggested that Trung Trac, the fighter, hunt the tiger. Trung Trac killed and skinned the beast, and Trung Nhi wrote a proclamation on the skin calling the people of Vietnam to rise against Governor Dinh and the Chinese overlords.

The sisters chose and personally trained thirty-six women as generals for their army of eighty thousand. One of their choices, Phung Thi Chinh, went into battle pregnant, gave birth on the battlefield, strapped the baby to her back, and fought her way back to safety.

In A.D. 40, the Trung sisters led their warriors in the liberation of sixty-five Vietnamese towns. Governor Dinh shaved his head and secretly fled Vietnam, taking with him the mantel of Chinese control in Vietnam. Trung Trac was proclaimed Trung Vuong, "She-King Trung."

The battles with the Chinese army waged constantly over the next several years until, in A.D. 43, the Chinese recaptured Vietnam. Rather than be taken by the Chinese, the Trung sisters committed suicide by drowning.

The second successful Vietnamese rebellion against the Chinese erupted in A.D. 248 and was led by a twenty-one-year-old woman named Trieu Thi Trinh, sometimes called "the Vietnamese Joan of Arc." She commanded an army of several thousand men and women.

Before her twenty-first birthday, she was victorious in more than thirty major battles and liberated Vietnam for a year. Trieu Thi Trinh is always depicted, sword in each hand, riding a war elephant into battle. Like the Trung sisters, she committed suicide when the Chinese retook Vietnam. Trieu Thi Trinh is remembered for a statement she made when her brother ventured to dissuade her involvement in warfare and revolution.

I will not resign myself to the lot of women, who bow their heads and become concubines. I wish to ride the tempest, tame the waves, kill the sharks. I have no desire to take abuse.[9]

Bui Thi Xuan, a Vietnamese woman general in the late 1700s, led troops in a rebellion that established, though briefly, the Tay Sons dynasty. When she was captured, her enemy, Emperor Gia Long, awarded her, in the grisly manner of her death, a compliment. She was trampled to death by elephants, but her heart, arms, liver, and lungs were fed to the Emperor's troops in his hope of imbuing his men with the spirit of the valiant woman general.

In the early twentieth century, the Vietnamese were again at war with a would-be invader, France, and over one million Vietnamese women participated. In 1907 a woman innkeeper named Nguyen Thi Ba poisoned to death over two hundred French soldiers as her part in the revolution, and in 1918 Hor Lhamo, a woman warrior from the north, rallied an army from the peasant villages and led them effectively against a feudal warlord who was backing the French.

In Nghe-Tinh Province in 1931, a guerrilla unit of 120 soldiers, 40 of them women, drove the French garrison out of the provincial capital. And, even though the French recaptured the town at a later date, the great success of the women in the battle spurred others to join the war. Ha Que, in 1945, rallied the first all-woman guerrilla unit in the province and, during the same period, Nguyen Thi Ngia, age twenty-three, led the troops that took Sadec, an important center south of Saigon. When she was captured by the French and tortured, she cut off her tongue rather than reveal secrets.

In the early 1940s, Ming Khai was tortured by the French for leading anti-French troops in Nam Ky. She wrote in her blood a poem on her prison cell wall, the last lines of which are: "The sword is my child, the gun is my husband." Today in Vietnam, Ming Khai's name is often borrowed by various women's work groups and military units.

The youngest woman warrior in the Vietnamese revolution, Vo Thi Sau, joined a guerrilla unit at age fourteen and killed thirteen French soldiers in hand-to-hand combat within the first few months of her warrior career. The French put her to death without a trial, making her the youngest woman to be executed in Vietnam. Her name became a rallying cry for the women who joined in the final victorious assault against the French in 1954 at Dien Bien Phu.

The ultimate defeat of the French was accelerated by a constant artillery barrage against their positions. This tactic was rendered possible by the women who carried the heavy ammunition and artillery from the Chinese border several hundred miles over the mountains.

More often than not, the warrior women of Vietnam fought their battles in defense of their own villages and homes. Rachem H'Ban, a woman of the Jarai tribe, spontaneously led a successful skirmish when eleven of President Diem's troops entered her village and harassed her people, stealing their food and raping young women.

After taking all weapons, the soldiers herded the villagers together. When the leader of the enemy troops shot a young man in the leg, Rachem H'Ban called to the women in their native language to arm themselves with torches from the house fires. The women quickly responded and barraged the soldiers with flaming debris. Rachem attacked the leader, knocked his gun from his hand, and strangled him to death. The villagers, mostly women, clubbed five soldiers to death and chased the others away. After the battle, both men and women elected Rachem H'Ban as village militia commander.

One of the most powerful women warriors of modern Vietnamese history, Madame Dinh of Ben Tre, entered the resistance against the French in 1937 at the age of seventeen. Captured with her husband and tortured by the French, she escaped after her husband was killed by their captors. She raised an army of rebellion in her home province of Ben Tre and drove out thirteen thousand of Diem's troops. Further, she successfully defended the province against the massive counterattack launched by the French.

Her skillful military leadership earned her the position of deputy commander of the People's Liberation armed forces, soldiers who attacked major enemy concentrations, dealt with the opposition's mobile forces, and initiated all offensive operations. Forty percent of the regimental commanders in the army were women.

Madame Dinh offered the following comment on the role of women in the Vietnamese army of liberation. Although undocumented, it testifies to the vital part they played.

> With their bows and arrows, booby traps, spiked pits, homemade guns, muskets, mines and grenades, our women killed the enemy in many places and at many times. . . . In 1965, when the U.S. sent troops into the South on a massive scale, the movement to have women join the armed forces increased. . . . For instance, the women guerrillas of Chu Chi district destroyed ninety-nine vehicles in the first six months of 1966. The Quang Nam women guerrillas swam the Bau Nuoc Lon River to attack U.S. troops. After killing twenty-one of them, they swam back to their areas and resumed farming as if nothing had happened. Mrs. Ngo thi May alone killed twenty-five American soldiers and won the Anti-U.S. Elite Fighter title three times. . . . In the first three months of 1968, some

ten thousand women joined the armed forces in central Trung Bo. In Huang Nam and Phu Yen, more than five hundred women carried out dangerous missions as members of guerrilla units. In Nam Bo, 40 percent of the women joined guerrilla formations . . . the guerrilla women of Tri Thien, Cho Lai, Lam Dong, Back Ai, Ben Tre, etc. also fought very heroically and wiped out more than a thousand enemy troops. The Hue women's self-defense unit defeated a U.S. Marine Battalion during the Tet offensive, and the Le Thi Rieng women's self-defense unit fought on the Saigon streets and wiped out one hundred security agents.[10]

Ut Tich left her children with relatives in her home village, joined a guerrilla force, and quickly rose to the position of commander. In 1965 in one of her many famous fights, Ut Tich killed thirty-five Saigon troops and shot down a helicopter. An expert at ambush, she frequently entered Saigon and attacked military barracks. She died in battle in 1970.

Ho Te Que, called "Tiger Lady," fought against the Vietcong. The mother of seven, she led Vietnamese Army raids with her trademark .45 automatic strapped to her hip. Some Vietcong prisoners spoke of the Tiger Lady as if she were a demon war goddess. She was killed in action in 1965.

In the same year, Captain Hui Po Yung, a physical education teacher before the war, led her unit of the Min Top women's army against the Vietcong to the south. Because of the admixture of European blood introduced via three generations of a local Swedish mining venture, the women of the Min Top region were larger and stronger than other Vietnamese women. One of the many famous women of the Min Top army, Dho Minde, could run forty-five miles nonstop. In one memorable demonstration, she shot the limb from a tree on which a Vietcong guerrilla was hiding. When the soldier fell at her feet, she calmly cut his throat with her boot knife.

The women's army of Min Top boasted a unit of markswomen led by Ding Le Tunn, a half-French Vietnamese woman. Her unit specialized in wounding the enemy with one shot, closing on him, and beating him to death with a rifle butt to preserve bullets. Some military observers from Western countries have commented that the only fighting women of modern times to compare with the Vietnamese are some of the Kikuyu women of Africa who fought with the Mau Mau in Kenya in the 1950s.

On the Vietcong side in 1965, a woman warrior named Ta Thi Kieu and another woman single-handedly defeated a thirty-man Saigon garrison. Ta Thi Kieu, who had led more than thirty-three combats, was attacking a fortress when the men of her unit became scattered after a brief firefight outside the redoubt. Ta Thi Kieu and her partner boldly walked toward the fort, believing the army to be behind them. Demonstrating the command presence developed in her martial life, Ta Thi Kieu announced in a loud voice, "The liberation forces are here!" The garrison troops believed her and relinquished their weapons.

A Vietnamese officer offered these comments about the women who accompanied him to flush out nests of Vietcong in a coastal area.

> Most of these women had volunteered for the best reason in the world—they had a score to settle. These were women who had lost their entire families in the Tet Offensive, had seen them lined up against the walls and shot. These women were imbued with a deep and almost boiling hatred, hatred at the very soul, the kind of hatred that if it were directed at me I'd want to move to another planet.[11]

Japan

The Japanese archipelago, consisting of the four large islands—Honshu, Shikoku, Kyushu, and Hokkaido—and hundrds of smaller ones, lies 110 miles east of Korea. Human occupation is evident from about thirty thousand years ago, although the crude stone artifacts that suggest this antiquity are few and controversial. About ten thousand years ago, Japanese natives were making pottery of the Jomon type, and between A.D. 200 and 300, an influx of Koreans introduced to the Japanese armor-clad, sword-wielding horsemen, the warrior predecessors of the aristocratic samurai military caste of historic Japan's feudal era. By A.D. 300, the Japanese had turned increasingly to rice cultivation and were in possession of bronze technology and an elaborate entombing tradition, which created large burial mounds called *kofun*. The tomb of Emperor Nintoku is about 120 feet high and 1,500 feet long. During this time, female rule was not uncommon in Japan. In fact, in one of the first exposés of Japanese life, the "Accounts of the Three Kingdoms" in A.D. 267, a Chinese envoy notes that a woman, Himiko of Yamatai, was considered the supreme ruler.

The samurai caste, the hereditary military elites of the country, produced many of the female rulers. The beloved Japanese war epic, *Heike Monogatari*, features many women warriors.

A nineteenth-century Japanese commentator on the samurai code, Bushido ("the Way of the Warrior"), wrote:

> Under Bushido, girls learned to repress their feelings, to harden their nerves and to excel in weaponry. This was usually the *naginata* (a halbred-like weapon). The Bushido woman had no overlord, so she learned to defend herself. Fencing kept her in good

health, gave her speed and endurance. The women following the
Bushido Code carried *kai-ken* (long-bladed daggers). They carried
these in their bosoms for defense, or if need be to commit *sepukua*
(ritual suicide). It was a tradition that their greatest domestic quality was in the education of their sons.[12]

Women of the samurai were trained in self-defense, and, comparable to
wedding customs of the Teutonic tribes described by Tacitus, daggers were
common wedding presents. In the Kanto (Tokyo area and northward)
women functioned as *djito*, "policemen" of the large rural estates.

The *naginata* was a weapon of choice for many samurai women because of its effectiveness against the sword, the preeminent "male weapon"
of the samurai. With its length a woman could keep a swordsman at bay,
and with its sharp heavy blade she could make slashing attacks. Many
famous female *naginata* fighters have been recorded in Japanese history.

Over a thousand years ago, Empress Jingo-Kogo, expert with the
sword, bow, and *naginata*, led her forces against Korea and, though pregnant at the time, took command. The king of the Korean kingdom of Silla
surrendered almost immediately when he saw the empress and her troops
approaching. She ordered that her spear be mounted at the gate of the
palace of the humbled Korean king as a memorial to her triumph. Empress
Jingo-Kogo ruled for seventy years.

Often the women warriors of Japan were involved in *kataki-uchi*,
"honorable revenge." Tora Gozen of Oiso, a famed sword fighter, helped
the Soga clan in *kataki-uchi* in the late 1100s. During the same period,
Miyagino and her sister Shinobu, with sword in hand, fought a government official who had unjustly executed their father.

Tomoe Gozen was the most famous woman warrior of medieval Japan.
In one battle, after she had killed several enemies in single combat, the
leader of the attacking force, Uchida Iyeyoshi, attempted to capture
Tomoe himself. During the skirmish, with swords flashing, her sleeve was
torn off as her attacker sought to drag her from her horse. Infuriated, she
wheeled her charger and severed Uchida's head, a trophy she later presented to her husband. In another battle, after many hours of fighting, she
was one of the last seven warriors standing. A later account depicted her
solo *naginata* defense of an important bridge against dozens of attackers.

Shizuka Gozen, mistress of the national hero Yoshitsune, accompanied
her lover in many battles in the late twelfth century and was conspicuous
in the defense of Horikawa Castle in 1185.

The twelfth century witnessed the winning of Japan by the first Minamoto shogun. In his bloody rise to power, his wife Masaki Hojo rode
with him as his most able general. When he died, she appointed her son

to the position of shogun and ruled as queen regent in his name. Because she had shaved her head after the death of her husband, she came to be known as the "Nun General." She was never defeated in battle.

Koman was a twelfth-century Japanese woman warrior involved in many daring exploits. At a battle between the Taira and the Minamoto on Lake Biwa, Koman saved the Minamoto banner from capture by swimming to shore with it in her teeth while Taira arrows rained around her. While employed by Lord Settsu as a traveling companion and bodyguard for his wife and two children, Koman was attacked by a band of outlaws. She drew her sword, threw away her scabbard, and shouted to Lady Settsu, "Follow me to death!" The lord's wife drew her short sword and went to Koman's side. When the fight was over, the lady had killed four men but was mortally wounded; Koman, uninjured, had downed six attackers. Also in the twelfth century, the great General Yoritomo was saved from death by the action of a Zen nun named Ike Gozen, who came to his defense with her *naginata*.

The young Emperor Antoku was saved in 1185 by the mistress of Tomotori, who repelled would-be assassins with a *naginata*; Tamaori Hime, wife of Atsumori, engaged the opposition on the beach during the Taira War; and Tenji-no-Tsubone fought beside her lover Sagami Goro in the sea battle of Dan-no-ura. In 1189 Fujinoye defended Takadachi Castle, and in public combat on the palace stairs, armed with *naginata* and sword, she defeated Yemeto Juro and Nagasawa Uyemen-taro. Itagaki led three thousand of her Taira clan warriors into battle against ten thousand of the Heike in 1199. When the great Shogun Yoritomo died, his wife Hojo Masa-Ko took control of the government. Born the daughter of a samurai family in 1157, she functioned well in a world of military men and maintained the loyalty of the army.

In April of 1201, members of the Taira clan fought for their lives defending Echigo Castle against overwhelming forces. Hangaku, a samurai's daughter and an excellent archer, dressed in soldier's attire, stood on the highest tower of the castle and launched her arrows into the enemy host with telling effect. Desperate to negate her firepower, they shot her in the back, a very unsamurai act.

Fighting with the *naginata*, the wife of Takebashi Jinkuro fought her way out of an ambush in 1570. Fifteen years later, the wife of Okumra Nagatomi was with him at Suemori Castle when they were attacked by a fifteen-thousand-man army loyal to Oda Nobunaga. Lady Nagatomi strapped on her sword and, with two attendants, mounted the walls where she remained day and night, encouraging the defenders, noting acts of bravery for later reward, and generally inspiring the Nagatomi soldiers with her courage and spirit.

At about the same time in Hitachi Prefecture, Ashitaka Castle, stronghold of Lord Okami Nakatsukasa, was attacked by soldiers of Lord Shigetsune. As the aggressors penetrated the family quarters, Lady Okami Nakatsukasa ordered the noncombatants huddled with her to rip up the tatami (woven rice straw floor mats) and the wood and paper walls and follow her onto the battlements. There she ignited this refuse and poured it down upon the attackers. The elite troops of Lord Shigetsune had no defense against the rain of fire generated by the Lady of Ashitaka Castle and they backed away from the walls.

Izumi-no-Okuni wandered the streets and alleys of Kyoto in the sixteenth century carrying the long and short sword reserved for members of the samurai caste and dressed in the traveling clothes of a *ronin*, a "cloud man" or out-of-work samurai. She created a form of popular musical drama, *Onna Kabuki*, in which women acted the parts of both men and women. Okuni's kabuki proved so bawdy that authorities feared for the corruption of public morals and suppressed the all-female show in favor of a version in which males play both male and female parts, the most common contemporary form of the still-popular entertainment.

The early seventeenth century witnessed the valor of Lady Kamitsuken Katana. Wife of a rich land-owning lord, the lady trained castle women in martial arts and led them into battle.

The panache of the Asian female warrior tradition, a narrative that ranges grandly from the warrior empresses of old China to the fighting Khatuns of Mongolia, the Trung sisters of Vietnam, and the Siamese female elite guards of the nineteenth century, is nicely summed up by the image of Lady Yatsushiro, medieval Japanese woman warrior, who fought with sword and *naginata* and rode into battle, while pregnant, with her pet fighting-wolf Nokaze racing at her side.

Hyderabad refused to become part of the Republic of India when India gained its independence in 1947. Here, members of the Hyderabad Women's Legion, mostly daughters of military officers and government officials, learn to shoot. Their efforts failed, though, and Hyderabad surrendered to Indian troops in 1948.

UPI/Corbis-Bettmann

CHAPTER 4

India: Kali's Daughters

India's varied topography, its high mountains, vast river systems, and lush plains and jungles with their promise of endless plenty, has long been a magnet to nomadic invaders. Sometime after 1200 B.C. Aryan invaders from north of the Black and Caspian Seas poured into India through the passes of the Hindu Kush Mountains and up the valley of the Indus River. They came as chariot-riding warrior pastoralists, led by a raja, or chief. Cattle husbandry was their passion; the animals served not only as the basis of their diet but also as money. Raiding a neighbor's herd was considered a worthwhile endeavor; hence, warfare was rampant.

The raiders quickly conquered the native inhabitants and in time formed the basis of the classical civilization of India. It would be a world of men, but at the outset women had many prerogatives. They could influence choices made by their families concerning whom they would marry, and they participated in religious cermonies and played important roles in social affairs. Further, they were allowed to remarry at the death of their husbands. These freedoms would be lost in the centuries to come but were witnessed and recorded by the first non-Indian travelers into the region.

The Greek chronicler Strabo, one of the earliest Westerners to penetrate India, noted that the noblewomen of the Indian courts were trained to handle weapons and routinely accompanied the male warriors into battle. Such women at times rose to absolute control of their domains as observed in the states of Malabar, Travancor, and Attinga by early travelers.

Centuries before the time of Christ, Alexander the Great swept through the Middle East at the head of his Macedonian cavalry, conquering Egypt, Persia, and numerous lesser kingdoms. In 326 B.C., he charged at the western portals of India and was met at the Battle of Hydaspes by King Porus and his allies. One of the Indian commanders on the field that day was the woman warrior Queen Masaga, embodiment of Kali, the Indian goddess of war.[1]

Two hundred years before Alexander's attack on India, Queen Nayanika was ruler and military commander of the Satavahana Empire of the Deccan region (south-central India). The princes of the Deccan, particularly the royal houses of the capital city of Hyderabad, in a centuries-old tradition, maintained a female guard of Urdu-Begani, or "camp followers," who possessed legendary courage and devotion.

In 300 B.C., Princess Kumaradevi married Prince Chandragupta, and they ruled their two kingdoms as co-regents. Both were of the Kshatriya, or warrior caste, where the military/executive function of the warriors was instilled in women as thoroughly as in men. This training of women continued in the Mauryan Dynasty founded by Kumaradevi and Chandragupta. A long tradition of women warriors in the Kerala state is reflected in the weapons art called Theyyan, which is still centered in the city of Malabar. And in southern India, the Nayars maintained a small female army, which, in a history that spanned centuries, was never defeated in battle until it faced the guns of the British army.

The Rajput caste (Kshatriya), with their strong emphasis on martial women, fielded armies that always comprised at least one all-woman troop. The unique way they tied their saris enabled them to ride in battle. As with the other castes and local populations mentioned, the women of the Rajput commonly studied martial arts and fencing.

Queen Orrisa assumed regency when her son died in the late ninth century and immediately involved herself in military adventuring. Queen Kurmadevi of Mevad commanded her armies on the battlefield in the late twelfth century. Queen Didday of Kashmir ruled as full sovereign for twenty-two years, and Queen Jawahirbai fought and died at the head of her army.

South in Sri Lanka, Queen Sugala led her armies against the southern king, her nephew. When pressed by the royal forces, she guided her forces into the mountains, where she built a number of forts. Sugala held out against the king's army for ten years and is remembered in Sri Lankan history as "Sugala the rebel queen fearless."

In the thirteenth century, Sultana Raziyya ruled in Delhi. A Persian historian who met her wrote, "Sultan Raziyya was a great sovereign, and sagacious, just, beneficent, the patron of learned, a dispenser of justice, the cherisher of her subjects, and of warlike talent."[2] When her father named her as his successor just before his death, rioting broke out in the city. Raziyya saw to the quelling of the riots, personally riding as a soldier to pacify her city. She tamed the potentially disruptive bureaucrats and nobles by creating and dispersing a variety of impressive-sounding royal appointments.

As she solidified her power, she dressed like a man, wearing a turban, trousers, coat, and sword, and she appeared in public unveiled. The sultana believed this masculine image would strengthen her control of her empire. Both she and her husband died in battle in 1240 while leading her troops in a bid to suppress another rebellion.

In the fourteenth century, Queen Padmini, a Rajput of Chitor, responded impressively to the insult of a Muslim enemy commander. Her husband, Rama, was captured in a skirmish outside the walls of Chitor and taken to the mogul's camp. Queen Padmini soon received a letter in which the mogul contemptuously suggested that he would return her husband alive and unharmed if she would become his mistress. In answer, she led a hand-picked squad of fifty-nine men in a surprise attack against the mogul's camp, killed him, and returned her husband to safety.

Chitor was a scene of many heroic exploits of India's women warriors. In one losing defensive fight, Queen Karnavatti, dressed in armor, defended the city for several months with the aid of a retinue of women warriors. When all seemed lost, she ordered a great fire built. As the flames leapt high, she walked into them, followed by her female captains.

Queen Durgautti of Gurrah, Hindustan, like the aforementioned Queen Padmini, battled a mogul, Asaph Khan. He assailed her with an army of six thousand horsemen and twelve thousand infantrymen. She responded with fifteen hundred war elephants and a six-thousand-man cavalry. Armed with a lance and a bow and arrow, Queen Durgautti rode a war elephant in the front lines and crushed the khan's army.

Her domains were so rich a prize, however, that Asaph Khan reorganized his army and, with additional artillery pieces, again struck at Queen Durgautti. Assisted by her son, she experienced success until he fell, which caused a general panic among the troops. They retreated; however, the queen drove her war elephant at the Muslim army and rallied her men for one more try.

As the two sides engaged, Durgautti was hit in the eye with an arrow. She broke the arrow shaft off, leaving the point in her eye, and continued her charge. When she was hit again, she demanded her elephant handler kill her for fear that she might be taken by the enemy. He refused, so she wrenched the dagger from him and killed herself.[3]

Queen Nur Jehan faced the Mogul General Mohabat Khan in the early 1600s with more success than that experienced by the heroic Durgautti.[4] For twenty years she remained the de facto leader of Hindustan, ruling for Sultan Jehangir. All responsibility of empire fell to her, including the wars aimed at his empire by Mohabat Khan.

The queen, mounting a strong offense, gathered her army and set out to intercept the slowly approaching Mohabat. The chronicles portray her riding in the *hoodah* of a war elephant with a bow and four large quivers of arrows tied to the inside.

In her excitement to engage the enemy, she moved far in advance of her army with her sons and a few guards, even fording a small river. When the mogul's soldiers opened fire with arrows and muskets, her retainers fled across the river, but Queen Nur Jehan emptied four quivers of war arrows at the enemy as she stood on her elephant's back. The queen's inspired troops counterattacked and defeated the army of Mohabat Khan.

Women warriors also fought on the side of the Muslim invaders. Juliana D'Acosta, "the Warrior Nanny," was born in Bengal, the daughter of a Portuguese trader named Augustin Diaz D'Acosta.[5] After being shipwrecked as a young woman, she was invited by Mogul Aurangzebe, in whose country she found herself, to be the governess of his son, Behadur Shah. Several years later, her student, now named Shah Aulum, succeeded his father and was straightaway challenged by his brothers.

Juliana mounted a war elephant and went into battle at the side of Shah Aulum, advising him and assisting in the command of his troops. Their success was complete, and the grateful Shah Aulum honored Juliana with the title of princess and a powerful marriage arrangement with a high-placed noble of the shah's court. Until she died in 1733, the shah ensured that Juliana lived in luxury, never forgetting her role in gaining him his throne.

In the late 1600s and early 1700s, many noblewomen of the Maratha warrior caste led their armies against the British invaders. Queen Anubai and Queen Ahalyabai were among those Indian noblewomen observed by the British with their troops in the forefront of the fighting. The warrior Marathan princesses also served as notable stateswomen. An Anglo-Indian officer of long standing once observed to English philosopher and economist John Stuart Mill that, if a Hindu principality was vigilantly and economically governed, if order was preserved without oppression, if cultivation was extending and people were prosperous, in three cases out of four, it was under a woman's rule.[6]

Rani (queen) Tarabai of Kolhapur, the daughter of Hambirrao Mohite, a famous Marathan cavalry commander, made her presence felt in eighteenth-century India. In the late 1600s she married Rajaram, a man who, like his father, King Shivaji, dreamed of freeing India from the power of the Muslims. But, after many engagements, he was lost in battle with the armies of the Mogul Aurangzebe, and Tarabai assumed regency for her son.

The mogul's army had left to Queen Tarabai a devastated domain. By 1704 the Maratha strongholds and towns belonged to him, so Tarabai, rather than fight for her own cities, dispatched raids deep into his territory. This tactic confused the mogul, who had expected the queen to attempt to wrest her country from his grasp in a last stand. She sensed his confusion and struck both militarily and financially through judicious use of bribes to Muslim garrison commanders. Panhala (west-central India) was won back through bribes, and Tarabai established it as her command center. She launched attacks from Panhala, retook Satara and the other fortresses of the Maratha, and Aurangzebe retreated with heavy losses. Perhaps hastened by his battering at the hands of Tarabai, he died shortly thereafter in March of 1707.

The queen, expecting the Muslims to come again, rebuilt her strongholds as the sons of Aurangzebe fought over their father's empire. When the dust cleared, Azim Shag was in control. He released from prison a young man named Shahu, who claimed to be the son of Tarabai's husband by a second wife, and sent him south with a military escort to claim his throne from Tarabai.

Although the queen insisted that the man was an imposter, the Marathan nobles were divided, and Satara fell to Shahu, as did Panhala and other important centers. Tarabai sent her armies, under the leadership of two of her chief generals, to confront Shahu's forces in the Poona district, while she rode to her neighbor, the ruler of Savantwadi, and begged for assistance. He provided her with a small army, which she led back to Panhala, and in 1710 she recaptured the city and established a new Maratha capital in the neighboring town of Kolhapur.

Shahu's victories faded as Tarabai, with a newly established base and renewed confidence in her allies, made inroads into his bid for power. Within a year, however, the tide turned once more. One of Tarabai's trusted generals was bribed by an agent of Shahu, and he turned over the Poona, the heart of Maratha territory, to Queen Tarabai's enemies. That, coupled with Shahu's appointment of a new military adviser, the famous Balaji Vishvanath, who immediately upgraded the army, led to the capture of Tarabai and her son. The power of money worked once again, and shortly after their imprisonment the queen and her son escaped. She quickly regrouped her army and retook Satara.

An observer in the early 1700s who saw Rani Tarabai in battle recounts, "Tara Bae did wonders that day, and was admired of all beholders. Men found it difficult to believe that the strong arm which sent them reeling from the saddle was that of a lady."[7]

A British observer on the scene at Satara wrote of Queen Tarabai's actions when disgruntled soldiers attempted to raise a rebellion against her.

> She sternly repressed an attempted mutiny of the garrison by beheading the leader. Such was her superhuman strength of will and vigour that his fellow-conspirators, thinking her an evil spirit, and therefore invincible, let themselves be executed without resistance.[8]

She died in battle against a British soldier she had engaged in single combat. Queen Tarabai fought according to the code of the elite warriors, whereas the British trooper, not encumbered by aristocratic codes of honor, stabbed her in the back.[9]

Mercenary soldiers from various parts of the world were also drawn into the wars in which the Indians strove to drive the British from their homeland. A mysterious German soldier of fortune plays a role in the account of warrior Farzana Somru, daughter of a mogul nobleman named Najaf Khan. Walter Reinhard, known as "the Somber" because of his fits of deep depression, fought in the forces of Najaf Khan against the British in the late eighteenth century. His nom de guerre became shortened and molded by dialect into "Somru."

Farzana Somru joined him in battle after they were married. They fought so effectively together that Najaf Khan, the emperor of Delhi, awarded them a noble's estate near Sarahana complete with a garrison of soldiers under their command. "The Somber" was killed in 1778, leaving Farzana, at age twenty-eight, as sole owner of Sarahana and commander of her own army.

Two years later, when rebels attempted to overthrow Mogul Shah Alam, he requested aid from Farzana, and she led her troops to protect his power. Seven years later, the embattled shah again called on Farzana, and again she saved him. The populace came to believe that she had supernatural power and that by spreading out her scarf in battle she could destroy her enemies. She died, the queen of Sarahana, at the age of eighty-six.[10]

In the mid-1800s the British confronted another woman warrior when they ventured to take the city of Lucknow. Hazrat Mahal, the Muslim queen regent of Oudh, held the British from their objective through her ferocious energy and military genius. According to the reports of newsman W. H. Russell of *The Times* (London), Hazrat commanded an army of women soldiers who guarded her personal quarters and command centers wearing military jackets and white duck trousers, with muskets and bayonets, cross belts, and cartridge boxes. He concluded with a statement of admiration for their "mental power."[11] John Low of the East India Company wrote of Hazrat: "[She is] . . . one of those tigress women, more virile than their husbands, who when finding themselves in a position to gratify their lust for power, have played a considerable part in Oriental history."[12]

The violence of the Indian revolution forced another Indian queen, the Rani Lakshmibai of Jhansi, into action against the British. The noble princess, born Manukarnika in 1830 and reared in a palace in Benares, was educated not only in the basics of reading, writing, history, and mathematics, but also in riding, sword fighting, and archery. Married about

1842 to the Raja of Jhansi, the rani soon came to dominate the weak-willed raja.

When their marriage failed to produce a son, the raja, with the rani's blessing, adopted one and designated him heir apparent. The British did not honor the raja's wishes that his adopted son succeed him with the rani as regent and annexed Jhansi after the raja's death on November 21, 1853. Furious, the Rani Lakshmibai appealed the British decision. The exchanges between the rani and the empire were disrupted by the outbreak of the Indian revolution, and for a time the rani was left alone to rule Jhansi. Her warrior nature emerged as she commanded her troops in a number of skirmishes against local groups she felt were infringing on her territory.

In 1857, a massacre of British men, women, and children in Jhansi by Indian rebel fighters turned the anger of the British against Rani Lakshmibai. The British at Star Fort in Jhansi had surrendered, had laid down their arms, and were walking from the fort when the rebel leader ordered them shot. The government in London claimed they had appealed to Rani Lakshmibai to relieve the embattled garrison of British soldiers and military families and that she had instead given the rebels money, horses, and supplies. She replied that the rebels were threatening to blow up her palace if she did not pay their blackmail.

As warfare became her prime preoccupation, she wore a costume of her own design that blended her image of herself as queen and warrior. She put away her costly saris and donned jodhpurs and a silk blouse with a low-cut bodice. On her head was a red silk turban and her hands were heavy with gold and diamond rings. A sword with a jewel-encrusted scabbard hung at her hip, and two silver pistols rested in her sash.

She practiced martial arts daily with particular emphasis on fighting and shooting from horseback. One of her stable managers, Turab Ali, a rare witness to the rani's practice sessions, later described her practicing with swords in both hands while guiding her horse with the reins in her teeth. The rani would need this practice. At the beginning of the new year, Sir Hugh Rose set out with British forces to take Jhansi.

Rani Lakshmibai raised an army of fourteen thousand and set them to work enhancing the defenses of Jhansi. The British surrounded the fortress town on March 20, 1858, and prepared their siege. The rani gave orders to her soldiers and organized the women of Jhansi to be part of the defense. The British describe watching the women of the city firing batteries, carrying ammunition, and relieving men on the battlements. And, in the midst of it all, the rani, her banner proudly flying from the highest turret, fought along the walls with her troops. One of the British units she faced, the Fourteenth Light Dragoons, noted in their historical records that she was "a perfect Amazon in bravery . . . just the sort of daredevil woman soldiers admire."[13]

Seeing that Jhansi would fall, the rani slipped out of the fortress with several of her guards and rode for the rebel stronghold of her neighbor, Tatya Tope at Kalpi. Her absence was discovered by the British, who pursued her. A better rider, the rani astride a champion stallion soon outdistanced all but one, Lieutenant Bowker. The Indian accounts state that the two fought with swords at Bhander, a crossroads where the rani had stopped for nourishment. The queen disabled Bowker and continued into Kalpi, ultimately traveling over one hundred miles in a twenty-four-hour period.

Rani Lakshmibai was welcomed as a hero by the warriors of Kalpi, the armies of the various Indian nobles who had joined the rebel cause. She enhanced her reputation by leading troops to take the British fortress at Gwalior, a much needed morale boost for the rebels. On this occasion, Rao Sahib, the rebel commander, presented Rani Lakshmibai with a fabulous pearl necklace he had "liberated" from the treasury at Gwalior as a token of gratitude for her contributions. Rao Sahib's "gift of honor" was vindicated shortly thereafter when the rani led a successful defense of Kalpi against the British when Tatya Tope was away raising new troops.

The rani of Jhansi fought her last battle on June 15, 1859. On the morning of the final British attack against Gwalior, she dressed in armor, belted on her sword and pistols, and rallied her soldiers with the parting words, "If killed in battle, we enter heaven, and if victorious, we rule the earth."

The rani commanded the defense of the eastern side of the city. She fought on foot and on horseback, moving fearlessly into breaches in the walls to stop the rush of the British infantry. Sometime on the second day of the battle, Rani Lakshmibai was killed. Lord Canning, present at the battle, wrote in a notebook found after his death in 1862 that the rani was shot in the back by a trooper of the Eighth Hussars. When the mortally wounded rani turned on the soldier and fired at him, he ran her through with his sword.

She was taken into the fortress by her troops. According to the legends surrounding this battle, she died after distributing the famous pearls to those who had stood by her. She was cremated, and her ashes were buried with great ceremony in Gwalior. Sir Hugh Rose wrote in his epitaph, "The Rani was remarkable for her bravery, cleverness, and perseverance; her generosity to her subordinates was unbounded. These qualities combined with her rank, rendered her the most dangerous of all the rebel leaders." The squadron commander of the Eighth Hussars added that "in her death, the rebels lost their bravest and best military leader."[14]

During the time that the rani of Jhansi led her soldiers against the British, Prince Ranjeet Singh of Lahore had a female guard composed of 150 women. They carried bows and arrows and, richly uniformed, rode white chargers in formal parade. During the same time, at Lucknow, travelers' accounts describe a body of female soldiers uniformed in red tunics and green trousers, carrying muskets and swords. Court accounts reveal that the shifting of various power factions at the highest levels of government were often driven by the influence of the female army.[15]

The tradition of the women warriors of India has continued into the twentieth century. The struggle against the British in the 1900s led some Indian women into roles of terrorist and assassin. Madame Chand, a leader of the Indian Independence Movement, called on the Indians living in Europe to practice with firearms so they could "shoot the English out of the land we love." She died in her midseventies believed by some of her followers to have been a reincarnation of the war goddess Kali.

Bengal produced notable female terrorists, who as a group were "elite, articulate, unique, and few in number."[16] Bina Dass was one of five female assassins working for independence in the 1930s. One of the youngest Indian freedom fighters, Rani Gaidinliu, joined the cause in the 1920s at age thirteen and was leading guerrilla fighting units by age sixteen. Captured by the British and jailed for fourteen years, she was freed by Nehru in 1947. And lastly, in World War II, Colonel Lakshmi Swaminathan commanded an all-woman battalion called the Rani Jhansi Regiment of the Indian National Army in a successful attack against an enemy force in Burma.

In conclusion, the impact of Phoolan Devi reveals the continuing presence of the Indian woman warrior. Richard Corliss, writing in the August 14, 1995, issue of *Time*, opens his article "Outlawed!" with:

> Rape victim. Marauder. Murderer. Superstar! Phoolan Devi, an outcast Hindu woman, became a folk hero as head of a band of outlaws preying on India's corrupt elite. Part Joan of Arc, part Ma Barker, on Feb. 14, 1981, she staged her own St. Valentine's Day massacre, leading the slaughter of 22 villagers she suspected of aiding her enemies. Yet her surrender, in 1983, was on her own terms, to the cheers of 10,000 supporters. On her release from prison last year [1994], three political parties asked her to run for office.[17]

Like many women warriors, Hannah Snell disguised herself as a man to go to war. In the mideighteenth century, she joined England's Frazer Marines to search for her lost husband. When her unit shipped to India, she was among the first to face fire in the battle for Pondicherry. At one point during the battle, Snell spent seven consecutive nights on picket duty and endured several injuries. After she retired from the military in 1750, Snell published her autobiography, went on a lecture tour, and opened an inn named "The Woman Warrior."

CHAPTER 5

British Isles: Queen by the Wrath of God

Though the British Isles had been inhabited from earliest times, the coming of the Celts in the fourth century B.C. inaugurated one of the most dynamic chapters in the history of those fabled islands. Originating in the steppes of western Asia, ancestors of the Celts lived along the Danube River in the third millennium B.C. Perhaps responding to the chaos of the titanic battles of Middle Eastern empires, which erupted with increasing regularity, Celtic pioneers moved west and north into Europe.

About 700 B.C. somewhere north of the Alps, the Celts learned the mysteries of iron working. Soon, their metal plows, iron-shod chariot wheels, and long swords created an elite warrior caste in which warfare and wealth were based on metal. Farm tools of metal made intensive agriculture successful, providing a subsistence base for warfare and exploration. Metal weapons convinced the Romans, after confronting the Celtic swords, to strengthen their shields and exchange their leather helmets for metal ones. In 100 B.C., the Greek geographer Strabo wrote of the Celts, "The whole race is madly fond of war, high-spirited and quick to do battle."[1] He was referring to women as well as men.

In one of the earliest recorded accounts of warfare against Celtic tribes, the Roman general Ammianus Marcellinus wrote that the Celts were:

> . . . quarrelsome and arrogant in the extreme. In a fight any one of them can resist several strangers at a time, with no other help than his wife's who is even more formidable, neck veins swollen with rage, swinging their robust and snow-white arms, using their feet and their fists and landing blows that seem triggered off by a catapult.[2]

The ancient traveler Diodorus of Sicily wrote, "Among the Gauls the women are nearly as tall as the men, who they rival in courage," and

51

Chadwick, in *The Celts*, noted that ". . . women warriors were an institutionalized part of Celtic life. . . ."[3] Plutarch, an observer when the Roman legions tangled with Celtic tribesmen at Aque Sextiae in 102 B.C., wrote that "the fight had been no less fierce with the women than with the men themselves . . . the women charged with swords and axes and fell upon their opponents uttering a hideous outcry." Dio Cassius recorded that the Romans found the bodies of women warriors clad in armor among the corpses that covered the battlefields along the Danube where the Romans engaged two Germanic tribes, the Marcomanni and the Quadi.[4]

The oral tradition in Ireland has carried from ancient times a story, *The Tain*, about a cattle raid. In this most venerated work of Irish traditional culture, the central character is Queen Medb, a woman warrior. Leader of her own army, she boasted to the king of Ireland, "I outdid them in grace and giving, and battle and warlike combat."[5]

The Tain revolves around the queen and her bellicose behavior toward her father, the King of Ireland, and her husband, King Ailill. She taunted her husband with her greater private fortune, which entitled her to control the castles under his sway.

Medb attempted to acquire a prize bull, the Brown Bull of Cualnge, to further discomfort her husband. In Celtic times, cattle provided the measure of value and a prime medium of exchange; therefore, possession of the prize bull would give her the largest bank note as well as a source of more prize cattle.

Medb offered the bull's owner, Dare, son of Fiachna, land, chariots, and even herself for a night or two. When Dare replied that he would rather keep his bull, the outraged queen declared war on Ulster.

Modern researchers are reassessing the question of Queen Medb's historical reality. Boulding wrote:

> . . . I am inclined to think there really was a Queen Mab (Maeve, Medb) of Connaught in western Ireland. . . . For Medb we even have a description of her position in a battle formation. There may also have been a "military academy" for young men and women run by the woman, Scathach. There are many references to her, and she was apparently a prophetess as well as a military strategist and teacher.[6]

Chadwick agrees with Boulding and adds that ". . . there remain a few historians who habitually deny the likelihood of such women having existed outside of epics and fairy tales, though it requires lead-lined blinders to hold such a belief in light of the evidence."[7]

A contemporary of Queen Medb, Aife, Queen of Alba (modern Scotland), led a troop of women warriors and like her sister, Scathach of Skye, with whom she often joined forces, directed a martial arts academy for elite young men and women.[8]

Celtic tribal custom stipulated the socioeconomic status of the Celtic women warriors, particularly those of the upper classes. Three kinds of marriage centered on the relative financial worth of the bride and groom independent of each other. Queen Medb was referring to this law when she harangued her husband in *The Tain*. If a married woman possessed a greater fortune than her husband, she controlled everything.

The ancient Irish viewed the king primarily as a military commander and defender of the realm. When a queen superseded her husband's wealth—as Queen Medb was busy doing when she attempted to acquire the champion bull—she assumed responsibility for the defense of the kingdom. The model relationship between Irish king and queen also applied at the level of lord and lady of private manors and estates, thus explaining the not unusual appearance of Irish noblewomen in military roles. Noblewomen, therefore, received martial arts instruction as part of their education. This same arrangement was practiced at the time among the Bretons and the Welsh.

An additional insight into the warrior woman's role in ancient Celtic society is revealed in the narrative of Macha Moup Guadh, "Macha of the Red Tresses." In 377 B.C. Ireland, kingship was bequeathed through the female line, and at the death of her father, King Aedh Ruadh, the seventy-sixth king of Ireland, Macha was requested to name a successor. She named herself to the shocked surprise of her brothers, who straightaway declared war on her. Macha killed one of them and captured her five nephews. The second brother's anger was assuaged when she married him, though she kept for herself the rule of Ireland. The Venerable Bede notes that the ancient Picts (allies of the Scots), like the early Irish, also tended to select a king from a female royal line.[9]

In A.D. 43 after several centuries of dominance and power, the death knell of Celtic suzerainty sounded when the Roman Emperor Claudius dispatched General Julius Caesar to conquer Britain. At first, some of the Celtic tribes accepted the tribute relationship with Rome; their nobles carefully cultivated the Roman overlords, while other tribes remained unrelentingly belligerent. Cartimandua, Queen of Brigantes (modern Wales), represents the first reaction, and Boudicea, Queen of the Iceni, the second.

In A.D. 51, Queen Cartimandua clarified her policy toward the Romans with one gesture. When the famed Celtic rebel war leader Caratacus fled to her for sanctuary, she arrested him and delivered him to the Romans, employing the opportunity to reaffirm her grateful acceptance of Rome's "protection."

Cartimandua further demonstrated her astute sense of survival a year or so later when her consort Venutius bid to raise a rebellion against her.

She imprisoned his brother, and Venutius responded, as she knew he would, by leading an army to his brother's aid—the gesture Cartimandua required to rouse the Romans to her defense. She explained that if Venutius controlled her kingdom, the Romans would no longer have a "flexible" client queen to manage but rather a rebellious nobleman. With Rome's assistance, she held her throne. While Venutius organized another attack, Cartimandua took his armor bearer Vellocatus as her consort; when Venutius advanced the second time, she sent Vellocatus against him and once more summoned the Romans to her aid.

Queen Cartimandua's Brigantes confederacy accepted a situation where, though they acknowledged the overlordship of Rome, they maintained control of their lands and vassals. The Iceni tribe, centered in modern Norfolk and the north of Suffolk, however, was on a collision course with the Roman invaders.

In A.D. 44, after defeating a British lord named Cassivellaunus, Caesar overcame several local tribes, one of them "the great Iceni," by heavy-handed diplomacy. The newly appointed Roman governor of Britain, Ostorius Scapula, had experienced dangerous hostility from the native population and rising guerrilla actions against the Roman garrisons, and he ordered a general disarmament. It was noted at the time that the Iceni were particularly strident in their protest of this action.

Iceni noblewoman Boudicea entered the story in A.D. 49, when she married Prasutagus, king of the Iceni. Under King Prasutagus and Queen Boudicea, the Iceni contrived to endure their tense relationship with the Romans for the next decade. But when King Prasutagus died in A.D. 60 and his will (in which half the Iceni territory was left to the Roman emperor, as was customary to ensure security of the lands, and half to Queen Boudicea) was not honored by the Roman procurator Catus Decianus, the Iceni hatred toward the Romans became a bomb waiting to be ignited.

The situation exploded into open rebellion when Catus Decianus sent his representatives to enforce his claim on the entire Iceni kingdom and was challenged by Queen Boudicea. The Romans publicly flogged her and raped her two teenage daughters. An understandably furious Boudicea vowed to destroy the Romans and organized the Iceni and allied tribes for rebellion.

The Roman writers Tacitus and Dio Cassius witnessed the events surrounding Boudicea's rebellion and interviewed witnesses in developing their accounts. Tacitus was privy to the inner workings of the Roman colonial government because his father-in-law, who would finally confront Boudicea and her Britons in a decisive battle, was a member of Governor Suetonius's staff.

Dio Cassius portrayed Queen Boudicea as tall and powerfully built with a mass of curly red hair that fell to her waist. Her loud voice commanded, and her eyes blazed with intensity. As she addressed her warriors prior to her first raid, Boudicea wore a multicolored tunic over which she had draped a thick cape fastened with a large piece of jewelry. Around her neck hung the famous Celtic torque, a thick golden choker. She addressed her troops from the back of her war chariot, gesturing violently with her spear as she fired their spirits for the fight.

As Boudicea's army of over one hundred thousand was massing, the procurator Catus Decianus ("he whose rapacity had driven the province to war" in Tacitus's words) fled to Gaul with all his staff, effectively leaving the Romans with no central government to confront her.[10]

In A.D. 60, Queen Boudicea struck at Camulodunum (Colchester). The town lay helpless before her, largely because the Romans could not conceive of their local vassals, no matter how rancorous, organizing an assault against a Roman town. Boudicea's warriors slaughtered the inhabitants and set the town on fire, a fire that burned with such intensity that to this day archaeologists and local builders encounter, ten or more feet below the surface, a red layer, which is indicative of a horrendous fire capable of melting brick.

Camulodunum in ruins, Boudicea turned her forces toward London. The Roman commander of the Ninth Legion, Petilius Cerialis, led his troops to the relief of Camulodunum but was ambushed by Boudicea's warriors north of the city and defeated.

The military governor of Britain, Suetonius, was campaigning against rebels in the north, but upon learning that the procurator had fled, marched his legions to defend London against Queen Boudicea's army. On arriving, however, his expert eye discerned that London was incapable of an effective defense against the thousands of warriors following the Iceni queen. He abandoned the city to her to find a more suitable battleground. Tacitus, at the scene at the time, wrote in his *Annals*:

> He decided to sacrifice the one town to save the general situation. Undeflected by the prayers and tears of those who begged for his help, he gave the signal to move, taking into his column any who could join it. Those who were unfit for war because of their sex, or too aged to go or too fond of the place to leave, were butchered by the enemy. The same massacre took place at the city of Verulamium (St. Albans), for the barbarian British, happiest when looting and unenthusiastic about real effort, bypassed the forts and the garrisons and headed for the spots where they knew the most undefended booty lay. Something like 70,000 Roman citizens and other friends of Rome died in the places I have mentioned. The Britons took no prisoners, sold no captives as slaves and went in

for none of the usual trading of war. They wasted no time in getting down to the bloody business of hanging, burning, and crucifying.[11]

Dio Cassius's account of Queen Boudicea's massacre in London is even more gruesome than that of Tacitus.

Those who were taken captive by the Britons were subjected to every known outrage. The worst and most bestial atrocity committed by their captors was the following. They hung up naked the noblest and most distinguished women and then cut off their breasts and sewed them to their mouths, in order to make the victim appear to be eating them. Afterwards they impaled the women on sharp skewers run lengthwise through their entire body.[12]

The warriors following Queen Boudicea included both men and women. General Suetonius, when speaking to his troops before a battle with Boudicea, scornfully stated, as Tacitus recorded it, that the Britons' ranks comprised more women than fighting men.

The Romans had massed an army of ten thousand as Suetonius maneuvered for the best position to encounter Boudicea's hosts. He hoped that her alliance would disintegrate, as had happened to the Britons who endeavored to stop Julius Caesar, but with Boudicea in charge the Britons not only did not disband, they actually grew in number and went on the offensive against Suetonius. Eventually, running short of supplies and realizing that his strategic retreats were exhausting his army, Suetonius made his stand.

The site of the battlefield is unknown, although many sites vie for this distinction, but the particulars of the battle were recorded. Suetonius, outnumbered almost twenty to one, positioned his legions in a small valley that opened onto a plain, forcing the Britons to approach up a slight rise. Boudicea's forces, estimated at over two hundred thousand, came thundering in wild disarray as was their custom. Behind them, in hundreds of wagons and chariots, rode the wives and children, prepared to watch their warriors deal the final blow to the boxed-in and outnumbered Romans.

The Roman military machine, however, had been honed in thousands of victorious battles that had led to the establishment of one of the world's greatest empires. When Boudicea ordered the charge, the Romans waited until the Britons reached javelin range and were fatigued by their uphill run. The sudden rain of heavy javelins, followed immediately by the disciplined quick-marching advance of the Roman phalanxes, pushed the Britons into the caravan that had followed them. Caught between the Romans and the chaos of carts, milling horses, and cattle, Boudicea's army was slaughtered by the Romans. Tacitus stated that eighty thousand dead Britons, men and women, littered the battlefield. Boudicea's fate is not known with any precision; however, most commentators relate that she committed suicide after her defeat.

What Boudicea and her warriors could not accomplish, the invasions of the Germanic Saxons and Angles in the first century A.D. did—the banishment of Roman influence in Britain, a military exercise in which Anglo-Saxon men and women participated.

The Saxon male warriors of the first century after Christ regarded their wives as equal partners in the struggle for existence. The marriage ritual comprised practical and symbolic elements that foreshadowed the relationship. In the ancient wedding rite, husbands of the Germanic tribes provided their wives with oxen, a horse and bridle, and a shield and spear or sword; she, in return, presented him with an article of armor or weaponry.[13]

Throughout the recorded history of the Angles and the Saxons, accounts describe women seizing control of territory and effectively defending their claim with massed armed force. In 722, for example, Aethelburg, estranged wife of King Ine of Wessex, led her army in the destruction of Taunton, one of King Ine's towns. Several decades later, the Anglo-Saxon Queen Cynethryth of the midland kingdom of Mercia, wife of King Offa, inherited in widowhood a large domain, which she ruled as lady abbess and defended with force against attacks by the soldiers of Archbishop Wulfed. The fate of the kingdom of Mercia became almost constantly enmeshed with the activities of women warriors following her example. Queen Cynethryth is celebrated in history as the only Anglo-Saxon queen who coined money bearing her own likeness.[14]

The image of women warriors is evoked in this Anglo-Saxon "charm" against a stitch, or a sudden, sharp pain.

> Loud were they, lo, loud, when they rode over the barrow.
> Bold were they, when they rode over the land.
> Shield thyself now and you might escape this violent attack.
> I stood under the linden, under the lightshield when the Mighty
>   Women made ready their strength.
> They sent forth screaming spears.[15]

Aethelflaed, the queen of Mercia in the late ninth and early tenth centuries, vowed a life of chastity after nearly dying in childbirth and applied her energies to the military pursuits of her husband. Their primary problem was the invading Danes and their occupation of Mercian territory.

Their second difficulty held the key to the solution of the first—the need to unite Mercia into a coherent kingdom.

"The Lady of the Mercians" accompanied her husband in battle until his death in 912. Afterward, she joined the efforts of her father, Alfred the Great, to dislodge and weaken the Danes. Her military employment of the warriors from the western Midlands enabled her brother, King Edward of Wessex, to thwart the Viking warriors. Her strategies led to the taking of Wales, victory over the Viking settlements in eastern England, and the ultimate consolidation of Mercia.

The Welsh drew Aethelflaed's ire for their assistance, or seeming assistance, to the Danes. She conducted battles against the Welsh and, after a string of victories, forced them into the status of tribute-paying vassals. In 918, she took the town of Derby from the Danes; in 920, she commanded the capture of Leicester and York.

She constructed the fortress towns of Warwick and Stafford and restored the Roman wall at Chester. Salmonson noted, "Had Aethelflaed not been the daughter of Alfred the Great, we might not have any knowledge whatsoever of the greatest military commander in medieval England."[16] The Mercians decided "lady" and "queen" insufficiently portrayed her luster and dubbed her "lord" and "king." She died in battle against the Danes at Tamworth in 922.

*　*　*

In the tenth century, an eminent figure among the Danes, Cnut of Denmark, conquered portions of England and Norway. In *Romeo and Juliet* fashion, he fell in love with an English noblewoman, Aelfgifu of Northampton, and she with him. Although King Cnut entered a politically advantageous marriage with the sister of the Duke of Normandy, he retained his devotion and respect for Aelfgifu and begat two children with her. The eldest he placed on the throne of Norway, with Aelfgifu as queen regent. Her rule was so fraught with violence and blood that forever after her name became synonymous with the worst of times.

Queen Aelfgifu was driven from Norway after the death of King Cnut. Her power was such, however, that she returned to England and convinced the nobles to select her second son, Harold Harefoot, as king. Another woman warrior, Emma of Normandy, queen of Ethelred the Unready, king of England, rejected Harefoot's suitability and successfully warred against him to support her own son's claim to the throne.

In 1075 in Norfolk, the home country of Boudicea's Iceni, a young woman named Emma was forced into military action when her husband, the rebel earl of Norfolk, was compelled to flee to France. She held his central fortress at Norwich against the royal troops and effectively proved that she could not be driven from her castle. Ultimately tiring of the game, she accepted surrender terms in which, in exchange for the castle, she received safe conduct to her husband in France. In the same period, Matilda of Ramsbury, mistress of Bishop Roger of Salisbury, held his castle at Devizes in his absence.

Castle defense against sieges and storming assaults required complex knowledge of arms possibilities (what holds the advantage, three swordsmen or two pikemen; could a light cavalry charge be successful against massed archers; etc.) and an ability to inspire confidence and morale under pressure. This type of warfare, very often faced by women warriors of the British Isles and elsewhere, was a complex psychophysical assault in which frenzied attacks would be followed by several days and nights of bombardment as prelude to a week of apparent neglect, which was punctuated by another attack at a different place on the walls. The defense commanders had to be adept at reading strategy in the deployment and arms of the enemy. Not only were they required to understand the nature of siege warfare, they had to transcend conventional siege thinking, that being the only difference in a relative standoff.

Women defenders knew the techniques of warfare, and many possessed the nerve and intelligence required for success. They understood the terrible burden placed upon them when ordered by their husbands to hold the fortress in their absence at all cost. Warfare was the major occupation of the lords of the estates, and their successes—expressed in booty, tribute, and ransom—provided a high standard of living for their queens and courts.

When the lord relinquished command of the castle to the queen, he was entrusting both of their futures and, as was often the case, the lives of his heirs to the military skills, courage, and good judgment of the lady of the castle. The resources in manpower and munitions left for the lady were often pitifully inadequate for a major defensive fight. In some cases, with less than a dozen guards, pages, stable boys, family members, and ladies-in-waiting, the lady of the castle had to resist an army of several hundred.

* * *

In 1114 German Emperor Henry V married the daughter of King Henry I of England, a twelve-year-old girl named Maud. Maud's brother William, heir to the throne of England, drowned six years later, leaving Maud, the only surviving child of the king, the inheritor of the British throne. When her husband died in 1125, she moved to her father's castle in England, where he groomed her to be queen.

Stephen of Blois, King Henry's nephew, protested and had himself crowned king, thereby initiating a succession war that would involve Maud and him in twenty years of carnage. Assisting Stephen was his wife,

Queen Matilda "the Good," a woman warrior who, like Queen Maud, led both castle defenses and sieges. Maud had a warrior on her side—her mother, Queen Adeliza, who joined with her in September 1139 when Queen Maud landed in southern England to organize war against Stephen.

Stephen attacked without delay, laying siege to Maud and her fighters in Arundel Castle. She conducted a stout defense, which moved Stephen, who did not want history to remember him as a knight who attacked the manor of two highborn women, to offer them safe conduct to a nearby ally. Later, Maud captured Stephen and chained him in Bristol Castle, despite the pleas of Queen Matilda the Good and her son.

Next, Queen Maud turned her attention to the town of Winchester, which was under the authority of Stephen's brother, Bishop Henry of Blois, and offered him a straightforward proposition: either leave his brother's cause and join her or she would "lead all the hosts of England against him at once."[17] Henry complied, and with her newfound military strength Queen Maud rode roughshod over the church and nobility, confiscating estates, reneging on royal agreements, and bleeding both of their treasuries as fast as she could.

Her old foe, Queen Matilda the Good, rallying support for her imprisoned husband's cause, blocked Maud in her castle at Winchester. Maud escaped to Gloucester, her brother's town, with only one companion. To avoid Stephen and Matilda's supporters, she was compelled to enter her sanctuary wrapped in a loose shroud, disguised as a corpse.

Her brother Richard aided her escape to her primary castle at Oxford, where she once again was besieged by the newly released Stephen. As winter descended, Maud's garrison weakened in the face of Stephen's pressure, but one day, looking from her tower over the snowy fields, Maud had an inspiration. The white bed linens were made into clothing, and on a snowy night in late December 1142, Maud led her camouflaged followers through King Stephen's front lines and six miles of darkness to Abingdon, where she acquired horses to complete her escape. In 1154 when Stephen died, his son Henry II was crowned king of England. Maud, accepting defeat, moved to Normandy, where she led a quiet life until her death in 1167.

During Maud's struggle with Stephen of Blois, local Welsh princes in the south were locked in battle with the invading Normans; true to type, the lesser nobles seized the opportunity to mount coups. In 1136, one such usurper was supported by a prince named Gruffyd ap Thys, who was accompanied in battle by his wife, Lady Gwenllian, at the head of her personal army. She also led her warriors at the struggle for Cydeli but later fell in battle. The battlefield at which she died is today called Maes Gwenllian.

In 1160, Nicola de La Haye was honored for her martial skill by being named the sheriff of Lincolnshire. A baroness and hereditary castellan of Lincoln, Nicola developed her stalwart reputation by excelling in all aspects of warfare. She was effective in leading offensive engagements and in defending besieged Lincoln Castle.[18]

Kildrummy Castle in Scotland was held by Lady Christian Bruce against David the Strathboie during the time of Edward I (1239–1307). When David was killed in battle, his widow staged a successful defense of his castle at Lochindorb against three thousand angry Scot supporters of Lady Bruce.

The sisters of Lady Christian Bruce—Marjory Bruce, Mary Bruce, and Isobel, Countess of Buchan—can also be numbered as women warriors of the Scottish nobility. Mary Bruce, when captured by the English, was placed in a sturdy cage in a tower at Roxburgh Castle, where she languished for eight years until a prisoner exchange set her free.[19]

Christian's sister Isobel left her husband, the earl of Buchan, to go to war for the Bruce, despite the earl's disapproval. Adding injury to insult, she appropriated his prize war horses and many of his knights when she left, leading her husband to issue a warrant for her death.

The lady was not to be obstructed. She was of the line of Macduff, that noble lineage that eternally had held the right and duty to induct a Scottish king. On Sunday, March 29, the countess and the nobles installed Bruce in the Scottish chair of state at Scone. When Isobel was ultimately captured, King Edward ordered her delivered to Berwick with these instructions:

> Let her be closely confined in an abode of stone and iron made in the shape of a cross and let her be hung up out of doors in the open air at Berwick, that both in life and after her death, she may be a spectacle and eternal reproach to travelers.[20]

That women warriors were taken seriously by the male warriors of the time is affirmed by the presence of women in tournament fighting. A British chronicle distributed in 1348 stated:

> . . . when the tournaments were held, in every place a company of ladies appeared in the diverse and marvelous dress of a man, to number sometimes of about forty, sometimes fifty, ladies from the more handsome and the more beautiful, but not the better ones, of the entire kingdom; in divided tunics, with small hoods, even having across their stomachs, below the middle, knives which they vulgarly called daggers, placed in pouches from above. Thus they came on excellent chargers or other horses splendidly adorned, to

the place of the tournament, and in such manner they spent and wasted their riches and injured their bodies with abuses and with ludicrous wantonness.[21]

Knight Richard Shaw wrote of fighting a Flemish knight whom he barely bested—he received wounds, and the Flemish fighter died. When aides opened the dead warrior's armor, they found a female. Her true identity was never discovered.

Agnes Hotot of the House of Dudley wielded a lance in a contest of arms with a man whom her father had challenged for some perceived insult. The father was ill on the day of the duel, so Agnes donned his armor and overcame her opponent, exposing her breasts to let him know that he had been beaten by a woman.

In Scotland in 1334, Lady Agnes "Black Agnes" Randolph, wife of the earl of Dunbar, fought in defense of Castle Dunbar in her husband's absence. Her adversary was England's earl of Salisbury, a specialist in military engineering and technology. For five months the English general laid siege to Dunbar and directed some of the most advanced machinery of warfare that had appeared in England. Black Agnes, leading her troops, withstood him and after each bombardment ordered her maids to dust the furniture and shake the rugs in her chambers. This act of normalcy was tailored to irritate Salisbury as he attempted to terrorize the inhabitants of Dunbar with his mines and cannon.

When the bombardment failed, Salisbury's men built a *testudo* or "tortoise," a wheeled covered shed under which his men worked battering rams. Agnes observed the apparatus for a period before ordering her men to swing a large rock over the edge of the battlements with a makeshift crane and drop it on the *testudo*. As Salisbury's men fled the crushed war machine, Agnes commanded that fire be dropped on the remains.

Salisbury next bribed a guard to admit a small raiding party and him into the castle. The guard proved more loyal to Agnes, and the lady almost trapped the English earl within her walls.

Finally, Salisbury brought Agnes's brother, the Earl of Moray, from prison to Castle Dunbar. He displayed the earl and threatened to kill him if she did not capitulate. Her response came in two parts. First, because the castle did not belong to her, she could not surrender it. Second, because her brother had no children, his death would simply assure that she would inherit the earldom of Moray and with it even greater power. Salisbury reluctantly returned the earl of Moray to prison.

On June 10, 1338, Salisbury withdrew from Castle Dunbar. Agnes passed away in 1369. A small poem crafted by some members of Salisbury's army conveys his attitude about Black Agnes:

She kept stir in tower and trench,
    that brawling, boisterous Scottish wench.
Came I early, came I late,
    I found Agnes at the gate.[22]

The English side in the struggle with the Scots in the fourteenth century boasted one of the most famous warriors of the time, Philippa of Hainault, queen of England, wife of Edward III. On October 12, 1346, Philippa assumed the role of commander in chief in England, while her husband, fighting on the continent, laid siege to Calais. She battled David the Bruce, king of the Scots, who was invading northern England in King Edward's absence.

Placing field command of her twelve-thousand-soldier army in the hands of Lord Percy, Queen Philippa rode with him to advise and direct as commander in chief. David the Bruce's and Queen Philippa's forces joined battle at Neville's Cross, a site near Durham. The Scots were destroyed; more than fifteen thousand died at the hands of the English, and David the Bruce was captured by Philippa and placed in the tower of London.

Queen Philippa wished to personally inform her husband Edward in France that she had captured the Scottish king, so she hurried to his encampment outside the besieged city of Calais, where she was given a thunderous welcome for her victory by the English army. In Edward's field tent, Philippa put her mark on history once more, not as a war leader this time, but as an exemplar of honor and compassion. Edward had, a few days before Philippa's arrival, agreed with the mayor of Calais that he would drop the siege if the six ringleaders of the rebellion were turned over, barefooted and bareheaded, with hangman's nooses around their necks and the keys to the city in their hands.

Within the city, six heroic men volunteered to appear before Edward, knowing that they were walking to their deaths. When Philippa learned of their selfless gesture to save the citizens of Calais, she knelt before her husband and asked for the lives of the six, basing her argument on points of honor, compassion, and humanity. His reply, recorded by a scribe at the time:

Ah, Madam. I could have wished you had been anywhere but here. Your prayers are so forcible that I cannot resist them. To you, then, I give them up.[23]

Queen Philippa took the hostages to her quarters, where she gave them a feast, new clothing, money, and their freedom. To Philippa's credit may be added the founding of Queen's College at Oxford and the patronage of

Chaucer. One of her most significant long-term projects, the support of a Flemish textile-making colony in Norwich in 1335, was the basis of the world-famous textile industries in the British Isles today.[24]

In fifteenth-century England, the War of the Roses, that struggle between the Houses of York and Lancaster for rights to the throne of England, was powerfully animated by one of the leading enemies of the Yorkists, Margaret of Anjou, daughter of King Rene of Naples and Sicily and wife of King Henry VI of England. Margaret's strong will quickly led her to dominate her husband, and in time, with the assistance of the duke of Suffolk, she took de facto control of England. She led her troops in twelve straight victories during the war of succession, including the defeat and death of the duke of York and the defeat of the earl of Warwick at St. Albans. However, when she went against Edward, her forces were overcome, but she did manage to escape.

In France, having convinced King Louis XI to rearm her, Margaret returned to England, took the field, and was defeated once again by Yorkist forces. She took refuge with her young son in the forest, where she met a bandit chief who aided her escape to France. She gathered yet another army and returned to England.

She landed near Weymouth and was forced into battle with Lancastrian forces led by Edward of York, later to be King Edward IV. Margaret lost again and was imprisoned for four years until King Louis XI paid fifty thousand crowns for her ransom. He elicited from her a public promise that she would never again go to war. Queen Margaret of Anjou passed away several years later in 1482.[25]

A contemporary of Margaret's, Mary of Guelders, Queen of Scotland, experienced Queen Margaret's generosity in 1460 when, newly widowed, the Scottish queen found herself in charge of the wars raging between England and her homeland. With Margaret of Anjou's support, she carried off a successful siege against Roxburgh and forced the surrender of Berwick.

In 1558, Elizabeth I became the queen of England. Her reign was one of the high-water marks in English cultural history. It was the time of William Shakespeare, the rise of the Anglican Church, and the development of the world-conquering English navy. Elizabeth herself had moments as a woman warrior; in fact, she was quite commonly seen in that light. For example, in 1588 at Tilbury, she appeared before her troops to encourage them in their impending encounter with the Spanish Armada. A chronicler of the time described Elizabeth "habited like an Amazonia Queen, Buskind and plumed, having a golden Truncheon, Gantlet and Gorget; Armes sufficient to express her high and magnanimous spirit."[26]

In 1571 Margaret Campbell, lady of Towie, was summoned by Captain Kerr, the queen's representative, to surrender Castle Corgarff. When Lady

Margaret refused, Kerr reviled her in coarse language. The lady of Towie showed her annoyance at this arrogance by pulling a pistol from the belt of her guard and shooting Captain Kerr in the leg. Infuriated, Kerr swore that he would burn Castle Corgarff and all its inhabitants with no hope of quarter. The lady of Towie replied with a scornful laugh.

Kerr directed his men to stack combustibles around the lady's tower and set it afire. When Margaret tried to lower her young daughter in a basket, Kerr impaled the child on his lance. Castle Corgarff was eventually reduced to a pile of smoking rubble, and Margaret Campbell, lady of Towie, her stepson, her three children, and her domestics—thirty-eight in all—were burned alive. The event became a rallying cry for the Scots.[27]

Women were also active in piracy during this time. In the late sixteenth century, Grace O'Malley (also Granny Wale, Graun'ya, Granuaile), an Irish pirate captain known as "the Queen of the West," preyed on English and Spanish shipping. It is said that she buried over nine tons of treasure along the Irish coast.

Grace was born at sea in 1530 into a family of pirates and entrepreneurs centered on Clare Island, off the coast of County Mayo. The family's legitimate and illegitimate wealth was protected by a series of fortresses and fortified harbors where the O'Malley fleet berthed in safety.

As a young girl, Grace exhibited the qualities that endeared her to her buccaneer father when she hunted a brood of eagles that had been attacking the lambs in one of his flocks. In her fight with the powerful birds, she was raked across the forehead with sharp talons, leaving a pattern of scars that marked her for life.

Her father, though having a son, trained Grace in land and sea warfare and groomed her to inherit his fleet, castles, and fortune. She so successfully raided the lucrative sea trade moving between Cork and Spain that Queen Elizabeth I of England put a five-hundred-pound bounty on her head and sent troops to take her central castle. The English soldiers were turned back. Queen Elizabeth never sought to engage Grace in sea battles, because she was advised that the Queen of the West would destroy the English navy.

In 1583 Grace's second husband finally persuaded her to end her war against Queen Elizabeth and become her ally. The English queen invited Grace to London to cement their alliance; on the way, she gave birth to a son whom she named Tibbot of the Ships. Several days later, a Turkish warship attacked her. True to form, Grace appeared on deck with pistols in each hand to assist in repelling the boarders.

One of her greatest victories came in her sixtieth year when her fleet engaged the Spanish off the coast of Shark Island.

... she came on deck in her nightgown, her gray hair flying loose down her back, the scars on her face livid, brandishing a sword in one hand and a pistol in the other. Her appearance was so alarming that the Spaniards dropped their weapons, believing they were being attacked by a fiend.[28]

Grace, it was said, possessed powerful connections throughout the British government. Though often arrested, her "pull" always assured her quick release. Still pirating in her sixties, she grew tired of her rough and rowdy life and retired to her castle on Clare Island, where she was eventually buried. "This was a notorious woman in all the coasts of Ireland,"[29] wrote Sir Henry Sidney of Grace in 1577.

Grace O'Malley was not the only woman pirate troubling Queen Elizabeth in the sixteenth century. Lady Killigrew of Cornwall, the wife of Sir John Killigrew, the leader of several pirate syndicates operating along the coast of Great Britain, also drew the English queen's attention. Sir John and his wife were friendly with Elizabeth because the queen preferred open communication with the local pirates so that in times of war she could license them as privateers and thereby augment her navy. (This had been one of her motives in making peace with Grace O'Malley.) Sir John, in fact, carried a number of impressive titles granted him by the queen— vice-admiral of Cornwall, royal governor of Pendennis Castle, and president of the commissioners for piracy. As long as the Killigrews refrained from preying on Queen Elizabeth's friends, they were free to pursue their buccaneer ways.

In the spring of 1582, however, a prize anchored in Falmouth harbor that Lady Killigrew could not resist, a rich German merchantman under the protection of the English queen. Killigrew selected a small band of her best fighters and stole alongside the merchantman in the dark. When Lady Killigrew was finished, the German ship was hers, and its entire crew had been put to the sword.

Queen Elizabeth ordered the lady and her two male captains arrested. The three were tried, convicted, and sentenced to hang. In the end, the two captains did hang, but Lady Killigrew was given a short jail term. Queen Elizabeth could not bring herself to alienate the Killigrews and their potential fleets of English privateers.[30]

One of the most bloodthirsty of the English female pirates, Maria Lindsey of Plymouth, fell in love with pirate captain Eric Cobham and married him the day after they met. They immediately set off in his fourteen-gun cutter for a life of piracy.

Maria enjoyed killing. She always took part in boarding parties and thrived on the blood and gore. Once she used a captain and first mate from a captured vessel for target practice, emptying eight pistols into them from a distance of twenty feet. In another instance, when the Cobhams had taken a British prize, she admired the flare of a British officer's uniform and had him stripped on deck. After running the hapless young man through with her sword, she donned his uniform, a costume that became her trademark. When the original became tattered, she ordered new ones made from its pattern.

In her twentieth year of pirating, Maria led a triumphant attack against an East India merchantman off the coast of Scotland and chained the survivors on the deck. As they huddled under the watchful eye of her crew, she cooked a big pot of stew in the galley below for the captives. They ate heartily and all died within a few hours. Maria Cobham's stew, of course, was poisoned.

Eric and Maria retired to an estate near Le Havre. They had two sons and a daughter, and Eric became a pillar of the community. When the local judge died, the mayor asked Eric to replace him! Maria, on the other hand, could not find contentment in her new life on land. She continued to wear her officer's uniform and spent many hours sailing her yacht.

One day, Maria went for a walk along the sea with a bottle of poison in her pocket. Eric later found the empty bottle and her cape at the edge of a steep cliff. Two days later, the body of Maria Cobham washed ashore.[31]

In February of 1544, the English attacked the Scottish coastal village of Maxton. Among the citizens killed in the invasion were the family and fiance of Maid Lilliard of Maxton. To avenge her loved ones, Lilliard enlisted with the Scottish forces of the earl of Angus, called "Red Douglas" because of his hair.

Maid Lilliard was there when Red Douglas counterattacked the English at Melrose and later at Jedburgh. Her last battle came when the Scots assaulted the English forces of Lord Evers at Ancrum Moor. The English were routed, and Lord Evers was killed by Lilliard. They found her body beside his on the moor, so mangled that observers were amazed that she could have fought Evers to the death in such a critically wounded condition.

The scene of the battle came to be known by the locals as "Lilliard's Edge." A folk rhyme celebrates the maid of Maxton:

> Fair Maiden Lilliard lies under this stane,
> Little was her stature, but great was her fame;
> Upon the English loons she laid many thumps,
> And when her legs were cutted off,
> She fought upon her stumps.[32]

In the sixteenth and seventeenth centuries, urban observers took note of the "Roaring Girls" phenomenon. Averell, in his *Marvailous Combat*, describes women "who from the top to the toe, are so disguised, that though they be in sexe Women, yet in attire they appear to be men."[33] The chamberlain records carried this account dated January 25, 1620: "Yesterday the bishop of London called together all his Clergie about this towne, and told them he had express commandment from the king to will them to inveigh vehemently and bitterly in their sermons against the insolence of our women, and they're wearing brode brimd hats, pointed dublets, theyre haire cut short or shorne and some of them stillettaes or poinard [knives and daggers], such other trinckets of like moment."[34]

The cover girl smoking a pipe and carrying a sword, pictured in the *Roaring Girls*, a book published in London in 1611, depicted a real, historically verifiable model of the type. Mary Firth, also known as Moll Cutpurse, lived in the late sixteenth and early seventeenth centuries. Her name appears in a number of lawsuits of the period. In her confession recorded in the Consistory of London Corrections Book of 1605–1606, she admits to "frequenting alehouses, taverns, tobacco shops and associating with ruffianly, swaggering and lewd company, namely with cutpurses, blasphemers, drunkards, and others of bad note."[35]

She appeared in court again in 1621 on a charge of wrongful arrest. Mary claimed that because of her reputation for locating stolen goods, she was asked by a friend to find a certain pickpocket and regain the purloined items. Mary sought to represent herself as an underworld policeman to rationalize her high-handed manner with the plaintiffs.

During the English Civil War, Mary single-handedly robbed the commander in chief of the parliamentarian forces, General Fairfax, even though he was an excellent swordsman in the company of an armed guard. She not only slew several guards but also killed the general's horse so she could not be followed. She relieved Fairfax of his purse but was soon captured and sentenced to be hanged. A bribe of two thousand pounds in gold won her release, and Mary returned to a life of robbery. She died in her mid-seventies, a wealthy woman.

*   *   *

John Calvin, born in 1509, was a French leader of the Reformation who separated from Rome after the rise of Lutheranism and established his own church in Switzerland. In 1536, he published his theology in *The Institutes of the Christian Religion*, one of the most popular books of the day. One of his central ideas was the notion of predestination, the belief that God alone directs everything that happens. This tenet easily expanded to a revolutionary theme: obey temporal authority but only to the degree that it does not disagree with the primary authority of God as revealed in the Bible. This thinking, in that it offered a moral method of challenging the princes, contributed to the revolutions of the 1600s and 1700s. The people of the Netherlands and Scotland became some of the most strident advocates of the radical views of John Calvin.

The attempts by King Charles I to foist the Church of England's prayer book on the Calvinist Church of Scotland was one of several missteps by the English king that led to the English Civil War. Charles also opposed the Puritans in the English Parliament when they argued for limitations on the king's prerogatives and further purification (hence "Puritans") of Catholic symbols and rituals from the Church of England. Charles responded with a renewed affirmation in his belief in the divine right of kings and marriage to a Catholic princess—Henrietta Maria, sister of France's King Louis XIII. King Charles's continual demands for money from Parliament, his use of force to extract "loans" from the nobles, and his leading of troops into the House of Commons in an attempt to arrest five of its members led to the outbreak of civil war.

Charles depended on his army of cavaliers under the direction of Prince Rupert, the king's nephew, and General Ralph Hopton to demonstrate the might of the Royalists. The anti-Royalists, the Roundheads, drew their support from the Puritans and from Parliament and organized their armies under the brilliant commander Oliver Cromwell. The Royalists found their strength among the nobles in the west and north, whereas the Parliamentarian forces depended on the east and south. The Scots invaded England in 1640, and the Irish rebelled against England in 1641. After four years of internecine conflict, the Royalists surrendered in May 1646. During the English Civil War, women warriors were found on both sides of the conflict, acquitting themselves with valor and determination.

The English at Berwick were attacked on June 5, 1639, by the Calvinist militant leader Lady Ann Cunningham, daggers in her belt and pistols attached to her saddle. She rode at the head of a troop of female cavalry fighters, each one a crack pistol shot.

Lady Cunningham's son, the marques of Hamilton, drew her special fury after he dared to disagree with her about certain religious issues. She threatened to shoot him if he appeared before her in battle and to this end kept several golden bullets with her at all times.[36]

The English Civil War also found Anne Dymoke fighting in Cromwell's forces in Scotland in 1657. Adopting a not uncommon ploy, she entered service disguised as a male with her husband, John Evison. She played the part of Stephen Evison, John's brother.

After her husband was lost at sea, Anne, still masquerading as Stephen Evison, enlisted as a soldier under a Major Tolhurst. She proved such a courageous fighter that, when her sex was eventually discovered, she was allowed to continue soldiering with her unit. Mary, countess of Falconburg, the daughter of Oliver Cromwell, also held warrior credentials as a cavalry leader.

In the seventeenth century, Anne Howard, fighting for the Royalists, won a reputation as a fearless special agent. Her fellow Royalist, Lucy Apsley Hutchinson, gained renown as a warrior after she defended Nottingham from anti-Royalists.

In 1642, the anti-Royalists under Sir Walter Erle and Sir Thomas Trenchard set their sights on Corfe Castle, a key Royalist fortress. The manor and castle had recently been purchased by Sir John Banks, the king's attorney general; at the time Trenchard and Erle marched toward Corfe, Sir John was en route to join the king at York. Lady Mary Banks, her daughters, and five soldiers occupied the castle of Corfe in May 1642 when the anti-Royalist army surrounded them and demanded their cannons. By way of reply, Lady Mary mounted the rampart and fired her largest cannon into the anti-Royalist forces.

She ordered the war drum of the castle beaten, and fifty of her tenants came to Corfe's defense. But, as the days wore on and food ran low, Lady Mary agreed to surrender her cannons if the rebels would leave her in peace. The cannons were removed, but neither side trusted the other. Lady Mary secretly raised more supporters and stocked her castle, while the anti-Royalists, feeling that they had removed Lady Mary's only potential threat, prepared to break their word and take her castle.

The commanders of the anti-Royalist forces led three hundred men against Corfe, bombarding the castle with Lady Mary's own cannons. After furious fighting, the rebels withdrew. But on June 23, hidden by a thick fog, they entered the town, surrounded the castle, and positioned a cannon in the ruins of a church close to the castle walls. Lady Mary and less than a hundred of her family and friends continued to hold on, even as the cannon pounded Corfe's walls to gravel.

The earl of Warwick, Sir Walter Erle's superior officer, became frustrated at Erle's lack of success against Lady Mary. He ordered extra rations of rum for his troops and promised that he would personally give twenty pounds to the first man to scale Corfe's walls.

Aware that a major attack was impending, Lady Mary and her entourage prepared to fight from the upper levels of the castle, while Captain Lawrence stationed the men who had come to Lady Mary's aid on the ground-floor levels.

The rebel attack against Captain Lawrence's position was met by small arms fire from ground level and bombardment with stones, boiling oil, and hot embers from Lady Mary's fighters above. The rebels were repeatedly rebuffed as they threw themselves against Corfe. When news arrived that Sir John Banks and Royalist troops were en route, the attackers fled, leaving behind over one hundred horses, which were promptly confiscated by Lady Banks for her personal stable. Lady Mary Banks had held Corfe for six weeks, outnumbered by more than fifty to one. A hundred of her enemy's men were dead compared to only two of hers.

For a few years after this victorious defense of her castle, Lady Banks was left in peace. However, when the marchioness of Wincester was removed from Basing House and Lathom House was later captured after Countess Derby's strong defense, General Fairfax sent a regiment of cavalry and two regiments of infantry to take Corfe Castle from Lady Banks. She was still holding out by February of the following year. Treachery won the day for the attacking forces, and Corfe Castle fell and was later destroyed. Lady Banks died five years after the fall of Corfe.

A female parliamentary champion found herself invested by Royalist forces in her family stronghold in the midseventeenth century. Brilliana Conway, the daughter of the lieutenant governor of the Netherlands, was born in 1600. She married Sir Robert Harley in 1623 and took up residence at her husband's family center at Brampton Bryan near Hereford.

In 1642 while her husband was at Westminster, the Royalist governor of Hereford demanded that Lady Harley surrender Brampton Bryan Castle. She refused, of course, and the Royalist men isolated the fortress and cut off its food supply by commandeering all of Harley's livestock. Three months later, Lady Harley was again summoned to surrender, and once more she refused. To a succeeding request that she abandon her castle, she commented, "I do not know that it is my husband's pleasure that I should entertain soldiers in his house."

By the third week in August, a stalemate ensued; the Royalists could not take the castle and Lady Harley would not surrender it. Fortunately, General Fairfax appeared with a force, which relieved the siege. Lady Harley died several months later from the strain that the long siege had placed on her health.

A saying of the time proclaimed that "Three women ruined the Kingdom: Eve, the queen, and the Countess of Derby."[37] Charlotte de la Tremoille, countess of Derby, was a Royalist heroine, the French Huguenot daughter of the duc de Thouars and wife of the earl of Derby, owner of Lathom House. During her life, Lathom House, with its walls six feet thick and moat over twenty feet wide and six feet deep, served as a fortress. Nine towers were located at strategic points along the walls, and six pieces of artillery were placed in each tower. To further enhance its effectiveness, the great castle sat at the pinnacle of an elevation.

Early in 1643, the earl of Derby was touring on the Isle of Man by request of the queen. Lady Derby was left in charge of Lathom House and two of the couple's seven children, Lady Mary and Lady Catherine. Parliamentary General Sir Thomas Fairfax, feeling that Lord Derby's absence would facilitate his taking of Lathom House with minimal bloodshed, on February 28 sent orders carried by one Captain Markland for Lady Derby to abandon her castle.

Lady Derby's riposte noted that because the general occupied a lesser social rank than she, a more fitting arrangement would be that he surrender his army to her. Nevertheless, she continued, she was prepared to receive the attackers' "utmost violence, trusting in God both for protection and deliverance."

Fairfax's army answered with a bombardment of Lathom. Their mortars threw eighty-pound stones. In a matter of days, the great walls of Lathom House were crumbling under the assault. Further, the attackers had diverted the water flow into the castle and driven off the cattle and domestic livestock that provided Lathom House with sustenance. Fairfax offered Lady Derby and her daughters safe passage if she would surrender, but the countess replied that it was "more noble to preserve my liberty by arms than to buy peace with slavery."

When the fall of Lathom House appeared imminent, Colonel Rigby, one of the Parliamentarian commanders, invited the townspeople to observe his final attack on the fortress. He moved his mortars forward and postured for his audience. Observing that the pompous colonel was more attentive to his audience than to her, Lady Derby dispatched her troops on a lightning sortie in which they successfully pulled his mortars into Lathom House.

With the military details in the hands of Captain Farmer, Lady Derby provided the attitude and command presence that permitted Lathom House to resist the besiegers three more months until a strong force under Prince Rupert finally arrived. One commentator noted, "It is evident that without a woman of the lofty courage—one might add the aristocratic arrogance—of the Countess of Derby, Lathom House would have fallen to the enemy almost immediately."[38] Lady Charlotte, countess of Derby, died in 1664.

In the southwest of England, the Parliamentary forces were driving against Basing House, the only remaining Royalist garrison in the area, which was defended by Honora, marchioness of Wincester. Oliver Cromwell himself arrived on the scene to observe the anti-Royalist army under Sir William Waller. When Sir William proposed safe conduct for the marchioness and her children, her response, in the mode of the countess of Derby in her exchanges with General Fairfax, withered the mere general with arch and regal disdain.

The marchioness directed her officers and worked with her ladies as they cast bullets from lead they had stripped from the roofs and turrets of

Basing House. The gallant defenders held Cromwell off for three months but were forced to treat for surrender terms in the end. The marchioness was permitted to attend her wounded husband in the Tower of London, and Basing House was destroyed by the Parliamentary forces.

One year later, another English noblewoman, Lady Blanche Arundel, in the absence of her husband who was fighting near Oxford, was attacked in her Castle Wardour by Sir Edward Hungerford in command of thirteen hundred Parliamentary troops. Lady Blanche had twenty-five men in the garrison at Castle Wardour along with her ladies-in-waiting. She deployed the men and organized the young women of her retinue to assist the men in the coming fight.

Sir Edward made his official demand for the surrender of Castle Wardour on May 2, 1643. Lady Blanche replied that she had been ordered by her husband to hold the castle and she intended to do so. In response, Sir Edward bombarded Wardour for six days and nights. At sporadic intervals, he sent parties against the walls of Wardour, but throughout it all the defenders under the leadership of Lady Blanche held fast. Finally, when the cannons had taken their toll on the castle walls and with no assistance on the horizon, Lady Blanche arranged the surrender of Wardour, the prime term being that no one under her protection be harmed. Sir Edward, with profound respect for Lady Blanche's courageous defense, agreed.

The Lady of Wardour died October 29, 1649, and was buried in a chapel in Castle Wardour beside her husband. Today, the inscription on her tomb can still be read.

> This lady as distinguished by her courage as for the splendor of her birth, bravely defended, in the absence of her husband, the castle of Wardour, with a spirit above her sex, for nine days, with a few men, against Sir Edward Hungerford, Edmund Ludlow, and their army, and then delivered it up on Honourable terms. R.I.P "Who shall find a valiant woman? The price of her is as things brought from afar off, and from the uttermost coast. The heart of her husband trusteth in her. . ." Proverbs 31.[39]

Many Parliamentary women warriors are recorded from this time. At the siege of Bristol by Prince Rupert, Mary Smith stayed on the battlements and helped build the fortifications, while Joan Batten and Dorothy Hazzard fought at the Frome Gate. Two hundred women came to Parliamentary Commander Colonel Fiennes requesting to join his ranks in battle, and in 1643 the imperious Prince Rupert was turned back at the village of Lyme on the Dorset coast by a village defense force, which included four hundred women. Observers note that, after the siege of

Lyme was lifted and Rupert had withdrawn, the women destroyed Rupert's earthworks so that they could not be used again to attack Lyme. It took them a week.[40]

In 1644, Mrs. Peirson, daughter of the earl of Carnwath, obtained a commission from the earl of Newcastle to head a company of cavalry. She joined General Montrose as he marched to Dumfries.

During the civil wars in England, Countess Portland led the defense of Carisbrooke Castle while standing at a cannon emplacement on the battlements. Lady Mary Winter held Lidney House, near Gloucester, against the Parliamentary commander Colonel Massey.

On the Royalist side, Irish women enhanced their already legendary reputation among the English for violence. Armed with short swords, they fought so viciously at the siege of Nantwich that the Parliamentary commander suggested that they should all be killed immediately and their bodies thrown into the sea. Instead, General Fairfax used them in a later prisoner exchange.

Fifty years later, a woman disguised as a man joined a Scottish regiment as an infantryman to look for her husband. She found him ten years later after she had participated in a number of battles and had been wounded several times. She fought under many names, including Kit Welsh, Christian Davies, Christian Ross, and Kit Cavanagh. When her fighting days were over, she stayed with the army as a cook and became known as "Mother Ross." She retired in 1708 with an army pension and was given a military funeral when she died.

In 1695, English King William III led his troops against Namur, the most heavily defended town in Belgium. The British prevailed, and, fighting in their ranks, Ensign Robert Cornelius displayed conspicuous heroism and received several wounds. When the doctors dressed the soldier's injuries, they discovered that Robert was a female. The young woman disclosed that she had joined the army disguised as a man and had been quickly promoted to sergeant and then to ensign. After the Peace of Ryswick ended his wars in Europe, King William III showed his appreciation of Ensign Cornelius's contributions to his victories by granting her a military pension.

An unknown Englishwoman was serving with the French army as a trooper under Marshal Catinant. This young warrior was repeatedly witnessed performing acts of bravery during cavalry skirmishes and was promoted to the rank of gentleman of horse. Louis XIV granted her a full military pension when her fighting days were over.

In some cases, an absent husband set the woman warrior in motion, not to defend but to attack. In the early 1700s, Anne Keith, Lady Methven, a battleship sailor for a number of years, was called by her husband to defend his estates while he was campaigning in service to his lord. She used the opportunity to deploy his soldiers against her political enemies.

She is described at the head of sixty knights carrying on her left arm a light horseman's carbine and in her right hand a sword. In a letter to her husband, she wrote:

> Comfort yourself in this, that if the fanatics chance to kill me, it shall not be for nought. I was wounded for our gracious King, and now in the strength of the Lord God of heaven, I'll hazard my person with the men I may command, before the rebels rest where they have power.[41]

Lady Methven's military excellence bound to her the fighting men of Tippermalloch, Bachilton, and Busby. Anne Keith, Lady Methven, died some years later in a riding accident.

Mary Ann Talbot, born in London in 1778, was, as Lady Methven had been in her early years, a British sailor. She first joined the 823d Regiment, disguised as a drummer boy, to follow her husband to war. After deserting the army, she joined the navy and served aboard Lord Howe's command ship as part of a gunnery crew in the war with France. After being wounded by grapeshot, she was assigned to the *Vesuvius* as a midshipman. Upon retiring from the navy, she received a pension of twenty pounds a year. She died in 1808.

A few years later, in 1821, ex-infantry warrior Phoebe Hessel died at the age of 108. Almost all that is known of her is found on her tombstone in the graveyard of St. Nicholas Church in Brighton, England.

> In Memory of Phoebe Hessel: born at Stepney in the year 1713. She served for many years as a private soldier in the 5th Regiment of foot in different parts of Europe, and in the year 1645 fought under the command of the Duke of Cumberland at the Battle of Fontenoy, where she received a Bayonet wound in the arm. Her long life, which commenced in the time of Queen Anne, extended to the reign of George IV, by whose munificence she received comfort and support in her later years. She died at Brighton, where she long resided, December 12, 1821.[42]

Also in the Battle of Fontenoy, Mary Ralphson, "Trooper Mary," a Scotswoman of the Third Dragoons, fought alongside her husband. She was born in Scotland in 1698 and married Ralph Ralphson of the Third Dragoons. She was cited for her strong performance at the Battle of Fontenoy under the command of the Duke of Cumberland. Trooper Mary fought at Dettingen in 1743, at Culloden in 1746, and in many lesser actions.

One of Trooper Mary's fellow Scots, Flora Macdonald, is often described as the most famous of the eighteenth-century adventuresses. She devised and carried off almost single-handedly the escape of Bonnie Prince Charlie to France in 1745. In 1776 she fought with her husband in the American Revolution, and, during the return voyage to England, she fought with sword and pistol in repelling an attack by a French warship.

In the mideighteenth century, a Britishwoman named Hannah Snell, *aka* "James Gray," joined the Frazer Marines disguised as a man to search for her lost husband. Her unit shipped for India aboard the *Swallow*, and she was immediately thrown into the battle for Pondicherry. In the first assault group to cross a river, Hannah waded chest deep under fire from the French batteries. She spent two weeks fighting in the trenches and seven consecutive nights as a frontline picket. For her efforts, she received six bullets in her right leg, five in her left, and one in her stomach. By doctoring the stomach wound herself, she maintained her disguise.

After her recovery she was assigned to the *Tartar Pink* and later to the *Eltham*. At first, her shipmates teased her for her lack of beard and called her "Miss Molly Gray"; however, her courage and toughness soon earned her the nickname "Hearty Jimmy." When she retired from the military in 1750, she published her autobiography and launched a speaking tour of England and Europe. With the proceeds she opened an inn, which she named the Woman Warrior.[43]

As the nineteenth century dawned, French General Napoleon Bonaparte commanded the stage of European politics. Before he was thirty years old, fueled by his fame as a popular military hero, he had joined in an overthrow of the Directory, the five-man executive council who had followed in the footsteps of Robespierre and the Reign of Terror, and by 1804 he had summoned Pope Pius VII from Rome to crown him emperor of France. By 1812, Napoleon controlled most of Europe; however, the British Isles had not fallen under his sway. He had made his major strike against Great Britain in October of 1805, engaging the British admiral Lord Nelson off the southern coast of Spain at the Battle of Trafalgar. Nelson mauled the French navy, rendering it impotent as a future threat to Great Britain.

As the French threat still loomed on the continent, a black woman, sailing under the name "William Brown," served aboard the British warship *Queen Charlotte*. She carried the rank of "Captain of the Maintop," a position occupied only by the most skilled sailors in the British navy. She held this rank for eleven years.

Tom Bowling, a boatswain's mate on a British man-of-war for over twenty years, was found to be a woman after she was arrested on shore for theft. Anne Johnson of Great Britain served for seven years on the crew of an English ship in the early 1800s. Her mother died in the Napoleonic Wars while fighting as part of a gun crew aboard a British warship.

Hanah Witney, an Irishwoman, fought for six years in the British navy. Ann Mills, "with sword in one hand and a Frenchman's head in the other,"[44] served on the frigate *Maidstone*, and an unknown woman who called herself Paul Daniel worked on various warships.

In the early 1800s, Napoleon's forces attempted to invade England at a small village called Fishguard. The people of the little town moved into action with one great bluff and some real face-to-face fighting. As the men armed themselves to fight along the docks and walls, the women, wearing red shawls, red blankets, and red dresses, marched in tight formation along the ridge behind the village, convincing the French commander that English reinforcements were approaching. He withdrew, but not before Jemima Nicholas captured seven French soldiers. Her tombstone can be found at Fishguard.[45]

Mary Dixon, a sixteen-year British infantry veteran, was one of the many women who died in battle at Waterloo. How could a woman, typically smaller and lighter boned than a man, survive for sixteen years, as Mary did, involved with frontline infantry warfare and hand-to-hand combat? First, of course, highly developed martial arts skills, wit, and courage can go a long way in nullifying a height and weight disadvantage. Second, the women who became warriors were usually healthy, vigorous women who enjoyed rigorous physical activity such as riding, hunting, and warfare.

It must be remembered that some women can display truly awesome physical strength. Nineteenth-century circus strongwomen provide many examples. Mrs. Josephine Blatt of Hoboken, New Jersey, who performed under the name "Minerva," stood six feet and weighed over two hundred pounds. Mrs. Blatt performed a harness lift of twenty-three men who weighed, including the platform and lifting chains, 3,546 pounds!

Austrian Katie Sandwina was the unchallenged "Strongest Woman in Europe" in the late 1800s. As a teenager, she twisted steel bars in her family's vaudeville act. At her peak strength, she could form herself into a human bridge on which could stand forty men and horses. Her weight-lifting exercises involved jerking more than 280 pounds over her head, and she could lift her husband over her head with one hand.[46]

*　　*　　*

Constance, Countess Markievicz (her Polish husband's name), a crack shot and excellent horsewoman, was born in Ireland in 1868 and grew up with a passion to free Ireland from British control. She organized a Boy

Scout troop in 1909 and trained the boys to fight against the British. In April of 1916, as a member of the Citizen Army, she fired on British police when they raided a rebel headquarters. Second in command, she shot several British snipers and organized the building of better defenses. When her group was forced to retreat to the College of Surgeons, she joined her snipers on the roof.

On April 29, the Irish leaders surrendered, and the countess was sentenced to death. Her sentence was later commuted to life and then nullified in June 1917, so she roamed free once more to harass the British. She was jailed and released several more times between 1917 and 1927, when she died fighting with the Irish Republican Army. Irish poet Sean O'Casey said that she was "clothed with physical courage as with a garment." The British government deployed British machine gunners to her funeral to prevent supporters from firing a volley of honor over her coffin.[47]

In the early twentieth century, as Great Britian faced attack by Germany, British women were drawn into support service for the military. They were drilled at Kitchener with the male recruits and endured the same training regimen, including weapons and hand-to-hand combat instruction. Present in every town, these female military groups were not seen as nurse or secretarial corps and were urged to practice shooting as often as possible. The Italian press reported in 1915 that a British woman, Countess Castlereagh, headed a four-hundred-woman regiment that accompanied the British army to the continent. The countess's regiment worked in communications, commissary, and munitions services. In addition, a group of London women formed a mounted guard, which was seriously prepared to do battle with the Germans if they invaded the British Isles.[48]

The art of the warrior often resides as much in the mind and wit as in the muscles. During World War II, Eveline Cardwell lived alone in a remote section of Yorkshire; her son and husband were away at war when a farmhand delivered the news that a Nazi paratrooper had landed in her pasture. As the soldier struggled with his parachute harness, Mrs. Cardwell ran up behind him unarmed and loudly ordered him to throw his sidearm on the ground and raise his hands. To her immense surprise, he did. She marched the chagrined Nazi paratrooper, at the point of his own gun, to the local police station. Mrs. Cardwell was awarded the British Empire Medal.

British women aided the war effort on the continent. Mary Lindell, an English Red Cross nurse who had married the Comte de Milleville in Paris, established in August 1940 an "escape line," a network of agents who helped people escape from behind German lines. After guiding several downed Allied pilots to safety, Lindell was captured by the Gestapo.

A year later she escaped to London, where she joined British intelligence. In October 1942 she reentered Nazi-occupied France and reestablished an escape line in the city of Lyons. Although the British were unable to offer her direct assistance, she saved the lives of fifteen airmen and soldiers, including the only two survivors of a British commando raid that crippled seven German ships in the harbor at Bordeaux in December 1942.

Second engineer on the S.S. *Bonita* during World War II, Britisher Victoria A. Drummond was awarded the British M.B.E., Lloyd's Silver Medal, the Coronation Medal, the War Medal, and five campaign stars.[49]

Pearl Witherington, a British intelligence agent, parachuted into France in the fall of 1943 to coordinate with local resistance forces and act as courier. In the spring of 1944, the resistance leader was captured, and Pearl assumed leadership in half of his territory. Her maquis (partisan fighters) grew to include 3,500 fighters and were responsible for the death of 1,000 Nazi soldiers in a four-month period.[50]

The spirt of the women warriors of the British Isles is captured in this heroic poem, *The Spear Lay*, from eleventh-century Ireland:

> We weave, we weave the web of the spear
>   as on goes the standards of the brave.
> All is sinister now to see.
> A cloud of blood moves over the sky and the
>   air is red with the blood of men
>   as the battle-women chant their song.[51]

The West African kingdom of Dahomey (now called Benin) had a famed women's army that lasted through the nineteenth century. Called the "king's wives," these women warriors lived apart from men in barracks on the palace grounds. European observers regarded them as excellent soldiers.

Corbis-Bettmann

CHAPTER 6

Africa: Mother of Nations

Greek myths informed the ancients that, long before raiding from their fortresses in the Caucasus Mountains, Amazons were centered in Africa. They were depicted as clad in red leather armor with snakeskin boots and shields. The most ancient contacts mention that the Amazons practiced animal husbandry but not horticulture.

Herodotus observed the remnants of a culture of women warriors in the sixth century B.C. when he traveled along the coast of North Africa. The following account from his journal, though clearly recorded through the eyes of a Greek, is noteworthy:

> Next to the Machlyans, there are the Ausans, who share the lake with them. Every year they celebrate a festival in honor of Athena, the virginal goddess. The girls are divided in two groups and fight with one another, proving, as they say, which ones were born of their nation. The maidens who die of their wounds are considered impure. Before ending the fight, they observe the following custom. The girls who conducted themselves with the greatest bravery are decorated with a Corinthian helmet, put on a chariot, and led all the way around the lake. I cannot say what weapons the Amazons used before the Greeks came to live near them. I believe, however, that they wore Egyptian arms, for I am of the opinion that shield and helmet were originated by the Egyptians and copied from them by the Greeks. The women's clothes and their shields with the image of Athena were copied by the Greeks from the Libyans though the Libyan images were clothes of leather. All the other things are the same.[1]

Herodotus added that the women were wearing red leather armor. Morocco, Libya, Algeria, and Tunisia are still known for red leather products.

When the Greek chronicler Strabo traveled into Libya about six hundred years after Herodotus, he found that "there have been several gener-

ations of belligerent women in Libya." He saw no women warriors, but
he did note that women ruled the country from the urban areas along the
coast. In the interior, and particularly into the Atlas Mountains regions,
the nomadic tribes were controlled by women, women who boasted of a
tradition of female warriors and armies.

Diodorus Siculus, another ancient traveler in North and West Africa,
asserts the existence of warlike women's nations in West Africa. He claims
to have been shown the graves of ten Amazon generals as well as three
burial mounds commemorating an ancient battle in which Myrine, captain of the Amazons in Libya, fought the Gorgons. The queen, after her
victory, ordered the dead placed in three funeral pyres, which were later
mounded with earthen tumuli. Modern explorers and scientists later confirmed many of Diodorus's observations.

French archaeologist Henri Lhote, working in the early 1930s and
again in the 1950s at Sefar in western Libya, discovered the "Fresco of
the Twelve Steps." In addition to images of elephants, giraffes, and other
animals, the ancient drawing portrayed a battle scene, which featured
bow-carrying women, thus adding some confirmation to the observations
of Herodotus, Strabo, and Diodorus.[2]

A classic account of Amazons is found in Homer's *Iliad*, his stirring epic
of the Trojan Wars, where he mentions them several times but does not describe their arrival at Troy. Less well-known, a more complete account of
the Trojan Wars, Arctinus of Miletus's epic *Aethiopis*, existed before the
Iliad. Whereas Homer ended his tale with the death of Hector, Arctinus
tells of the arrival of the Amazons at Troy, led by their queen Penthesilea
and accompanied by King Memnon and his armies from Ethiopia. The
connection of Africa and women warriors in Arctinus fits with the reports
of the ancient travelers.

Most scholars would dismiss the accounts of Herodotus, Strabo, and
Diodorous as compelling evidence to support the existence of women warriors in Africa, although all three ancient writers have proved accurate in
the great majority of their testable observations about life in the centuries
before Christ. As time progresses, the evidence supporting the presence of
a tradition of African women warriors grows in its persuasiveness.

An impressive series of Ethiopian warrior queens, queen regents, and
queen mothers, known as *kentakes* (Greek: Candace), are only now appearing to the light of history through the ongoing deciphering of the
Merotic script. They controlled what is now Ethiopia, Sudan, and parts of
Egypt. One of the earliest references to the *kentakes* comes from 332 B.C.
when Alexander the Great set his sights on the rich kingdom of Ethiopia.

The presiding *kentakes*, known in history as "Black Queen Candace of
Ethiopia," designed a battle plan to counter Alexander's advance. She

placed her armies and waited on a war elephant for the Macedonian conqueror to appear for battle. Alexander approached the field from a low ridge, but when he saw the Black Queen's army displayed in a brilliant military formation before him, he stopped. After studying the array of warriors waiting with such deadly precision and realizing that to challenge the *kentakes* could quite possibly be fatal, he turned his armies away from Ethiopia toward a successful campaign in Egypt.

Bas-reliefs dated to about 170 B.C. reveal *kentakes* Shenakdahkete, dressed in armor and wielding a spear in battle. She did not rule as queen regent or queen mother but as a fully independent ruler. Her husband was *her* consort. In bas-reliefs found in the ruins of building projects she commissioned, Shenakdahkete is portrayed both alone as well as with her husband and son, who would inherit the throne by her passing. The following African queens were known to the Greco-Roman world as the "Candaces": Amanirenas, Amanishakhete, Nawidemak, and Malegereabar.[3]

A hundred and fifty years after Alexander was repelled by the Black Queen, the Romans, under Patronius, the Roman governor of Egypt in 30 B.C., tried to conquer Ethiopia, and again a *kentakes* stopped them. Queen Amanirenas neutralized Patronius's army, defeated his garrison at Cyrene, and drove the Roman legions northward. Not only did the Romans fail to take her country, Queen Amanirenas took parts of theirs. A wall painting depicts her, armed with bow and arrows and spear, holding a tether attached to seven captives.

The *kentakes* of Ethiopia left many monuments to themselves. Amanishakhete, Nawidemak, and Malegereabar commissioned numerous bas-reliefs in the ancient site at Nagaa, picturing them armed with one and two swords, battling lions, and subduing enemy war leaders.

* * *

A medieval Arab writer, Magrizi, noted a corps of women lancers in the Beja tribes living between the Nile River and the Red Sea; d'Arnaud, in 1840, found a battalion of spearwomen protecting the King of Behr on the Upper Nile; and the explorer Pigafetta told of the women soldiers of the Monomotapa (modern Zimbabwe). Edward Lopez described a troop of women archers who served in the army of the King of Monomotapa. Denham saw the women of the Fellatah tribes fighting in battle with men. Henry Morton Stanley, in his famous search for Dr. Livingston, confronted a troop of riflewomen fighting for King Mtesa of Uganda.[4]

The Yoruba of West Africa, a tribe whose population numbers in the millions, possess a strong history of women military heroines and female armies. Likewise among the neighboring Hausa, women commanders led migrations, founded cities, and conquered their enemies. The trade routes through the western Sahara drew the Yoruba and the Hausa into Libya, perhaps establishing the antecedents of the women warriors encountered in northern Africa by the ancient Greeks. Their existence further confirms the observations of Diodorous noted earlier that women warriors were commonly found in West Africa.

In the Niger and Chad areas, the presence of women warriors and women-led martial kingdoms are well-documented. In the Transvaal regions, three successive warrior queens, Mujaji I, II, and III, reigned.

The Hausa Empire composed of seven states—Daura, Kano, Gobir, Zazzau, Katsina, Rano, and Garun Gabas—came into existence in A.D. 1050, the end product of continuous rule by a line of seventeen queens. In the sixteenth century, the Hausa Empire was led by Queen Aminatu (also known as Amina), the senior daughter of Queen Bakwa Turunku, the queen of Zazzau (later renamed Zaire after her youngest daughter).

Aminatu took control of the Hausa in 1536 and reigned until 1573. Her first efforts were directed toward territorial expansion; leading a twenty-thousand-man (and woman) army, she annexed several non-Hausa states. For thirty-four years, she commanded and protected her realm with a firm hand. The remnants of numerous fortresses seen in central Africa today are still identified with her name.

Queen Aminatu forged trade routes through the Sahara to North Africa, and tradition credits her with introducing the kola nut into local cultivation. Nigeria honored the eminent queen by erecting a life-sized equestrian statue of her, sword raised, on the grounds of the National Theater in Lagos. Modern citizens of West Africa have demonstrated their regard for the great Hausa queen by naming many educational institutions after her.

*   *   *

In 1563 Duarte Barbosa, a member of Vasco da Gama's expedition along the coast of Africa, published his memoirs detailing their experiences. He described meeting the King of Benamatapa, observing that he "always takes with him into the field, a great band of warriors, and five or six thousand women, who also bear arms and fight." He added, concerning these warriors, "those most renowned for bravery are the female legions, greatly valued by the Emperor, being the sinews of his military strength."[5]

The Mbundu peoples of Angola possessed the woman warrior tradition that in the seventeenth century produced the great Queen Jinga. The Igbo and Lozi in northwestern Zimbabwe had their "princess chiefs," as did the Bemba. Among the Kpelle, peoples of Liberia and Sierra Leone, rich and powerful women often became chiefs and commanders of armies. Mende and Lovedu women ruled many chiefdoms.

Women of the Bamileke and the Nupe, controllers of the food supply and at times the exclusive agents of trade and marketing, often rose to positions beyond their husbands, including chieftainships. Noble women of the Ashanti frequently maintained households separate from their husbands, as did the Bakeri women. Well into modern times, the women of the Kom of Cameroon mobilized into armed masses to redress wrongs.[6]

Feats of female military prowess are noted for the Lango of east central Africa as well as for the Mpororo, Latuka, Fanti, and Ubemba. Sir Richard Burton, traveling in Somalia in the nineteenth century, cited the women warriors and added, "in muscular strength and endurance, the women of Somal are far superior to their lords."[7]

Some African women warriors so impressed their people, and sometimes their enemies, that they were considered immortal or in possession of supernatural powers. In A.D. 350 Mujaji became the first queen of the Lovedu through her fame as a sorceress and rainmaker. Armed with a spear, she led her warriors in battle and was so effective as a warrior that the Lovedu thought her incapable of being killed. Mujaji, the rainmaker, not only directed armies but also ruled as a king, possessed a harem, and accepted in ritual marriage the daughters of prominent tribal chieftains.[8]

In A.D. 688, a black Jew whom the Arabs called Queen Dahia Al-Kahina, "the Sorceress," was queen of Carthage and Mauritania and leader of a confederation of Berber tribes. When her general, Kuseila, was killed in battle, Queen Dahia assumed command and repulsed the first Arab invasion. When Arab general Hassen-ben-Numan captured Carthage in 698, the Sorceress rallied her troops and retook the city.

Soon, however, the overwhelming might of the Islamic invaders ended the queen's fighting ability, and she converted her tactics to a scorched earth defense, laying waste to water supplies, animals, and crops to deny the Arab armies a foraging base. Her excessive efforts, however, disastrously affected the lives of her supporters, who abandoned her leadership. General Hassen-ben-Numan later returned and killed her in battle. Queen Dahia's legacy persists today in the ruined soils of southern Tunisia.[9]

Another black Jewish woman of warrior renown was Judith, queen of the Falashas (black Jews). She made war on Ethiopia and captured the sacred capital of Axum in A.D. 937. She hunted and killed members of the family of Solomon and the Queen of Sheba, thus forestalling threats to her rule from the noble line. Before she died in 977, she had captured almost all of Ethiopia.

A succession of warrior queens—in this case ending with madness—occurred in the central African region of the Congo in the late 1500s and early 1600s. Queen Mussasa, leading troops that included a female battalion, secured a kingdom along the Cunene River. Her daughter, Tembanduma, succeeded her in a revolt in which her mother was deposed.

Queen Tembanduma's sanity disintegrated slowly. She once tried to convince her people to train all girls in martial arts and to grind boys into an ointment that would ensure immortality for females in battle. When her women rebelled, she changed her order to include only captured male children.

In a battle, she lost an eye and was terribly disfigured. This hideous transformation produced an even more terrifying visage as she charged at the head of her troops. A chronicler who saw her in action wrote, "The . . . host that attacked old Lattaku was led by a ferocious giantess with one eye." She died after being poisoned by a lover.

The most famous African woman warrior of the seventeenth century was, without a doubt, Zinga Mbandi. She was born in 1580 in west-central Africa, daughter of the *ngola*, king of Ndongo.

Zinga Mbandi is first heard from in 1620 when on behalf of her brother, the *ngola*, she attempted to negotiate the independence of Ndongo with the Portuguese governor. She demanded the release of her father, exiled by the Portuguese to the Kwanza Islands, and solicited their help in driving out the Imbangalas, who had recently occupied a portion of territory claimed by Ndongo. Those observing her in these weighty negotiations were impressed by her energy and intelligence.

A vignette from Zinga's first encounter with the Portuguese summarizes what people who dealt with her came to expect. When she was ushered into the governor's reception room during her negotiations in Luanda in 1620, she found Governor de Sousa seated on a large chair, while the attendants, herself included, were left to stand. Without hesitation, she ordered a servant to his hands and knees and sat on him. Then, eye to eye with the governor, she introduced herself formally.

Zinga's perception of the Portuguese, gleaned from the intense hours of negotiation in Luanda, convinced her of their hostile intentions, despite their claim of friendship, and she responded by organizing a women's army and attacking their outposts. Her women's bows, arrows, and spears were no match for the weapons of the Portuguese soldiers, and she was defeated; however, the Portuguese would face Zinga many more times.

After the deaths of her brother and nephew—both rumored to have been murdered by her—she became the *ngola* of Ndongo, and the Portuguese sent their forces to destroy her. She countered with her men's and women's armies and sought an alliance with the Dutch, the Portuguese nemesis in Africa. When her forces were defeated, she was driven out of her territory, and a puppet king of the Portuguese was placed on the throne. Zinga marched her troops eastward and took the kingdom of

Matamba, which became the center of a war she waged against the Portuguese for eighteen years.

Women held more power than men at Zinga's court. Loth observes: "The women in the queen's retinue displayed military skills, strength and bravery; they learned to use weapons and went to war with the queen."[10]

Zinga was accompanied during these years by Captain Fuller and a company of sixty men whom the Dutch had placed under her command. Fuller described her during a ritual sacrifice as dressed in men's clothing draped in animal pelts with a sheathed sword dangling from a loop at her neck. A battle-ax hung from her belt, and she held her bow and arrows in one hand along with an iron bell, the mate of which was grasped in the other. She rang these bells as she leapt "according to the custom, now here, now there, as nimbly as the most active among her attendants." She then pulled a white feather through the hole in her nose, a sign for war, and moved toward her victim. The Dutch captain wrote that she cut off the man's head and "drank a great draught of his blood."

Fuller found Zinga's sexual practices worthy of note. She kept fifty or sixty young men in her palace as lovers; some of them she dressed in women's clothing. Still, he admitted that, though he abhorred her "devilish superstition and idolatry" and was repulsed by her human sacrifices and bizarre sexual practices, he found her "a cunning and prudent Virago, so much addicted to arms that she hardly used other exercises; and withal so generously valiant that she never hurt a Portuguese after quarter given, and commanded all her slaves and soldiers alike."

Zinga's withdrawal into the interior of her country disrupted the Portuguese slave trade and weakened their military by threatening supply lines from Luanda to her domain. The Portuguese, in pursuing Zinga, left Luanda vulnerable to the Dutch, who took it in 1641.

Queen Zinga moved her center to the Dande River, where she could ship her prisoners of war to the Dutch in Luanda and at the same time mount campaigns against the Portuguese puppet king in Ndongo. Her army, which contained a women's battalion, won victories against the Portuguese in 1643, 1647, and 1648, but in a later battle, when Zinga's sister was captured and imprisoned by the Portuguese, some of the fire went out of the queen. Perhaps feeling that the time was right or simply seeking to free her beloved sister, she made peace with the Portuguese in October of 1656.

When she died at eighty-one, her body was publicly displayed, dressed in her royal robes as the *ngola* of Ndongo, with her bow and arrows placed in her hands. As per her dying request, when her body was interred, she was recostumed as a Catholic nun with the bow and arrows replaced by a crucifix and rosary.

* * *

The island of Madagascar, lying off the southeast coast of Africa, is noted in this traveler's account from 1765:

> Women can be found on this island who are far superior in courage and virtue to others of their sex. The historians of the island refer to one Dian-Rhea, who brought the entire island under her scepter. Dian-Nong, Amboulee's princes gave countless proofs of her bravery and magnanimity. Several times she went to war at his side and saved his life more than once.[11]

When Europeans first contacted Madagascar, they found that the island had been previously ruled by a succession of queens: Ranavalona I, Rasoaherina, Ranavalona II, and Ranavalona.

In eighteenth-century southwest Africa, a Herero ruler named Kaipkire led her army in war against British slave traders; in the nineteenth century, the wars between the Herero and the German colonial forces, some of the most vicious colonial warfare to take place in Africa, saw many military actions by Herero women fighters. By 1919, Herero male and female resistance soldiers, fighting the modern well-equipped European army, forced a stalemate, and the Germans were compelled to gradually withdraw their efforts.

Many African women fought the evil of the slave trade, sometimes as leaders of armies and sometimes in small-scale acts of rebellion. One such account is derived from the journal of a ship's doctor on the English slaver *Robert* lying off the coast of Sierra Leone in 1721. According to the account, one of the African men who had been brought aboard as part of a thirty-person slave cargo was a resistance leader the British called Captain Tomba.

Realizing the necessity to act before the *Robert* sailed, Tomba quickly organized a mutiny; however, when the time came to strike at their captors, only Tomba, one man, and one woman were willing to fight for their freedom. The three rebels killed two of the crew before they were overpowered and chained.

The *Robert*'s doctor notes that Tomba and his male partner in rebellion were merely whipped and scarified, for they were valuable property. Three male conspirators were forced to eat the liver and heart of a British crewman who had been killed, after which they were shot. As for the woman rebel, the doctor writes, "The woman he hoisted up by her thumbs, whipp'd and slashed her with knives, before the other slaves till she died."[12]

Nandi, the mother of the great African leader Shaka Zulu, fought against slave traders. She was a great influence on Shaka's development as a war chief; when he became king of the Zulu, he created a women's army.

The king of Whydah in 1700 had four to five thousand women classified as wives who worked in the royal household and served as his personal guard. The king of Yoruba claimed that his wives, some of whom formed a battalion, could by holding hands stretch from one end of his country to another.

Among the Batlokwa in the early 1800s, Queen Mantatisi fought her enemies, the Matiwane and the Zulu, who under the great chief Shaka Zulu had displaced her people. She matched his tribes in military prowess with her armies and once even managed by sheer nerve to win a battle without an army. An enemy unit discovered her while she was visiting relatives in a rural village and prepared to attack. Queen Mantatisi quickly assembled the women and children in the town, set them in marching order, and led them straight at the enemy. The confused attackers, probably assuming the advancing lines to be Mantatisi's soldiers, fled.

In 1823 white missionaries from Cape Colony described the so-called Mantatee Horde. Queen Mantatisi (also Mantatee) was at that time directing her entire nation of fifty thousand on a march southward in search of a new homeland. She moved this large mass of humanity quickly and efficiently and absorbed lesser chiefdoms as she passed.[13]

Of all the female armies of the African kingdoms, the best documented is the Dahomey. This agricultural kingdom of coastal west-central Africa was described by F. E. Forbes in 1849 and 1850, by Sir Richard Francis Burton in the latter nineteenth century, and by preeminent American anthropologist Melville Herskovits in the early twentieth century. In the mid-1800s Forbes estimated that of the twelve thousand soldiers in the Dahomean army, five thousand were women. Almost twenty years later, Burton estimated that the women's army of the Dahomey numbered about 2,500.

Called *ahosi,* the "king's wives," the women warriors lived apart from men in barracks on the palace grounds. When not involved in fighting for their king, they spent time as all soldiers do—working, drilling, practicing war.

Forbes described the Dahomean women warriors on review.[14]

> All were armed, accoutered, and dressed as nearly as possible alike in blue and white tunics, short trousers and caps bearing the different devices of their regiments. They marched separate from the men with their own war drums, banners, war-stools, shields and ornamented human skulls provided unwillingly by previous enemies.

In their battle formation, the Fanti company, the elite women warriors, took the central position and were recognized by the small blue crocodiles sewn on white headbands that they wore when fighting. The comparison of the crocodile design of the Dahomean Fanti and the reptilian skin boots and shields associated with the ancient Greek description of the African Amazons is striking. The British consul at Dahomey from 1861 through 1865 noted that some of the elite Dahomey warrior women wore a strip of crocodile hide as part of their uniform.

In addition to the Fanti, the women's army was divided into a right and left wing, and each of the three corps was further divided into five arms. Each of the *agbarya*, or blunderbuss women, the biggest and strongest women of the army, was attended by an assistant carrying ammunition. Within the *agbarya* were three small elite groups: the *zo-hu-nun*, carbineers; the *gan'u-nlan*, or "sure to kill company"; and the *achi*, bayoneteers.

The second arm of the women's army was known as "elephant huntresses," the bravest women in the army. The third group was called the *nyekplo-hen-to*, or "razor women," specialists in the use of light swords. The fourth arm was the largest group, the frontline infantry armed with tower muskets.

The exotic fifth arm, the *go-hen-to*, the youngest women in the army for the most part, were archers who fired complexly barbed poisoned arrows. They were distinguished by scanty attire that permitted them more freedom of movement in battle, an ivory bracelet on the left arm, a tattoo extending to the middle of the leg, and a knife lashed to the inside of the wrist.

The Dahomean women warriors were not an archaic decoration at the king's court. In 1728 under King Gezo, they attacked and defeated the kingdoms of Whydahs and Popos; in 1840, the men and women of the Dahomey army attacked the Mahee, who were surrounded by prickly bush "barbed wire" at their fortress at Attahapahms. Early on the morning of the second day, the women's unit captured the fort, including the Mahee king, his family, and a number of important ministers. Likewise, women soldiers died with the men in the unsuccessful attempt to take Abeokuta in 1864. But even in defeat, the women stood their ground while the men fled. Captain Duncan of the Life Guards noted, "On a campaign I would prefer the women of that country, as soldiers, to the men."[15] The Dahomey would agree. Dahomey culture viewed women as the more disciplined of the sexes and the most capable of withstanding the rigors of war.

In the 1850s, Captain Duncan made these observations concerning the Dahomean female army:

The speed of these women, despite the fact they are carrying a long Danish musket, a short sword and a sort of club, would astonish a European. Generally speaking these female warriors are an extremely impressive sight. The women are very agile, and, thanks to the constant exercise which they have here and elsewhere, including their work in the home and in the fields, can withstand considerable physical stress. One of the female officers of the king's corp, who I was introduced to, was called Adadimo. In each of the last two annual military campaigns she had taken a male prisoner and the king had rewarded her with promotion and the present of two female slaves. Adadimo is a tall, slim woman, quite pretty, about 22 years old and of a quiet unassuming personality.[16]

Duncan later investigated Adadimo's claim and found it truthful. The belief in women's superiority on the battlefield was held by a number of African societies.

Woman warrior Seh-Dong-Hong-Beh commanded the female forces at Abeokuta and led the attack against the Egba fortress, the center of resistance. European accounts describe her standing before six thousand female fighters, her body oiled and spear raised, as she shouted the order to advance. The European cannons in the fort decimated her battalion, and only a sixth of her command returned from Abeokuta.

In 1889 Nausica, the Dahomean king's favorite woman warrior, danced for the French ambassador Bayol. A year later, she died fighting the French, falling by a cannon she had just captured. The decline of the Dahomean woman warrior tradition resulted from the English colonial policy of excluding women from combat roles.

*   *   *

Madame Yoko held sway in the nineteenth century by controlling the fourteen-tribe Kpa Mende Confederacy, the largest in Sierra Leone. In her time, fifteen percent of all tribes in the Sierra Leone were ruled by women chiefs.[17]

In 1862, a woman named Nehanda Nyakasikana was born in central Zimbabwe. Affectionately called *Nbuya* (grandmother) Nehanda by the citizens of her country, she became one of the foremost religious leaders in Zimbabwe in the late nineteenth century and, in response to the burdensome British colonial presence, a leader in the patriotic war for independence.

Nehanda established her headquarters at Musaka, an impregnable mountain stronghold. She directed her warriors at the farms, mines, and businesses of local white settlers and entered battle with them. One white observer at the time wrote: "At the present moment, Nehanda is the most powerful wizard in Mashonaland and has the power of ordering all the people who rose lately and her orders would in every case be obeyed." She was captured in December 1897 by the British, charged with instigating rebellion and murder, and executed April 27.[18]

On the other side of Africa in the same era, the British had to face another fighting woman, Yaa Asantewa of the Ashanti, now the modern state of Ghana. She ascended to the role of queen mother during the time of the British protectorate of the Gold Coast (west-central Africa). She found the British presence humiliating and, finally, on March 28, 1900, after a major diplomatic gaff by the British governor, Lord Hodgson, concerning the Golden Stool, the sacred symbol of the Ashanti nation, unendurable.

The most highly revered emblem of the Ashanti, the golden stool upon which the king sits, is believed to contain the souls of all deceased Ashanti. It is particularly associated with Osai Tutu, the "George Washington of the Ashanti." The insensitive British governor, to make a point about British dominance, demanded to sit on the golden stool. Yaa Asantewa's outrage at this sacrilege sparked rebellion.

According to a modern elementary school history book, *Ghana: A History for Primary Schools*, she said at the time:

> No white men could have dared to speak to chiefs of the Ashanti in the way the Governor spoke to you chiefs this morning. Is it true that the bravery of Ashanti is no more? I cannot believe it. Yea, it cannot be! I must say this, if you the men of Ashanti will not go forward, we the women will. I shall call upon my fellow women. We will fight the white men. We will fight till the last of us falls![19]

Within three days, Yaa Asantewa had mobilized her warriors and laid siege to the British mission in its fort at Kumasi, and for three months they were helpless before her. The British were compelled to import several thousand troops and major artillery pieces to break the siege and capture the queen of the Ashanti and her supporters. Most of her chiefs were given probation with a prisoner-of-war status, while Yaa Asantewa, the most dangerous Ashanti leader as far as the British were concerned, was exiled to the Seychelle Islands off Africa's east coast, where she died twenty years later.

Twentieth-century wars of liberation proved a fertile ground for women warriors. They composed an integral part of the Algerian independence movement, and the French captured, killed, and executed them, as they did the male combatants.

In the 1950s, women comprised five percent of the guerrillas who fought in the Mau Mau war to liberate Kenya from British control, a war fought mainly by warriors of the Kikuyu. At first, Kikuyu men resisted the presence of women; they had no woman warrior tradition. But in the first years of war, the women proved themselves sufficiently, and guerrilla leaders in 1953 agreed that, depending on military excellence, women could be promoted to the rank of colonel.

Wanjiru Nyarmaratu, a Mau Mau woman fighter, joined the revolution as a teenager, initially carrying supplies to the male guerrillas. She raised money and collected clothing, medicine, and scrap metal for making weapons. In time, her expertise impressed the upper-level leadership who allowed her to recruit fighters and dispatch them to the various regiments as they were required. As an acknowledgment of her excellence in the Mau Mau military effort, she was appointed a judge of the Mau Mau court, which passed sentences, including the death penalty, on anti-Mau Mau crimes. Some of the executioners of the military court were female.

The African woman warrior tradition has flourished into modern times. When Dr. Hastings Bando founded the modern state of Malawi in 1964, he did so with the military support of a five-thousand-strong all-woman army, warriors who were crucial in maintaining internal order and in guarding the dangerous border with Tanzania. Teurai Ropa Nhongo, "the Blood Spiller," led guerrilla fighters in the Zimbabwe liberation movement of the 1970s. Two days after she commanded a successful fight against a Rhodesian contingent, she gave birth to her daughter. And, as late as 1987 in Uganda, Alice Lakwena inspired her Holy Spirit Movement to war in a popular uprising.[20]

Simón Bolívar, South America's greatest hero, led the revolution that freed Venezuela, Colombia, Ecuador, Peru, and Bolivia from Spanish rule in 1819. Many women fought alongside Bolívar, including Delores Rodriguez, who served as a sapper in the war for Peruvian independence.

CHAPTER 7

Latin America: Las Guerreras

The women warriors of Latin America first appear in Western history in a letter written by Christopher Columbus on February 15, 1493, which he sent to Queen Isabella from the New World. After describing for his sponsor the wonders of his discovery, he offered comments on many topics, including women of the Carib Indian culture. "They use no feminine exercises, but bows and arrows of cane . . . and they arm themselves and cover themselves with plates of copper, of which they have plenty." In the report from his second voyage, he described being attacked by female archers on the island of Guadeloupe.[1]

The Spanish conquistador, Francisco Pizarro, confronted women warriors in 1531 when he landed at Tumbes and encountered the Inca Empire of Tawantinsuyu.[2] The chroniclers of Pizarro's many battles with the Inca made frequent mention of women in battle. One of his captains, Diego de Almagrom, encountered Indians massed for battle in the district of Liribamba as he returned to Quito from Cuzco. With their horses, armor, and harquebuses, the Spanish won the day, but with great difficulty largely because of the presence of Indian women slingers who took a heavy toll on them.

In another battle, after the Spanish had executed Inca Ataw Wallpa, his generals brought an Indian army of twelve thousand, including large contingents of women warriors, against the Spanish. Unmarried noblewomen, the daughters of Inca lords, were most visible in major battles with the Inca army, but as de Almagrom's experience points out, the women of the villages would also mount serious military resistance.

The presence of women in Inca war, while quite effective, was necessitated by ritual. Ancient Inca belief held that warfare, including both men and women combatants, was an essential feature of ritual petitions to the sun god for protection against epidemics and natural disasters. If the real

95

thing did not happen, the peoples of the Andes region would generate a ritual war between villages. Olivia Harris, an anthropologist who studied the Laymi Indians of the central Bolivian highlands, writes:

> While she is unmarried, a girl will sing, dance, get drunk. She will fight against other girls in the ritual fights, *tinku* that take place at big fiestas. In particular, the presence of unmarried girls is essential for the success of the group of male warriors who go together to the *tinku*. This same group of warriors and unmarried girls, known as *wayli*, has an important ritual function for the community, since it is they who interceded with the Sun-God for protection and pardon. The girls of the *wayli* have ritualized roles in battle: the girls act as standard bearers in the troop, carrying flags and sacred images; and they also help the majors maintain discipline in the ranks.[3]

In the Inca Coya Raymi, "the Festival of the Queen," women, as the central ritual figures, armed and prepared men for battle. Celebrated each fall, this important festival was directed to the moon, the wife of the sun, and formed a central part of the Inca woman's ritual life.

In the origin myth of the Inca, women played major roles as priestesses and ritual leaders in the first four generations of the royal line. The prestige of women was defended in the late 1500s when the Spanish viceroy commissioned a history of the Inca. Its findings were dismissed by an Inca noblewoman, Coya Cusi Huarque, queen of the independent state of Vilcabamba, because the writer failed to note that her lineage ranked higher than that of the puppet Inca king, whom the Spanish called Don Carlos.

Some years later, Pizarro, conqueror of the Inca, dispatched his brother Gonzalo Pizarro southward from the town of Quito to search for El Dorado, "the City of Gold." Gonzalo encountered a river with dense forests on either side and followed it eastward. When his supplies were eventually depleted and his men in danger of starving, he sent Captain Francisco de Orellana with several men, including a Dominican priest, to find food for the stricken expedition. The priest, Gaspar de Carvajal, left a written account of Orellana's explorations.

On New Year's Day 1542, Orellana was told by an Indian headman from a riverbank village that they were entering a country controlled by warlike women who would attack them. Orellana and his men were entirely prepared to believe this because tales of the Amazons were popular back in Spain.

Father Carvajal wrote that weeks later when the main assault came, he saw women warriors in the battle—classic Amazons, he was sure. "There came as many as twelve of them in front of all the Indian men as women captains. . . . The Indian men did not dare turn their backs, and anyone who did turn his back, the women felled with clubs right before us."

The Romans described the same ruthless behavior among various European tribeswomen they met in battle. And early colonists in the southeastern United States reported that in the Choctaw Indian ball game, which they called "the little brother of war," women armed with branches (precursors of the modern cheerleaders' pompons?) attacked male players who they felt were displaying cowardly behavior on the field of play.

Years later when Carvajal's account was published, the river that the original expedition had followed, the Marañon, was renamed the Amazon River. Some of the more experienced New World explorers criticized this name change, citing information that further extends our knowledge of the range of the women warriors of Latin America. South American explorer Antonio de Herrera stated:

> In regard to the Amazons, many have expressed the opinion that Captain Orellana ought not to have given this name to those women nor ought to have affirmed on such a slim foundation that they were Amazons, because in the Indies it was not a new thing that women should fight and draw their bows, as has been seen in some of the Windward Island in Cartagena and its neighborhood, where they showed themselves to be as valorous as the men.[4]

The Spanish soldiers, surprised by confronting female warriors in the New World, chose to believe they were fighting Amazons.[5] This decision elevated them to heroes, whereas to fight and die against mere women would have rendered them foolish.

In 1537, Ines Suarez sailed from Spain to search for her husband, who had been reported missing in Peru. After discovering that he had been killed, she settled in the town of Cuzco; shortly thereafter, she met Pedro de Valdivia, a military man who had been active with Pizarro's forces against the Inca. De Valdivia made an impression on Ines, who rode with him when he left Cuzco to join his army in Chile. Her martial exploits are noted in a variety of skirmishes involving his forces; in the wars against the Arucanian Indians, she was seen both nursing the wounded and fighting on the front lines.

In the mid-1600s, Peru boasted "the Valiant Ladies of Potosí," Doña Ana Lezama de Urinza and Doña Eustaquia de Sonza.[6] Doña Ana Lezama, adopted into the de Sonza household, developed a close friendship with the de Sonza daughter, Eustaquia, and in later years became her lover.

Both young women displayed a passionate interest in the fencing lessons provided for Eustaquia's brother and after the young man's death were allowed to pursue their interest. By age thirteen, they were studying with a sword master as well as learning to handle firearms.

As was befitting proper young women of their class and times, they were raised in virtual seclusion from the rough life of Potosí. In their late teens, however, they often dressed as men, slipping away from the de Sonza hacienda and plunging into the violent nightlife of the city for adventure and a test of their martial skills.

In one street fight against four men, Doña Ana was knocked out, and Doña Eustaquia warded off the attackers with her sword until Ana regained consciousness and jumped to her feet. Doña Ana recognized the man who had struck her down and attacked him with such ferocity that she cut through his shield and nearly severed his hand. The remaining three men fled. As dawn approached, the two women returned to the de Sonza home and found, after removing their light body armor, that both had numerous sword wounds.

For five years the lovers wandered Peru, engaging in fights and gaining great fame as swordswomen. They returned to Potosí after Doña Eustaquia's father died and willed them his estate. A few years later, Doña Ana died from a wound she received in another of her dangerous pastimes, bullfighting. Four months later, Doña Eustaquia died of grief.

It would have been interesting to witness the results if Ana and Estaquia had chanced to disturb the peace in the Chancay Valley. At the same time the "ladies of Potosí" fought on the streets, la Niña de la Hueca captained the encapado, a tough band of mounted police who patrolled the mountains and forests of Peru. La Niña was six feet tall, muscular, and expert with pistol and lance.[7]

Resistance to the Spanish brought many Indian women into warfare in the late eighteenth century. Baltazara Chuiza commanded fighters against the Spanish in Ecuador in 1778. In 1780 Cecilia and her brother, José Tupac Amaru, led an army against the invaders. José's wife, Micaela Bastidas, fought in the uprising, leading troops of men and women. Juana Robles captained armies in the Argentinian revolution, and in 1803 Lorenza Avemanay commanded Indians in a resistance against the Spanish in Ecuador. Juana Azurduy, fighting with her husband, led women's guerrilla forces in Bolivia. In Uruguay, Ana Monterrosso de Lavelleja, wife of an army commander, directed the guerrilla unit known as "the Thirty-three Orientales."

* * *

The greatest hero in South American history, Simón Bolívar, was born in Venezuela to a rich planter's son in 1783. At the age of thirty-eight, Bolívar, "el Libertador," led a ragged army in a six-year revolution that resulted in the independence of Venezuela, Colombia, Ecuador, Peru, and Bolivia from Spanish rule.

In the summer of 1821, Bolívar captured the ancient city of Quito, and one of its inhabitants, twenty-four-year-old Manuela Saenz, captivated Bolívar with her beauty, intelligence, and courage. In a love letter he wrote, "I too suffer from this searing fever, which consumes us like two children."[8] Astride a cavalry charger in colonel's regalia, fiercely hostile to his enemies and fiercely loyal to his cause, Manuela rode in battle as his companion and military adviser.

Many women served on battlefields and as spies and messengers in Argentina, Colombia, Peru, and Brazil during the wars of independence. Podicarpa Sala Varieta, fighter with Bolívar's forces, was later honored with a heroic statue. Three sisters, Las Ibañez, also worked in support of Bolívar's cause as spies and soldiers, and eighteen-year-old Dolores Rodriguez was a sapper (military engineer) in the war for Peruvian independence.

On the northern Atlantic coast of Colombia in the 1800s, black slave women, las Cimarronas, fought for their freedom in the Pelenques near the city of Cartagena. In the same area in 1501, Juan de la Cosa, sailing with Captain Rodrigo de Bastides, reports that he landed with a party many miles north of the Orinoco River, in the vicinity of present-day Cartagena, and was immediately attacked by a large group of Indians wielding spears and shooting poisoned arrows. The Indian raiding party comprised both men and women.

In Central America, Maria Candelaria organized an army and initiated a rebellion against the Spanish overlords. In the early 1800s during the Mexican War of Independence, Gertrudis Bocanegra raised and commanded an army of women. She was captured, tortured, and publicly executed in 1817.

Maria Graham in her *Journal of a Voyage to Brazil* writes that she met one Doña Maria de Jesús in the early 1800s. Dressed as a soldier, Doña Maria was a much-decorated infantry fighter. The emperor at Rio de Janiero granted her an ensign's commission and the Order of the Cross, which he himself fixed on her jacket.[9]

Less than fifty years later, Irish-born Elisa Alicia Lynch rode in battle with Francisco Solano Lopez, the self-styled liberator of Paraguay. Lynch, who had been raised in a military family and was an expert horsewoman, met Lopez in Paris and returned with him to South America. Shortly thereafter, Lopez, with Lynch at his side, retreated with his troops to Angostura, where the patriots awaited the attack of the Brazilian and Argentinean forces.

The assault came one day when "Ella," as Lynch liked to be called, was riding outside Angostura and spied the Brazilians and Argentines sweeping across the plain. Quickly turning to the women's camp to organize fighting groups, she ordered them to bring knives, pitchforks, axes—anything that would serve as a weapon. She grouped them into units of fifty and arranged these units in a long column.

As Lopez's men were driven back by the Argentine infantry and the Brazilian cavalry, another Paraguayan army suddenly appeared over the crest of a hill, with Elisa Alicia Lynch, dressed in a colonel's uniform and waving a sword, at their head. The Brazilians and Argentines panicked at the sight of a thousand fresh troops entering the fray and fled the field. This was Lynch's first military action but not her last.

By 1869, the tide had turned and Lopez camped in the hills with less than a hundred men, while his adversary the Marquis de Caxias, with sixty thousand troops, tightened his grip on the countryside. Elisa Lynch and her three sons had been taken prisoner and deported.

She traveled to England only to find that the man to whom Lopez had entrusted her money had spent it. When she tried to return to Paraguay in 1875, she was refused entry. Elisa Lynch, cavalry colonel, died in abject poverty and was buried in Paris in a pauper's grave.[10]

In the Mexican peasant armies of popular leaders such as Zapata and Villa rode women called *guachia*. Armed combatants, they proved equal to any male fighting unit. Adelita, inspiration for a famous Mexican folk song, was an actual warrior of the *guachia*.

The Mexican Revolution provides many well-documented cases of Latin American women warriors, beginning with the intrepid Mary Petre de Fernandez, wife of revolutionary leader Francisco Madero's adviser.[11] "The Plan de San Luís Potosí," written in San Antonio, Texas, by the exiled revolutionary government October 5, 1910, claimed that the recent election of President Díaz was unlawful and established Madero as the true "provisional president." Because Madero's agents in Texas were under scrutiny, Mary de Fernandez volunteered to smuggle the revolutionary document into Mexico.

In Mexico, Aquiles Serdan, with his wife, Carmen, as director of the women's revolutionary efforts, built a support base for the coming rebellion. Carmen Serdan and the Narvaez sisters—Guadalupe, Rosa, and María—recruited fighters, plotted strategy, and made and deployed weapons.

When their secret headquarters was surrounded on the morning of the planned uprising, Carmen, rifle in hand, urged the townspeople to join the revolution. In the fray that followed, her husband was killed, and she was wounded and taken prisoner. Though condemned to execution, she was later released and immediately contacted the Narvaez sisters to rejoin the war for independence.

Carmen Parra de Alaniz, before fighting for General Zapata, had organized an armed uprising in Casas Grandes, Chihuahua. She commanded three hundred men in the capture of Ciudad Juárez. Margarita Ortega, a demolition expert, who repeatedly risked her life carrying ammunition and dynamite through enemy lines, was shot on November 24, 1913.

One woman rebel commander, Margarita Neri, had such a frightening reputation that when the governor of Guerrero heard that she was approaching his city, he had himself shipped to safety in a packing crate. Neri, who claimed Dutch-Maya descent, led over one thousand men and women north, fighting through Tabasco and Chiapas, swearing that she would personally decapitate Diaz.

Maria Luisa Escobar, famous for her dynamiting talents, was killed in battle. Juana Luicio fought from a base in Guanajuato, and Maria Aquirre battled on the Costa Chica in Oaxaca. Margarita Mata commanded a rebel army in the state of San Luís Potosí. Artemisa Saenz Royo, a member of the "Red Battalion" of the Casa del Obrero Mundial, held the rank of colonel and was wounded several times. Ramona Flores led guerrilla fighters in the north and was promoted to chief of staff.

The following story, depicting the courage of women in battle, is recounted in every woman warrior tradition. In 1913 the federal forces held the key city of Tampico against the Constitutionalist army. Four of their best commanders had unsuccessfully led attacks against the city, finding the Federals too well-fortified. After a week the rebels, camped in the swamps around the city, grew dangerously fatigued. Piercing the pall of gloom, a woman grabbed a regimental banner, leapt on a wagon, and raised the battle flag over her head. "We've got to enter Tampico," she shouted, "no matter how. All of you who've got the nerve, follow me!" She ran toward the city with the rebels following and in the end took Tampico. This woman's lost identity remains a poignant symbol of the millions of women warriors who fought valiantly on every battlefield on earth—unknown.

Occasionally a woman warrior becomes known because she writes about her career or because, as in the case of Karla Ramírez of El Salvador, she tells her story. The following account is taken from an interview with Ramírez.

> One night the military took away my cousin, who was eighteen. We never knew why. Sometimes they take pictures of the corpses, however, and so that is how I know what they did to him: they burned him to death with torches. That was another reason I had to fight.
>
> In 1980, I realized I had to go to the mountains and help the campañeros to fight. . . . At first I was scared to go because I thought about what could happen to me and also because I had a baby son just four months old.
>
> Members of the organization came to my house at about five o'clock, when it was still dark. I took my *mochila*, my back pack, and went with them. My husband understood why I had to go. He was in the organization, too, but he had to stay in San Salva-

dor. . . . It was very hard to leave him. I cried. But I knew what I did was for my baby, not only for him, but for everybody, because for me everybody is my son.

In the mountains I learned how to crawl so the enemy couldn't see me coming close, and I learned to roll along the ground to avoid the bullets. I learned to climb, to protect myself, to hide from the enemy. I learned how to use all kinds of weapons, including the M-19.

The first mission I had was to stop a convoy of weapons along the highway. Every time there is a convoy we have to stop it because most of our weapons come from the military. There were twenty-five of us on my first mission. We went down the mountain on foot. You know the soldiers will start shooting right away and you have to be prepared for that.

When I saw that first convoy coming, I felt the hair on my skin stand up, I was so scared. But when they came close enough for me to see them, then I didn't feel any fear. When the soldiers saw us, they wanted to run away, but we had them surrounded and they had to fight.

I have fought many times, but that first time was not easy. I had to keep in mind that these are the people who had killed someone in my family, and as long as I kept thinking that, I knew I could kill them. While I was waiting, I thought "I cannot, cannot." Then when the convoy came, I knew I could. There is no choice but to kill. You have to demonstrate to your compañeros that you can. You know everybody is scared. If you ran away, others might do the same and it would be your fault.

It is hard to kill someone. I have to keep my compañeros in mind, a very special, very human feeling, and then I can do it. I have cried sometimes, for what I have had to do. . . . Men would cry too, sometimes, but no one would say anything to them about what they were feeling because they would be embarrassed. When I cry all those things that make me feel bad seem farther away, and I feel much better. . . . Most of all, I think about my son. I think about all the people who are waiting for the liberation of our country, and that every time I fight I help to win that struggle.

I stayed in the mountains for five months the first time and went on twenty missions. We didn't only fight, but went into the towns and took control of them.

In our group there are about two hundred and fifty women, and almost seven hundred men. A woman can become a leader the same as a man, and do everything a man can do. We hold the same desire in our hearts. We only want to have justice and liberty. I think the feeling I have is the same feeling that many women have, and if they have my feeling then they should go ahead and not be afraid to die to change things. If you die you leave behind your heart to the people who follow, to your child who comes after you.[12]

In Nicaragua in the late 1970s, women comprised thirty percent of the fighting force in the Sandinistas' final offensive against Anastasio Somoza supporters. The founder of the Sandinista National Liberation front, Commander Tomás Borge, in a speech given in 1980 noted: "Women were in the front line of battle, whether they threw homemade bombs or were in the trenches. They were in the leadership of military units on the firing line during the war."[13]

On January 20, 1981, Fidel Castro delivered a speech in Granma Province. The following excerpt offers an interesting insight into a guerrilla commander's appreciation of women warriors.

> I remember that when I organized the Mariana Grajales platoon [AUTHOR'S NOTE: Mariana Grajales, a black woman, was a rebel leader in Cuba's first war of independence]—in fact, I took part in the combat training of those comrades—some of the rebel fighters were furious because they didn't like the idea of a platoon made up of women. We had some spare M-1s, and the M-1 was considered a good light weapon and, therefore, we thought it would be the right one for the women. Some of our fighters wanted to know why they had Springfields while the women were going to get M-1s. On more than one occasion I got so annoyed that I would answer, "Because they are better fighters than you are." And the truth is that they showed it. A large group of women formed part of the troops that marched on Holguin. Near Holguin, a women's platoon engaged in a fierce battle with the army, and the platoon leader was wounded. As a general rule, when the platoon leader was wounded the men had the habit of retreating—which is not correct, but it had become practically a habit. The women's platoon had attacked a truck loaded with soldiers. When the platoon leader was wounded, they weren't discouraged. They went on fighting, wiped out the truckload and captured all the weapons. Their behavior was truly exceptional.[14]

The many cases of Latin American women warriors seem to cluster around their participation in wars of liberation, from the times of Inca resistance to the Spanish to the political struggles of the modern era. Lenin once commented, "The experience of all liberation movements has shown that the success of a revolution depends on how much the women take part in it."[15]

These antique coins depict the redoubtable Cleopatra the Great, who led a tumultuous life that included love affairs with Julius Caesar and Mark Antony, as well as an illustrious career as a war leader in the many power struggles she and her lovers faced.

Courtesy of American Numismatic Society

CHAPTER 8

Egypt: The Commander of Storms

About eight thousand years ago, hunters and gatherers roaming the banks of the Nile River encountered travelers from Abyssinia. In time the two groups melded to give rise to the Egyptians. The agricultural bounty provided by the Nile's annual flood made the Egyptians strong and numerous, while access to the Mediterranean and to the interior of Africa by way of the Nile provided trade contacts that enriched them. Four thousand years later, they were building great cities and pyramids.

At the heart of the classic Egyptian cultural system lived the pharaoh, the "God King." Pharaoh, sometimes a woman, centered the political, religious, economic, kinship, and military institutions of the state. Noblewomen often became important political figures as well as commanders of major military ventures. In fact, the lack of prohibition against Egyptian women participating in public affairs allowed even a commoner woman to gain power. During the Old Kingdom (3100–2345 B.C.), the prime minister of Egypt, second in power only to King Pepi I, was Nebet, a woman.

The first king of the First Dynasty, Ahamenes, married a woman warrior, Neith-Hetep, the first historical queen regent of Kemet, or Black Egypt. Her name, ironically, meant "the War-Goddess Is at Peace." Her military identity was proclaimed by the shield and crossed arrows of the war goddess Net, which always accompanied her name on monuments and public documents.[1]

Nitocris, a female ruler of Egypt about five thousand years ago, is remembered for the vengeance she wreaked when her husband, the king, was murdered. After assuming the vacant throne, she feigned confusion and indecision, convincing her husband's assassins to attend a banquet where she would forgive them and they, in turn, could offer needed advice about ruling in her husband's absence. The guests were ushered into an underground dining hall on the banks of the Nile. When they had finished their meal, Nitocris opened the gates connecting the Nile channel to the large room and drowned them. History remembers Nitocris's ruthlessness as a ruler and military commander, but she is also known for completing the third great pyramid, which her husband had begun. She became a central character in many Egyptian legends.

Egypt's rise to greatness was seriously threatened in the second millennium B.C. by the occupation of its northern territory by the Hyksos, chariot-driving warriors from Palestine. The ultimate liberation from this invasion came between 1580 and 1510 B.C. and was engineered largely by three Egyptian queens: a mother, daughter, and granddaughter.

Queen Tetisheri, ancestress of the succeeding dynasty, set the war machine in motion by formulating and executing military actions against the Hyksos from her base in Luxor, and her daughter Queen Ahotep warred against the Hyksos after her husband was killed in battle.[2] An Eighteenth Dynasty inscription concerning her reads: "She assembled her fugitives. She brought together her deserters. She pacified Upper Egypt. She subdued the rebels."

Queen Ahotep, ruling as regent for her young son Kamose, focused her energy on the continuing war to remove the Hyksos invaders. Not only did she successfully execute the offices of queen regent and commander in chief, but, as the first woman, she held the position of second prophet of Amun. One of the most powerful offices in the government, the second prophet directed all civil and religious functions.[3] Ahotep's daughter, Queen Thothmes, with her husband, Amose, finally drove the Hyksos out of Egypt forever.

The greatest woman pharaoh by all accounts, Hatshepsut (1505–1485 B.C.), whose name means "Chieftain of the Noble Women," ruled Egypt from 1490 to 1468 B.C. during the Eighteenth Dynasty. An absolute ruler, she reigned as a king, not as a queen regent, and to make her position clear, she sometimes dressed in male attire complete with a false beard and a wig.

Famous for a reign marked by peace and prosperity, Hatshepsut organized the first merchant expeditions to Punt (Somalia) and ensured that various plants brought back were adapted for use in Egypt. She engineered a number of major building programs, and her tomb at Deir el-Bahri remains a major tourist attraction in Egypt.

Despite her justly deserved reputation for peace and diplomacy, much of Hatshepsut's energy was directed toward the military, a favorite project being the building of a great navy for trade and warfare. She personally led her troops to quell a rebellion in Nubia. Eyewitness accounts of battles, offered by both Hatshepsut and others, reveal the little-known martial component to this great pharaoh's rich and complex career.

In Djehuty's stela, Senmut's tomb, and at Zoser-zosru, inscriptions tell of Hatshepsut's battle exploits. A scribe wrote:

> I followed the good god. The Living Horus. In Upper and Lower Egypt may she live! I saw her overthrow the Nubian Bowmen, their chiefs brought to her as living captives. I saw when she razed Nubia, I being in her Majesty's following.[4]

Beginning about 4000 B.C. and ending when Egypt fell to Alexander the Great in 332 B.C., thus ending Dynasty XXXI, the list of queen regents and female *horuses* (independent rulers) is impressive[5]:

Neith-hotep, queen regent in Dynasty I;
Mer-Neith, living *horus* and queen regent in Dynasty I;
Anchnesmerir, queen regent in Dynasty VI;
Nitocris, living *horus* in Dynasty VI;
Sobeknofru, living *horus* in Dynasty XII;
Ahotep, queen regent in Dynasty XVII;
Ahmose-Nefetere, queen regent in Dynasty XVII;
Hatshepsut, living *horus* and queen regent in Dynasty XVIII;
Mutemwia, queen regent in Dynasty XVIII;
Ta-wsret, queen regent in Dynasty XIX.

Egypt was conquered in the fourth century B.C. by Alexander the Great, who established as his governor the first in a long line of Greek Ptolemies, descendants of the original Macedonian general assigned to the province by the conqueror. By focusing on the women of the Ptolemy line, a sample can be crudely drawn to offer an insight into the activities of aristocratic women warriors in this period of Egyptian history.

Berenice I, half sister and later wife of Ptolemy I, fought beside her husband in the early fourth century B.C. and was renowned for savagery. She was widowed in early middle age and assumed the regency for her son, who was murdered shortly thereafter by her brother-in-law. The enraged queen pursued him and killed him with her own hands. Still not satisfied, she repeatedly drove her war chariot over his body until all traces of it were ground into the earth.

Arsinoe II Philadelphus, the daughter of Ptolemy I and Berenice I, followed in her mother's footsteps. Her reputation as a fighter was growing before she was married to the elderly Lysimachus, whom she soon controlled. When widowed in 275 B.C., she joined the military ventures her brother, Ptolemy II Philadelphus, was waging in Syria. She usurped his army after watching him lose battle after battle; with her planning and battlefield leadership, she reversed his losses.

She married her brother about 278 B.C. and soon controlled all of Egypt. At Mendes and at Fayyaum she garrisoned troops loyal to her, not only to protect the empire from invasion but also to maintain the power base needed to rule Egypt. With this security, Arsinoe II constructed new dikes and canals, created many acres of new farmland for the people, and led her armies to settle occasional revolts. The first Egyptian woman ruler to appear on coins, Queen Arsinoe also personally strengthened the Egyptian naval forces.[6] In the line of Ptolemy queens, she was surpassed only by the redoubtable Cleopatra the Great.

The death of Ptolemy I brought another Egyptian woman warrior into the field. Deidameia attacked and captured Ambracia to avenge Ptolemy's death. She was dazzling on the battlefield but did not live long enough to prove her military talents. She was assassinated while praying at a temple dedicated to the goddess Diana.

Berenice II of Cyrene began her military history in 247 B.C. by organizing an army and attacking the man to whom she was betrothed, a man she hated. Later, after marrying Ptolemy III Euergetes, she led her armies on numerous occasions. Her specialty was fighting from a chariot, and she was so expert that she defeated all of the male charioteers in the games of the Greek Olympiad and at a chariot race in Nemia.

Arsinoe II Cleopatra was the wife and sister of Ptolemy IV and mother of Ptolemy V. She demonstrated her warrior credentials in 217 B.C. when she led her cavalry to fight Antiochus the Great in Palestine.

The last of the great Ptolemaic women warriors, Cleopatra VII (Cleopatra the Great), was born in late 70 or early 69 B.C.[7] Though popularly regarded as an Egyptian, Cleopatra was actually Macedonian-Greek, a true daughter of the Ptolemies, a line that combined brilliance—they developed Alexandria as a cultural center surpassing even Rome—and psychotic violence.

Ptolemy I, called Soter, "the Savior of His People," was a brutal governor who, an ancient inscription tells us, maintained his power by "cutting off quantities of heads and shedding floods of blood."[8] Ptolemy II, named Philadelphus, "Man of Brotherly Love," killed his two brothers; Ptolemy IV killed his mother and her brother; Ptolemy VII, named Euergetes, "the Benefactor," killed masses of his own subjects indiscriminately "to teach them respect for their king"; Cleopatra the Great's father, Ptolemy XIII, called "the Flute Player," murdered his sister Berenice and then composed and performed a dirge for flute at her funeral.[9]

For over three centuries, noblewomen of the Macedonian line played a central role in the series of states that struggled back to life after the disintegration of the empire constructed by Alexander the Great. The most treacherous of them were the Cleopatras, a name common among ruling houses in Syria and Egypt. The sisters Cleopatra, daughters of Ptolemy VI of Egypt, cut a wide and bloody swath through ancient history.

One of them married three kings of Syria in succession, wedding the third while the second was held captive in Parthia. To stifle any suggestion that she had acted incorrectly, she killed the second when he returned, claiming that he had insulted her by taking a wife while in captivity. She then murdered her own son and the son of the second king by another wife because he claimed the throne. She was preparing to murder the youngest son of the second king when the youth discovered her intent and forced her to drink the cup of poison that she had prepared for him.

The sister of the Syrian murderess, also called Cleopatra, married her uncle, Ptolemy VII, but was soon left a widow with two sons. She favored her younger son and plotted to have him ascend the throne with her as regent, which necessitated the removal of the firstborn son. Her favorite apparently saw his mother as the true danger and murdered her. He took the throne by force, but the people of Alexandria rose against him and replaced him with the elder brother.

Cleopatra VII (Cleopatra the Great) was one of the six children of Ptolemy XII Auletes and Cleopatra V Trypanena. Her precocious energy and intelligence drew her to the throne, and she possibly coruled with her father in the months before his death. At her father's passing in 51 B.C., she was named coruler with her ten-year-old brother, Ptolemy XIII. In actuality, both coruled with Rome as the first among equals. The great Roman general Julius Caesar, in fact, was in Alexandria when Cleopatra and her brother came to the brink of war.

In 54 B.C., Cleopatra's brother, backed by court officials, drove her from Alexandria. She rode to the eastern frontiers and, with the vast wealth of the Ptolemies, raised an army and moved it toward Alexandria for a showdown with her brother Ptolemy XIII. Caesar, not wishing disruption in the Roman territory, demanded that Cleopatra and Ptolemy appear before him to reconcile their conflict. Ptolemy XIII refused to be commanded by a mere Roman general and surrounded Alexandria with twenty thousand troops, putting Caesar in a state of siege in the city's palace.

Cleopatra left her armies outside Alexandria and had herself smuggled into Caesar's presence wrapped in a bed sack. She charmed the general and acquired the loan of three Roman legions with which, added to her own army, she dispatched her brother as a threat and established her rule in Alexandria.

Cleopatra's sister, Arsinoe, also arrayed against Cleopatra at this time and prepared to war against her, in self-defense as she saw it. Cleopatra turned the issue over to Caesar, who sent his legions against Arsinoe and defeated her. He ordered Arsinoe taken to Rome and placed on public display as one of his trophies of war.

When Caesar returned to Rome, his mistress Cleopatra soon followed. She dreamed that through Caesar she could become empress of the Eastern Empire with her beloved Alexandria as its capital, but her dreams were shattered in 44 B.C. when he was assassinated. In the struggle for power that followed, Cleopatra met Mark Antony, friend of Caesar and one of the triumvirs who finally came to power.

Cleopatra soon controlled Mark Antony's head and heart. Her dream was reborn. In 36 B.C., Antony gave her Jericho and the island of Cyprus for a wedding present. Other lands westward toward India, including the fantastically rich Nabataean Arab kingdom, came to her as she wielded her power over Antony. For her part, she promised to provision the Roman expeditionary force setting out for war in Macedonia and to offer support to the Roman forces with her fleet whenever called upon to do so.

During the winter of 33–32 B.C., Antony and Cleopatra lived in Ephesus enjoying a life of nonstop revelry. Cleopatra dazzled the relatively provincial Antony with her sumptuous displays of entertainment in the Oriental style while filling his mind with fantasies of empire. Gradually, Antony drifted away from Rome and accepted the reality of Cleopatra's fantasy.

His military adviser Ahenobarbus argued that Cleopatra's constant presence in councils of war and policy was incorrect and distracting. He wanted Antony to dismiss her, but Canidius Crassus offered a strong counterargument. Cleopatra, he pointed out, had paid a major percentage of war cost, plus, of the five hundred ships in Antony's fleet, two hundred belonged to her. Finally, he reminded those critics of the queen that Cleopatra had ruled an immense empire for years unaided and that she possessed, at the very least, equal power to any of the kings allied to Antony's cause. Cleopatra stayed. Her presence was so central, furthermore, that when Roman Emperor Octavian responded to the threat posed by Antony and Cleopatra and declared war, he directed the missive not to Antony but to her.

Cleopatra participated with Antony in the councils of war leading up to the fateful sea battle at Actium. On September 2, 31 B.C., Antony, at the command of three hundred ships, and Cleopatra, in her purple-sailed command ship heading her personal fleet of two hundred vessels, met the Romans under Octavian.

The sea battle had raged for hours, neither side gaining the advantage, when Cleopatra's command ship pulled out of the battle and led the withdrawal of the Egyptian fleet back toward Egypt. Antony abandoned his command and followed her. She slowed to meet him, and he boarded her ship. They sailed to a southern island to await other survivors of the battle, and the few who appeared told of Octavian's complete victory. No one has ever explained what motivated Cleopatra's abandonment of the field at Actium. Once back in Alexandria, Antony withdrew in depression and spent days in a small cell overlooking the harbor at Alexandria, brooding on his fate.

While Antony ruminated, Cleopatra's fertile mind and inexhaustible energy coupled to implement a bold scheme. While she conceded the loss of an eastern empire, she still controlled great wealth and her fleet. She conceived of dragging her fleet across the desert to the Red Sea and setting out with her treasures, her family, her army, and her administrative staff to found a new kingdom far to the south. She might have made it if the desert Arabs, the bedouin, near the Red Sea had been more receptive. They burned half her fleet and forced her to cancel her grand scheme.

Antony was advised to murder Cleopatra and make peace with Rome, but he refused. At Cleopatra's urging, he proclaimed the Eastern Empire with Alexandria as its capital and ordered the buildup of armies, navies, and city defenses. For a time they succeeded in taking the fight to their enemy and carving out large sections of Roman territory; however, Octavian was not to be defeated. Cleopatra's charm did not work on the new emperor, and when she could not dissuade him from his plan to display her in his triumphant procession in Rome (as Bat Zabbai would be similarly displayed by Aurelian several centuries in the future), she died by her own hand on August 31, 30 B.C., at the age of thirty-nine.

In modern times, the tale of Cleopatra the Great is commonly interpreted as a story of romance. She is depicted as a seductress who turned the heads of Caesar and later Mark Antony through her beauty and feminine wiles. Such a view is typical of the contemporary reading of the histories of great warrior women. It is easier for historians, most of whom are men, to think of women sexually than militarily. A closer reading of the history of Cleopatra indicates that it was her armies and navies, her world-conquering ambition, and her savvy in the ways of war and politics that drew the Roman leaders to her. Beautiful women would be easy to access if one were Caesar or Mark Antony, but Cleopatra's attraction to the Romans was more powerful than the transient quality of beauty. First and foremost, Cleopatra the Great was a military asset to the Romans.

Women have taken part in many of the Middle East's most vicious wars. Today, all Israeli women serve two years in the military. This photograph shows Israeli women soldiers as they practice shooting Uzi submachine guns.

Reuters/Bettmann

CHAPTER 9

Middle East: More Blood Than You Can Drink

Women warriors appear in all of the ornate Middle Eastern civilizations that arose in the second millennium B.C. Over three thousand years ago, Rameses II of Egypt wrote of a female cavalry of the Mysian (Lydia) captained by women that went into battle against the Egyptians.[1]

Dating to about 1296 B.C., the biblical Deborah was called upon by the Israelites to guide them in their war against the Canaanite army of Jabon, led by his general Sisera. Deborah, a judge of Israel, whose duties included among others political and military advising, instructed the Israelite General Barak to raise an army of ten thousand troops and take the battle to Jabon. The discussion that ensued is recorded in Judges 4:8–9. "If thou wilt go with me, then I will go; but if thou wilt not go with me, then I will not go. And she said, 'I will surely go with thee: notwithstanding the journey that thou takest shall not be for thine honor; for the Lord shall sell Sisera into the hand of a woman.'"

Deborah's presence and guidance inspired the Israelites to victory over Jabon's army, but the Canaanite General Sisera nearly escaped. Deborah secured the assistance of Jael, the wife of a tribal general supposedly allied with Sisera. Jael lured Sisera into her tent and, after lulling him to sleep, drove a stake through his head. In true ancient warrior fashion, she proudly displayed his body to the Israelite General Barak.

Deborah's song of victory commemorating the battle with Lord Jabon's forces is one of the oldest Hebrew verses. "The people were oppressed in Israel, until you arose, Deborah, as the mother of Israel."

In later years when the Jews were threatened by Nebuchadnezzar II's General Holophernes, fresh from his victories in Egypt, another woman, Judith, would strike the decisive blow that turned the tide in favor of the greatly outnumbered Jewish resistance fighters. Using her beauty and charm to gain entrance into the quarters of General Holophernes, she encouraged him to drink himself into a stupor and then decapitated him with his own sword. With the general's head tucked under her shawl, she escaped to the Jewish lines. The next morning, the bewildered forces of Holophernes looked out to see their general's head mounted on a pole. Thus demoralized, the soldiers of Nebuchadnezzar II made easy prey for the Jewish forces.

In the late ninth and early eighth centuries B.C., Assyrian Queen Sammuramat secured the throne from her husband Ninus, ordered him killed, and seized control of the expansion of the Assyrian Empire (centered in modern-day Iraq). She fought her way to the oceans, thereby accessing foreign trade ports for landlocked Assyria. She conquered Babylon and constructed one of the seven wonders of the world, the Hanging Gardens of Babylon. Sammuramat conquered Ethiopia and Egypt, held Bactria—from the Hindu Kush to the Oxus River—against her husband's attack, and repulsed the armies of India. According to chroniclers of the time, Queen Sammuramat led an army of three hundred thousand foot soldiers, five thousand horse cavalry, and large contingents of camel-mounted cavalry and charioteers.

Her impressive record of accomplishment and conquest led the Greeks, who called her Semiramis, to fashion tales that she was descended from the gods, a not unusual fate for such earthshakers. Although the most mythologized of the Assyrian rulers, she left records of her accomplishments on stelae and a variety of self-glorifying monuments. On the platform that once held a statue of the great queen, she had written:

> Nature made me a woman yet I have raised myself to rival the greatest men. I swayed the scepter of Ninos; I extended my dominions to the river Hinamemes eastward; to the southward to the land of frankincense and myrrh; northward to Saccae and the Scythians. No Assyrian before me had seen an ocean, but I have seen four. I have built dams and fertilized the barren land with my rivers. I have built impregnable walls and roads to far places and with iron cut passages through mountains where previously

even wild animals could not pass. Various as were my deeds, I have yet found leisure hours to indulge myself with friends.[2]

A statue of the god Nebo in the British Museum bears the names of King Vul-Lush and his queen, Semiramis, "a princess of Babylon."[3]

While Sammuramat reigned, nomads to the north of her empire grew restless. The Persian Cyrus the Great organized these tribes and forced the Assyrian Empire under his sway, during which time his daughter Atossa involved herself in military adventures with him. She later married Darius the Great and gave birth to Xerxes. Historians tell us that Atossa had a strong influence over all these great men. Another of Darius's warrior daughters, Statira, was captured in a skirmish with Alexander the Great during his campaigns through Persia.

Assisted by Alexander in 344 B.C., warrior Queen Ada recaptured her throne city after it had fallen to her brother. Observers of her siege of the acropolis, where he was hiding, agreed that she delighted in personally seeing to her brother's destruction. Strabo wrote that the battle, for Queen Ada, was "a matter of anger and personal enmity."[4]

To the company of Atossa, Statira, and Sammuramat may be added Queen Pheretime of Cyrene (an ancient Greek city in Libya) and Queen Mother Amenstris, woman warrior nobles who for a time held various levels of control of the Persian Empire and its military might. Maria of Aetolia, Persian queen regent in the early fifth century B.C., led her army in battle and gained fame for the strict discipline she required of her armies.

The aforementioned Cyrus the Great, founder of the Persian Empire and conqueror of Assyria, met his end at the hands of a tribal chieftain—Tomyris, Queen of the Massagetae. In what is now eastern Iran, the Massagetae tribe was resisting Cyrus's plan for empire, so the king, to render the Massagetae an example to other uncooperative nations, led a campaign against them. Herodotus, the Greek historian, has left a detailed account of this historic encounter.

The Persian conqueror first sought to marry Tomyris, but she responded that her empire was being wooed, not she. When she heard his engineers were building bridges to expedite the movement of his army into her territory, she sent a message requesting that he desist. She concluded with: "Rule your own people, and try to bear the sight of me ruling mine."

Cyrus arranged a meeting with the queen's ambassadors and Tomyris's son Spargapises ostensibly to discuss peace terms, but the Persians killed the emissaries and captured Spargapises. This time Tomyris wrote to Cyrus:

> Glutton as you are for blood, you have no cause to be proud of this day's work, which has no smack of soldierly courage. . . . Give me back my son and get out of my country with your forces intact, and be content with your triumph over a third of the Massagetae. If you refuse, I swear by the Sun, our Master, to give you more blood than you can drink for all your gluttony.[5]

When her son was murdered in captivity, Queen Tomyris threw her forces against Cyrus's two-hundred-thousand-man army and destroyed it. Herodotus, a man of great experience in the ancient world, judged it to be the bloodiest battle he had witnessed. Not even a Persian messenger survived to carry the tale of the battle, and for years his people did not know what had become of Cyrus.

As her final act on the battlefield on the day of her victory, Queen Tomyris filled a large vessel with human blood and ordered Cyrus's head to be brought to her. She thrust it into the blood and, according to Herodotus, said, "Though I have conquered you and live, yet you have ruined me by treacherously taking my son. See now—I fulfill my threat, you have your fill of blood."[6]

Another woman warrior of the time, Zarina, queen of a Scythian tribe, conquered Media, in modern northwest Iran.[7] She commanded troops in numerous decisive battles and founded the city of Roxanace. From her fame the term *czar* was born.

Fifty years after the death of Cyrus the Great, the Persian king Xerxes warred against Greece. One of his allies, the Carian (southwestern Asia Minor) Queen Artemisia I, joined him with five warships. Herodotus tells us that the queen went into battle for no other reason than "her own spirit of adventure and her manly courage."[8]

Her most famous action occurred at the great naval engagement of Salamis when the Persian and Greek navies met in a decisive battle. Before the fight, Artemisia I had wisely advised Xerxes, in opposition to the advice of his other generals, not to engage the Greek naval power. She argued that the loss of his fleet would sacrifice his land army. To his detriment, Xerxes did not listen.

As the Greeks shattered the Persian attack, Artemisia I escaped the scene, pursued by the Greek general Ameninias. She demonstrated her creative knack for military tactics by ramming one of her own fleet rather than engaging Ameninias. Convinced that she must be one of his own, Ameninias returned to the battle. The Greek general not only lost the infamous Persian commander Artemisia I that day, but also the ten-thousand-drachma reward that the Greek army offered for her capture.

As the only of Xerxes's naval officers to survive the defeat of the Persian armada, she received his praise as the best of his generals and was rewarded with a complete suit of Greek armor for her gallant action. Her efforts during the battle inspired him to say, "My men have turned into women, my women into men."

Prior to her ill-fated partnership with King Xerxes, Queen Artemisia led her army in the defeat of her kingdom's archenemy, the island of Rhodes. The two countries had a long history of hostility, and after her husband's death the Rhodian war fleet attacked the queen at the fortress town of Halicarnassus.

Artemisia divided her troops, leaving one group in ambush positions in Halicarnassus and secretly leading the remainder from the city. She instructed the citizens to surrender the town when the Rhodians approached the gates.

When Artemisia received the signal that the Rhodians had entered the marketplace, she launched a surprise attack against the casually tended Rhodian fleet riding at anchor in the bay and then advanced toward Halicarnassus. Meanwhile, her forces hidden within the city sprang their part of the ambush, and the Rhodians were trapped between two arms of Artemisia's army.

Not satisfied, Queen Artemisia sailed the captured fleet back to Rhodes. The inhabitants, seeing the victory flags of their navy, opened the port and ran to the docks to greet their victorious forces. Artemisia's troops easily took the capital and leisurely captured the entire island.[9]

Middle Eastern history also acknowledges Artakama, the warrior daughter of the military governor of Bactria (eastern Iran), Artabazus; Aba, the daughter of Xenophanes, who warred with the military support of Mark Antony and Cleopatra the Great; and Rhodogune, the second-century B.C. Parthian queen who rushed from her bath without drying her hair upon hearing word of an impending revolt. She vowed to her servants that she would return from the battle and complete her bath later in the day. Queen Rhodogune led her soldiers into a war that lasted several years, and she did not bathe or brush her hair until she was declared victor. Thereafter, Parthian art depicted her with wild, flying hair.

In 50 B.C. the Greek traveler Strabo encountered Queen Pythodoris of Armenia, coruler with her husband Polemon, whose impressive warrior credentials convinced him that she was descended from the Amazons. Further to the east, several centuries later, Hypsicratea coruled the Persian Empire with her husband King Mithradates. With him, she drove the Persian armies against the legions of Rome, presenting a memorable figure with her closely shorn blonde hair, armor, helmet, and mail and armed with ax, lance, sword, and bow and arrows.

In the tenth century A.D., Adelaide of Susa was forced to defend not what she owned, but what she would inherit.[10] Daughter of the Marquis Olderic of Turin and Susa (southwestern Iran), Adelaide, in armor and mail with a sword at her side, challenged all who attempted to relieve her of her inheritance. She married Otto of Savoy and served with him as coruler. She became sole ruler after his death, when she assumed the office of queen regent for their young son.

In the eleventh century A.D. during the First Crusade, Armida of Damascus successfully defended her city. In the same century, Turkish princess Turfkan Khatun commanded her forces in a successful attack on the city of Ispahan and installed her four-year-old son as sultan. She defended her son's claim with force for many years.

Turfkan Khatun epitomizes a woman in Turkish history known as the *walide* sultan (queen mother), a noble position comparable to the *kentakes* of Ethiopia. The *walide* sultan played a conspicuous role in the coronation of her son, after which she was ceremoniously moved into the new king's palace.

The *walide* sultans powerfully affected Turkish policy by directly impinging on their sons' choices for various ministerial posts and vizierships. Powers in their own right, these women possessed their own fleets for personal trade and their own armies levied from the tenants who farmed the queen mother's land. Often, the incapability of the king (too young, old, debauched, weak-willed, or indifferent) would necessitate that all power be shifted to her. Such was the case with Nu Banu (died 1587) under Murad III, Safiyya (died 1609) under Mehmet III, Mah Peiker Kosem (died 1651) under Murad IV and Ibrahim I, and Tarkhan Khadijey (died 1683) under Mehmet IV.[11]

In the early twelfth century, Baldwin II, King of Jerusalem, having no sons, selected his daughter, Princess Melisende, as his successor. She became the vehicle by which the kingdom passed to her husband, Count Faulk V of Anjour, at their marriage. Several years later, however, King

Faulk died, leaving an only son, Baldwin III, for whom Queen Melisende served as queen regent. On Christmas Day in 1143, Baldwin III and Queen Melisende were crowned in Jerusalem.

In time Melisende and her son found themselves at odds, and Baldwin moved against his mother at Jerusalem. Though the city fell to him, the queen and her retinue retreated to the Tower of David, which she fortified. It was expected that, recognizing the hopelessness of her position, she would surrender and retire meekly to a convent. In fact, the situation only exacerbated Queen Melisende's defiance, and she relinquished her tower only after her son agreed to cede to her the city of Nablus and its surrounding lands and villages. She forced King Baldwin to swear an oath that he would never bother her again.

In 1157, while Baldwin III fought outside Antioch, Queen Melisende, on her own initiative, struck the cave fortress of el-Hablis from which the Muslims controlled the great expanses beyond the Jordan River. William of Tyre wrote that the success was based on the "planning and zeal" of Queen Melisende.[12]

Jerusalem was also the seat of Agnes, wife of King Amalric. When he died in the latter twelfth century, she moved quickly to cement her power over his realm by arranging marriages for the king's sisters to men of her choosing and filling all governmental positions with appointees loyal to her alone.

Queen Agnes retained such power that no one could move against her. In 1182, for example, when Raymond of Tripoli sought an audience with the new king against her wishes, she refused him entrance into "her" kingdom.

In 1832, as Ibrahim Pasha was about to invade Syria, he had to seek assurance of the neutrality of the powerful emir of Mar Elias, commander of a garrison of Armenian troops at an impregnable fortress in the wilds of Lebanon. This emir, sword-wearing practitioner of astrology and other arcane arts, was in fact Lady Hester Stanhope of England, daughter of the earl of Stanhope and Hester, daughter of the earl of Chatham.

From an early age Lady Stanhope felt powerfully that her destiny lay in Asia. In 1810, at the age of thirty-four, she traveled to the Near East, visiting Jerusalem, Damascus, and Palmyra, and in 1813 she took up residence in a deserted convent perched on a high stone prominence in the Lebanese desert. She hired an army of mercenaries to serve as her garrison and, according to all accounts, controlled her small army and her staff with an iron grip. In a decorated stable at her fortress, she kept two fine mares, upon which she planned to ride into Jerusalem with the Messiah in his next coming.[13] She died in her desert fortress at an advanced age.

In 1855, a Kurdish warrior called the Black Virgin led a thousand cavalry troops in the Crimean War and later fought against Russian forces under Omar Pasha in battles along the Danube River.

The warrior spirit of twentieth-century Persian women was demonstrated in 1911, when Russia issued an ultimatum to the Persian National Assembly in Teheran. As the assembly vacillated, three hundred women, many carrying pistols, stormed into the building and threatened the president with the death of their own husbands and sons if he submitted to cowardly terms.

Bracha Fuld, born in 1926, was at eighteen an officer and instructor of Jewish women soldiers. She commanded a number of military actions and fought in the Battle of Sarona. In her last fight, she commanded an eight-man unit assigned to protect a road upon which Jewish refugees attempted to elude the British and reach safety in Palestine. When her small unit was about to be overrun by the British, Bracha sent half of her squad to safety and carried on a suicidal night battle with the British tanks. She later died from injuries received in this fight. Today in Tel Aviv, Bracha Fuld Street commemorates her valor.

In Israel on May 19, 1941, emergency order no. 2 directed the formation of the Palmach, assault companies for infiltration, surprise attack, and assault. On November 29, 1947, the United Nations General Assembly voted to partition Palestine into Jewish and Arab states. On May 14, 1948, the British withdrew from their occupation of the area, and soon-to-be Prime Minister David Ben-Gurion proclaimed the new state of Israel. Less than a day later, the armies of Syria, Lebanon, Iraq, Egypt, and Transjordan attacked. By June 1948, the six-thousand-member Palmach included twelve hundred women with five women leading combat units. In the Battle of the Roads, women comprised one-third of the convoy escorts. Meir Pa'il, Knesset member and army colonel, stated, "Women were excellent . . . there was not a single incident of a female soldier not behaving correctly under fire."[14] Jewish women warriors fought in the struggle for independence and in the 1948 campaigns emerged as frontline combatants. However, when the Israeli Defense Forces were created in 1949, women were excluded from combat roles altogether.

The ancient legacy of the woman warrior was echoed as late as 1986 in the retinue of Benazir Bhutto, the woman claimant to Pakistani leadership. The crack female guards that surrounded Bhutto were termed Amazons.[15]

The success of individual women warriors in World War I prompted the creation of the first Russian all-woman battalions. Recognized for their bravery, heroism, and fighting skills, these units came to be known as "Battalions of Death."

Eastern Europe:
Battalions of Death

When the ancient Greeks sought to understand the nature of life, they looked to the gods, none a complete stranger to warfare, and there, at the foundations of their great civilization, powerful images of the woman warrior abounded. Aphrodite aided Ares at the Battle of Troy. Athena is described as having sprung fully armed from the head of Zeus and was invoked with Ares in any prayer or salutation to the gods of war. Athena, along with Hera and Aphrodite, formed the Areia, "women warriors."

Artemis Orthia enjoyed the distinction of favorite war goddess of the Spartans, the highly militarized elites who ruled in southern Greece and who offered figurines of warriors at her temples. She was the spiritual patron of the military training of the young men of Athens, and soldiers going into battle would invoke Apollo and her for success.

The Spartans were particularly interested in educating women to warfare. The great Spartan king, Lycurgus the Law-Giver, in the seventh century B.C., formally encouraged Spartan women to excel at javelin throwing, running, boxing, and wrestling. The wedding ritual of the Spartans necessitated the study of wrestling because "the wedding ceremony was preceded by a public wrestling match of the utterly naked couple."[1]

Single combat as a courtship ritual continues today in many societies. In modern Baroda, India, hundreds watched a wrestling match that would determine whom Hamida Banu would marry. The agreement stated that if she lost to her challenger, Bab Pahelwan, she would be his wife. And, if Bab Pahelwan lost, he would retire from professional wrestling. He lasted a minute and a half with the heavyweight Hamida Banu.[2]

Constant enmity between the Spartans and the Athenians runs throughout the history of ancient Greece. In the fourth century B.C., a young Spartan nobleman encouraged his sister Cynisca to enter her horses in the chariot race of the Olympic Games, because he felt confident that her victory would embarrass the Athenians. Cynisca's team won, and her victory is noted on inscriptions and victors' lists. In 268 B.C. and again in 264 B.C., the war horses of Bilistiche of Argos, concubine of Ptolemy II, won the Olympic four-horse chariot race. The noblewoman Euryleonis is also recorded as victorious in the Olympic chariot competitions.

As has been made apparent in this survey, throughout history and in every corner of the world, women warriors have generated ferocious defensive battles to hold their castles and towns. In the third century B.C., Princess Arachidamia led women soldiers in the defense of Lacedemon against the attack of Pyrrhus.

When another Spartan city was attacked by a large enemy force in 280 B.C., the senate determined to send the noble wives and children to safety in another town. As the men of the senate deliberated, a princess named Chelidonis drew her sword, swearing that she and the women of the town would not flee but would stand in the defense of the city. Chelidonis led the women in the successful battle with a slip noose looped around her neck, so that if her enemies dragged her over the wall in a fight, they would not take her alive.

Women warriors of the Athenian allies also stood against the Spartans. In the fifth century B.C., the Spartan Kings Cleomenes and Damaratas and their allies attacked the city of Argive. The soldiers of the town gave battle near their city but were devastated; seven thousand of them died. The Spartans turned toward the city for what they thought would be an easy entrance, but Princess Telesilla and her women warriors barred the gate and climbed the battlements to successfully challenge them. The yearly festival of Numenia was later created as a day on which men dress as women and women as men to commemorate the ancient victory.[3]

On the northern border of Greece lies Macedonia, where in the fourth century B.C. a great dynasty arose. Advances in the warring arts initiated by Philip and applied by his son Alexander the Great escalated Macedonia to a world empire. As was the case with the Cyrus/Darius line in Persia and the Ptolemies of Egypt, so too did women warriors populate the world of Philip of Macedonia and his son Alexander. A historian notes, ". . . that Macedonia women of the governing elite were disposed to violence is beyond question, for the records prove it."[4] Philip's first wife Eurydice, an Illyrian warrior princess, passed on the martial traditions and arts of her people to her daughter Cynane and her granddaughter, who took her grandmother's name when she rose to power.

Meda of Getae (modern eastern Bulgaria), Philip's second wife, was reared in the arts of leadership and war as were all noblewomen of her country. In 1977 Manolis Andronikos, a Greek archaeologist, excavated what he believes to be the tomb of Philip of Macedonia. In the chamber assigned to Queen Meda, no jewels, mirrors, or combs were found but rather armor, arrowheads, and other artifacts of war.[5]

Cynane, daughter of Eurydice and Philip, gained fame for her military skills, both as a general and a shock-troop fighter. She charged at the head of her troops in victory over the Illyrians and killed the Illyrian queen Caeria in single combat. In her spare time, she trained her daughter by Amyntas, Eurydice, in martial arts and military strategy.

She engaged the generals of the Macedonian Empire after the death of her half brother, Alexander the Great, when her rightful claim to the throne was denied and the generals divided the realm among themselves. Vastly outnumbered, her forces met the traitorous generals, who sought terms with her, fearing the damage she would do their armies if the issue were forced. Cynane refused surrender under any name, for the daughter of Philip and the rightful heir of Macedonia declared that she had "resolved upon a glorious death." She compelled the generals to fight her to the death—hers, it turned out.

Cynane's daughter, Eurydice II, married Philip III Arrhidaeus. He proved mentally incapable of ruling, a fact Cynane understood when she arranged the union. Eurydice II quickly overshadowed her husband and became the de facto ruler of the Macedonian Empire. She successfully defended her throne by arms, including warring against another woman, Olympias, who also claimed the throne.

The wife of Alexander the Great, Queen Cratesipolis of Sicyon, fought beside her husband and continued as a military commander after his death. She controlled several Greek cities and a large mercenary army and in the fourth century B.C. conquered Corinth in the name of Ptolemy I.[6]

In the land of Illyria (present-day Albania), home of Philip's first wife Eurydice, lived a pirate leader named Teuta, wife of King Agron of Illyria. Teuta seized rule of Illyria after her husband's death in 231 B.C.

Teuta and her people earned their livelihood through piracy. Comparable to the Vikings of a later time, they attacked ships and coastal towns in search of booty and tribute. King Agron and later Teuta instituted the policy of seizing the islands along the Greek coast.

Rome officially noticed Teuta's interference in their Adriatic trade. Their emissaries found her leading the siege of Issa, one of the few Greek islands still holding out against her. To their demand that she cease raiding their ships, Teuta responded that etiquette in her country forbade interfering with anyone's right to make a living. The Romans conveyed their irritation at her insolence, whereupon she ordered them killed.

Rome and Greece jointly declared war against Teuta and forced her withdrawal from a number of occupied islands. Her army held one stronghold so long that the Romans finally arranged a settlement in which they would pay her for not threatening the islands of the Greeks or their merchant ships. She accepted their money and commenced piracy against her other neighbors, as was her claimed right as an Illyrian, a right she was willing to challenge the Roman Empire to defend.[7]

North of the Macedonians and west of the Scythians, the Sarmatians, an equestrian nomadic nation, ranged in the fourth century B.C. The presence of women fighters and captains raised speculation among the Greeks concerning their ties to the legendary Amazons. Archaeological excavations of Sarmatian tombs in the twentieth century revealed women buried with armor, horses, and weapons, grave goods commonly denoting the military status of the interred.[8]

A Sarmatian warrior queen, Amage, ruled as co-regent with her incapacitated husband in the fourth century B.C. When a Scythian tribe pressed on her eastern borders, she dispatched a request to their leader that he turn back. When he refused, she led a hand-picked group of 120 Sarmatian warriors on a raid into Scythia. While her soldiers fought the palace guards, Amage entered the fortress, found the Scythian prince, and killed him in a sword duel. She ordered his family put to death excepting his son, whom she allowed to remain on his father's throne with the stipulation that he obey only her.

The Sarmatians remained a force several decades before the birth of Christ with women warriors still in evidence. Dynamis of Bosphorus, whose name translates fittingly enough "she who must be obeyed," is remembered for her association with the Sarmatians of that era.

Dynamis was married to King Asander, ruler by Roman acquiescence of the Cimmerian Bosphorus and successor to her aged father. Dynamis and her lover, Scribonius, led a revolt against Asander, and Dynamis assumed control. Rome found this act unacceptable, given the importance of control of the Bosphorus, and sent a neighboring king and Roman minion, Polemo of Pointus, to quell Dynamis's rebellion. Polemo was promised the governorship of the Cimmerian Bosphorus and Dynamis's hand in marriage if he succeeded.

Polemo defeated her resistance and soon controlled both the Bosphorus and, so he thought, Dynamis. She raised an army with the help of the Sarmatian warrior Aspurgus—whom she married despite Polemo's claim on her—and with her new husband conducted a series of battles that defeated Polemo, who was killed by Aspurgus in 8 B.C.

Once more in control, Dynamis considered her relationship with Rome and Augustus Caesar and elected to make peace with the Roman emperor. She became a Roman vassal, still in control of the Bosphorus and possessor of a title, "Friend of the Roman People." Queen Dynamis, "She Who Must Be Obeyed," died in A.D. 8 of old age.

North of Dynamis's realm in the Ukraine, women warriors have been shaping history for thousands of years, as they have in the Caucasus to the southeast. Women's armies were noted in Bohemia from the eighth century. The foundation of modern Ukrainian history was built upon the accomplishments of such warrior queens as Olga (ninth century A.D.), Queen Anna Michailivna (A.D. 1065), Princess Ivannie Ianka (twelfth century A.D.), Queen Polots'ka Predslava (A.D. 1173), and Queen Yaroslavna (A.D. 1185).[9]

Queen Olga of Kiev etched her warrior portrait for history in dealing with the Drevlians, a Slavic tribe living west of Kiev. After her husband, Prince Igor, was murdered in 945 while extracting onerous taxes from them, Olga swore vengeance. She began with the Drevlian ambassadors who were sent to convince her to marry their war chief Mal and abandon the throne of Kiev. The first group of messengers, so the story goes, she buried alive. The second, she boiled in their baths, and the third she ordered chopped into little pieces. Not yet satisfied, she armed herself and led her army to Iskorosen, the capital of the Drevlians.

The Drevlians proved effective at siege warfare and withstood Olga, who became increasingly impatient to finish the battle and return to Kiev. One day, she had a brilliant idea. She called off her skirmishers and walked to the city walls where in a loud voice she addressed the citizens of the embattled city. She told them that she had killed enough to avenge her husband and wanted to return home, but her royal honor demanded some token of tribute before she could leave. The Drevlians, thrilled to be so close to safety, offered her gold and treasure, but she refused, saying that she possessed enough gold. She requested one pigeon from each citizen of the town. The Drevlians, barely believing the token demand, hurried to their rooftop aviaries to comply, and before nightfall thousands of caged pigeons were delivered to her.

Olga issued orders to her captains and retired for a few hours before completing her revenge. Acting on her instructions, the soldiers tied small burning sticks to the pigeons' legs and released them. They promptly returned to their rooftop homes, which quickly set the entire city on fire. As the citizens fled, Queen Olga orchestrated their slaughter.

After vanquishing the Drevlians in 946, she traveled through her defeated foe's territory and built hunting lodges and palaces. The next year, she marched her armies north collecting tribute and confiscating more land. The *Russian Primary Chronicles* cite her as the first private landowner of Russia, and the chronicler adds, "Her hunting grounds, boundary posts, towns, and trading posts still exist throughout the whole region."[10]

Olga's Russia was a volatile mixture of native Slavic groups and Viking invaders, the Varangians, who had penetrated the heart of the country through its river systems. Historians indicate that the Varangian women stood with their men in wielding battle weapons.

In the time of Mahomet II (eighth century A.D.), the Turks attacked the capital of the island of Lemnos. Lady Marulla, daughter of the governor, was wounded and her father killed as the Turks approached the walls of the city. However, seeing that the defenders were withering under the Turkish assault, Lady Marulla drew her sword on the frontline Turkish fighters. Inspired by her leadership, the garrison rallied and threw back the Turkish threat.

The following day, a Venetian general arrived, prepared to relieve the siege of the capital, only to find a victory celebration in honor of Lady Marulla. After hearing from the citizens about Lady Marulla's exploits, the general commanded that each of his soldiers recognize her courage and valor with a gift.[11]

In the early tenth century, Zoe of Constantinople seized control after the death of her husband, Leo VI. She is remembered for her strong but enlightened reign and for her military successes. She smashed the rebellion of Constantine Ducas, brought the interminable wars with the Saracens to a close in a favorable peace, and forced the Bulgarians to relocate farther to the north of her territory.

On the other side of the Black Sea, south of the Caucasus and west of the Caspian Sea, Georgia rose to prominence in 1184. Queen Tamara, who had coruled with her father King Girgi for the six years before his death, wrested full control of the country.[12] Georgia's location was ideal. Mountains barred it from Russia to the north and the inhospitable high desert plateau of Armenia blocked hostile access from the south, yet coasts on two seas provided a trade network that reached into the Far East. Queen Tamara was last in succession of the Bagrationis clan, warriors who had fought into the Georgian valleys from northern Armenia in the late tenth century.

In her twenties when she succeeded to the throne, Queen Tamara was immediately forced to defend her title. She pacified the always troublesome noble houses with gifts and compliments and warred for her throne against two Russian princes, besting them in two major battles in 1191. In 1200, she quelled another rebellion. Throughout it all, she married a number of times and gave birth to several children to ensure succession to the throne.

Her skill at horsemanship and her courage continually impressed the Georgian nobles. When they were compelled to accompany her on hunts, she won their loyalty and simultaneously taught them respect for her martial talents.

Queen Tamara excelled at military tactics, devised successful battle plans, and functioned as an inspiring orator in rousing her troops before battle. Following the custom of her people, she marched barefoot at the head of her troops, a spiritual/military leader. She wore arms and commanded major troop advances and retreats during battles. After a reign of twenty-four years, during which she guided Georgia into its golden age, Queen Tamara died peacefully on January 18, 1212.

In 1603, John Cartwright wrote while traveling in Armenia that he found the people "to be industrious in all kinds of labor. . . . Their women very skillful and active in shooting and managing any sort of weapon."[13] This pattern of female activity was found throughout Armenia and eastward into Kurdish and Syrian areas as well as the Mongol regions of the steppes.

A woman warrior tradition was noted by anthropologist Sula Benet in 1974 while studying the Abkhazians, a people whose territory borders Tamara's Georgia. The Abkhazian social order was based on two principles: family affiliations and the right of each person to bear and use weapons. Both sexes were trained in horseback riding and weaponry, skills that differentiated a free person from a slave. Benet writes concerning Abkhazian women: ". . . in the past, she . . . was expected to take up arms bravely when necessary, to fight alongside the men and to be stoic and relentless."[14]

Two hundred years after the death of Queen Tamara of Georgia, fourteenth-century Bohemia was contested by a number of female warriors. Countess Margaret Maultasch of Tirol in 1342 directed her troops in a battle against the king of Bohemia, her husband. Later she married the son of Emperor Louis IV and joined him in a number of battles to discipline rebellious nobles and to defend territorial boundaries from encroachment by hostile neighbors.

In the same era Queen Sophia, widow of Wenceslas, held the throne of Bohemia. She was challenged by a self-proclaimed patriot named John Ziska and his women's army. In an engagement near Pilsen, his female warriors faced the professional army of Queen Sophia.

Ziska devised a plan to thwart Queen Sophia's heavy cavalry charge. As the mercenary knights rolled forward in their well-ordered battle lines, the anti-Royalist women stripped their veils, capes, scarves, and outer gowns and hung them over the low brush that covered the field. When the queen's cavalry reached the sea of cloth, the horses became entangled, and the cavalry charge broke up in confusion. Ziska's second order came, and the women descended on the knights, dragging them from their horses. Sophia's professionals were defeated by the Bohemian women's army.[15]

Some decades later in Bohemia, Queen Libussa and her nemesis, Queen Valeska, fought the "Bohemian Girls' War," a battle over the emerging nation of Bohemia. Libussa with her three sisters experienced early success.

Later, Queen Valeska won the kingdom from Libussa and instigated a cruel reign during which all Bohemian girls served compulsory military duty. Aeneas Piccolomini, later Pope Pius II, wrote in the *Historia Bohemica* that all men had their right eyes and thumbs removed to render them useless in battle.[16]

Meanwhile, far to the south, Helen Palaeologina married John II of Cyprus and attained total rule of the island in 1442. She occupied Constantinople in 1453 and controlled Cyprus long enough to pass it to her daughter Carolotta.

Whereas Helen of Cyprus rode with fortune, Marina Muizeck, sixteenth-century Russian empress, ended her very brief military career unceremoniously. She was dumped by rebellious peasants through a hastily cut hole in the thick ice of a frozen pond for donning armor and leading her troops to avenge the murder of her husband. Suffice it to say that swimming in armor (a martial art the Japanese samurai called *Tachi Oyogi*), even under the best of conditions, is an extremely arduous activity, one for which the courageous empress had apparently not trained.

Female martial activity emanated from some surprising sources; it was not unusual in world history for women warriors to be nuns. In the 1650s, Philothey Benizelos established a convent in Greece and so successfully attracted women students that the local governments feared her growing power. The women of the convent were armed and trained as fighters, for several times Philothey had been called to forcibly pacify rebellious tenants who protested the harsh taxes exacted by the convent managers.[17]

In the mideighteenth century, Catherine the Great of Russia shaped her legend. She served as a vigorous commander in chief to the Russian military establishment, and in times of war she wore a military uniform. Armed with both pistol and swords, Catherine walked the walls studying the enemy positions, accompanied by her similarly attired ladies-in-waiting. In a famous winter battle, she ordered her men to hack cannon shapes from ice and darken them with soot to mask the true quantity of her firepower.

She rose to power by accoutering herself as a soldier, mounting a warhorse, and leading her army against her husband's palace at Oranienbaum. He wisely ran away upon her approach.

Abbot speaks of her immense military ambitions:

> What her armies were doing was known to her each day, and her voice was incessantly calling upon her generals to press on. She carried the Russian frontier to the Black Sea. With Frederick the Great and Queen Maria Theresa of Austria, she overwhelmed Poland, taking the greatest part for herself. At the very threshold of her unexpected death, she was planning war upon almost all of

Europe—Constantinople, and Stockholm, Paris and Teheran were to be hers.[18]

* * *

The Greek woman warrior tradition continued into the eighteenth century with Lascarina Boubalina. Born in 1783, she developed into a Greek naval commander known as Capitanissa and, with her squadron of warships, attacked Turkish shipping in the Aegean and Mediterranean. After recapturing several Greek towns that had been occupied by the Turks, Lascarina Boubalina was murdered in her home at Spetsai in 1825.

Manto Mavrogenous of Mykonos captained two ships to clear pirates from the waters near her island. With that accomplished, she organized a small army and several times led her soldiers against the Turks. Statues of Captains Mavrogenous and Boubalina stand in the War Memorial in Athens.

Also fighting the Turks, Moscho Tzavella led an army of peasant women against the forces of the pasha and defeated him. On the other side, Turkish women frequently accompanied their husbands into battle.[19]

Between 1943 and 1947, during the Greek Civil War, Anna Dosa served as a commander in the Coronis campaign. Approximately one-fifth of the soldiers who fought in the Greek Civil War were female, and 250 Greek women were honored as resistance heroines during World War II. One stalwart warrior, Annetta of the Peloponnesus, single-handedly captured and disarmed a group of German soldiers.

* * *

Poland in the mid-1800s was pressing for its independence. Austria held Cracow and abused the population. A young Polish woman, nineteen-year-old Appolonia Jagiello, joined the insurrection against the Austrian overlords in 1846. Mounted on her charger and dressed in a Polish officer's uniform, she plunged into the thick of the fighting, saber drawn. The rebels, outnumbered ten to one, were crushed, and Jagiello went into hiding in Warsaw. Two years later the Polish patriots tried again to rise against the Austrian government in Cracow, and again Appolonia Jagiello appeared, sword in hand.

When the second uprising was quelled, she traveled to Vienna to study the Austrian state more closely. She fought with the Hungarians, who were also struggling with the Austrians, in battles at Widen and Eneszey, where the Hungarian army defeated the Austrians. For her heroics, she was promoted to the rank of lieutenant in the Hungarian army and joined the forces under General Klapka that captured the important city of Raab.

In 1848 when the Austrians defeated the Hungarians and the hope for independence all but vanished in Poland, Jagiello moved to the United States. She lived in Washington, D.C., honored as a true heroine until her death several years later.

*   *   *

Women warriors of nineteenth-century eastern Europe were ubiquitous at all levels of the military. Italian, Austrian, Georgian, Prussian, Greek, Turkish, and Russian armies all claimed women soldiers, women who fought and died in frontline combat and received the highest decorations for heroism and valor. Exemplary were Russian soldier Alexandra Dourova, who fought with the Fourth Hussars in the wars against Napoleon, and Thérèse Figuer, intrepid cavalry warrior on the French side, who had four horses shot from under her but continued her fight.

The Russians were attacked by the small army of Emilja Plater, daughter of Count Ksawery and Countess Anna Plater. At the age of twenty-five, she led several successful engagements against them.

In all phases of the anti-Tsarist revolution in the latter nineteenth century, women participated. In 1878 the so-called Era of Terror was triggered by Vera Zasulich when she assassinated a prison official, while Sofya Perovskaya led the assault team that killed Tsar Alexander II in 1881.[20] Trotsky, in his *History of the Russian Revolution*, noted that women directed the revolution's inception in St. Petersburg in 1917. Russian anti-Tsarist women fighters acted on military fronts all over Russia as line troops, military train conductors, snipers, demolition experts, spies, terrorists, and assassins. Vera Zasulich, for example, shot and killed the governor of St. Petersburg in 1876.

Fighting on the side of the tsar in 1914, Princess Eugenie Shakhovskaya filled many roles, including chief executioner of Kiev, member of the tsar's dreaded secret police, and first woman military aircraft pilot. Russian women fought in combat roles in World War I, and during the eight months of the provisional government that followed the monarchy in 1917, they served in women's battalions.

In 1915 nineteen-year-old Olga Krasilnikov, disguised as a young man, served in the Russian army on the eastern front in nineteen battles before she was seriously wounded and sent back to Moscow. She received the St. George Cross. Another Olga, Olga Serguievna Schidlowskaia, served as an infantry fighter with the Russian Fourth Hussars during this time.

The same year Olga Krasilnikov was fighting in Poland, Natalie Tychmini won the St. George Cross for bravery in a battle with Austrians at Opatow. She lent her fighting abilities to her country not only in World War I but again in World War II.

One of the last battles in World War I to witness the actions of Russian women warriors occurred on October 25, 1917, when a unit of fighting women from Petrograd defended the provisional government holed up in the Winter Palace. They opposed women in the Red Guards, the shock troops of the Bolshevik revolution.[21]

The success of women warriors stimulated the creation in 1917 of the first Russian all-woman battalion, which comprised 250 women, some as young as seventeen. According to Swiss observers, the women's battalion did well in its baptism of fire near Smorgon.[22] The experiment proved so successful that several other all-female "battalions of death" were later formed in Moscow, Odessa, Ekaterinodar, and Perm.

Marie Baktscharow, nicknamed "Yashka," captain of the first battalion of death, won medals for heroism on the front lines. In one of her most famous exploits, she crawled into the face of withering machine-gun fire to rescue several fallen comrades. It was she who first proposed the creation of the women's battalions. Marie once said, concerning her warrior life, "My country called me, and an irresistible force from within pulled me."[23] One young woman in Yashka's battalion said simply of her first battlefield experience, "I found myself next to a German and ran him through with my bayonet, shot him, and took his helmet for a memento." Another, Mariya Golubyova, had this to say after the war:

> I had no sensation except to rid my country of an enemy. There was no sentimentality. We were trying to kill them and they were trying to kill us—that is all. Any Russian girl or any American girl in the same position would have the same feeling.[24]

A male Austrian officer who had met the Russian women in battle later commented:

> Especially in attack did they show themselves to be brave and not infrequently blood-thirsty. Naturally we were quite far from feeling any knightly sentiments toward these Penthesileas [AUTHOR'S NOTE: Penthesileas was a mythical queen of the Amazons]. It is interesting to note that these female warriors did not wear trousers, but blue smocks. These were the first skirts we had ever seen that left the knee bare.[25]

Vera Butcharev, a captain in the Battalion of Death, achieved fame for her reckless courage in the face of enemy fire. The sisters Ludmilla and Volkensteii Kornilov also proved themselves effective warriors in Yashka's battalion.

Zoya Smirnow joined a group of twelve Russian girls, some as young as fourteen, who disguised themselves as boys and, emulating the battalions of death, went into battle as infantry. They killed numerous enemy soldiers in battles in Galicia and in the Carpathian Mountains.

A Dutchwoman, Jenny Merkus, and an Englishwoman, Flora Sandes, found a place in the lists of the women fighters in Eastern Europe. Jenny, called "the Amazon of Herzegovina," fought as a Bosnian cavalry warrior in their uprising against the Ottoman Turks.

In August of 1914, Flora Sandes of Suffolk, England, left her homeland for Serbia as a member of an ambulance company raised by Madame Mable Grouitch. Her fighting life began with the Fourth Company in a battle with the Bulgars on Mount Chukus. The Nashi Engleskinja, "our Englishwoman," was wounded by a grenade fragment in a later action and while recuperating in an army hospital was awarded the King George Star, the Serbian military's highest decoration, and promoted to sergeant major.

In mid-1918, Flora fought with her platoon as they repelled the Austrians and Germans. She retired from the Serbian army in 1922 and in September 1926 learned that a grateful Serbia had promoted her to captain of the Reserve Officer Corps.

When the Germans invaded Yugoslavia in 1939, Flora, who was then sixty-three years old, was called up as a captain in the Reserve Officer Corps. In 1945 the British Royal Air Force flew Captain Sandes back to Suffolk, where she died ten years later.[26]

Thousands of women fought in Eastern Europe in World War I, the great majority of them unknown and unsung. Following the lead of their Russian sisters, 2,400 Serbian women volunteered for an all-female company called "the League of Death." Other women fought in independent guerrilla units, and some, like Sophie Jowanowitsch and Milena Manditsch, simply joined the regular army.

* * *

Yugoslavia, a nation formed after World War I from the states of Serbia, Macedonia, Montenegro, Slovenia, Croatia, and Bosnia-Herzegovina, has a long history of women warriors. In 1389, Serbian Countess Milice resisted the Turks; and Macedonian, Serbian, and Montenegran women battled the Ottoman Turks in the early nineteenth century. In the uprising of 1804, women actively engaged in combat, and one group of Yugoslavian women warriors commandeered an enemy cannon barehanded. A battalion of women fought in a battle between the Turks and Montenegrans in 1858. The break up of Yugoslavia in 1990 and the resultant civil wars in several regions has provided more examples of women fighters.

The participation of women in warfare in this part of the world speaks to more than a spontaneous response to civil war. Montenegro, for example, had an ancient custom, the *kult majke* (cult of motherhood), that in its rule of respect for women permitted them to participate in warfare.[27]

In 1941, the Germans invaded Yugoslavia and installed Ante Pavelic, the founder of the Croatian Ustasha Party, as their puppet. The Ustasha governed Croatia until 1943, when the Germans commenced their horrific occupation. Thousands of Serbs were murdered by the Ustasha, while the Germans sent several hundred thousand Serbs to concentration camps. A Serbian army officer organized anti-Nazi guerrillas called Chetniks, and in June 1941 when the Germans invaded the Soviet Union, Tito, Communist party leader in Yugoslavia, called on all members of the party to oppose the Germans.

In Serbia, Macedonia, and Slovenia, over one hundred thousand women enlisted in partisan units. Seventy percent of the women warriors had not reached twenty, and most were Serbian.

The first women's partisan *ceta* (unit of several hundred) was organized in Tranavec in August 1942. After its first battle, an editorial in an underground Serbian newspaper described what happened.

> We looked with suspicion on the military skills of the women comrades, but all that doubt today has disappeared like summer light in the morning fog. On our way across Kordun, our II Partisan Shock Brigade, in whose rank was the *ceta* of young women, came into conflict with motorized, tank and infantry forces. In the fight which developed, the young partisan women, together with their partisan comrades, fearlessly attacked the enemy's horses, trucks, even the tanks, and the old experienced soldiers were amazed at the young peasant girls who only yesterday took rifle in hand.[28]

Ninety-two women were designated as national heroes by the Yugoslavian government. Danica Milosavljevic, who achieved the rank of second lieutenant, fought on the Salonika-Belgrade line in thirty-eight battles in just over six weeks. Milka Kufrin is celebrated for her part in sabotaging the Zagreb–Rijeka railroad. Every night for over seven months, she prowled the heavily guarded system of tracks, setting explosive charges directly under the Nazi guns.

Disguised as an old woman, she once destroyed a German tank by waiting beside the road as their military convoy passed. In the folds of her bulky dress were hidden two grenades and two Molotov cocktails. She escaped after her attack but was later killed in action.

The demolition expertise of two other women warriors should be noted. Red Army soldier Tanja Chesnieres attacked an important German command center, eliminating the guards, setting explosives, and killing an SS agent in hand-to-hand combat. The Gestapo became familiar with the demolition skills of Czech resistance fighter Elena Haas through her many successful sabotaging missions. The French resistance acknowledged her invaluable aid in destroying an important bridge used by the Nazis. She was killed in a raid against German positions in 1945.

Almost all of the couriers for the Yugoslavian Partisan forces were young women. On foot, bicycle, horseback, and motorcycle, they demonstrated their bravery again and again as they carried their messages over rugged mountainous terrain and through enemy lines.

One of the most ferocious woman warriors of the Yugoslav resistance, Mira, fought in a partisan guerrilla unit and was personally responsible for the death of several hundred German soldiers. The Nazis feared these women fighters because they often tortured their captives. Mira was killed when her unit was ambushed.

Kurt Strod, leader of the Czech resistance to Nazi occupation, owed his life to the courage of a woman fighter. He and Marja Kolzany were discovered by the Nazis as they prepared to dynamite a bridge in March 1940. German bullets hit Strod several times, and he went down. Marja Kolzany stayed with him, keeping the Nazis at bay with her machine gun until she could drag him to safety.[29]

Helen Ruz, member of the Voluntary Ukraine Legion, fought with her fiance, two brothers, and father in the front lines of all the major battles of her regiment. At the end of the war, she alone survived. She took from war two medals for her courage in battle and several broken bones.

Princess Wolonsky also lost her husband and brothers in the war. Driven by the need for vengeance, she disguised herself as a man and joined the infantry, quickly distinguishing herself in action at Wolhynia. As with other women warriors who fought in disguise, Princess Wolonsky lived with the fear that medical treatment necessitated by battle wounds would reveal her secret. She was discovered in this fashion and sent to Kiev but later fled, donned her disguise, and returned to the battle, where she fought for several more years undetected.

The Cossacks have a long and proud fighting tradition, which speaks of the prowess of both men and women. In World War I, Olga Kokovtseva captained the Sixth Regiment of the Ural Cossacks and received several battle wounds as well as the St. George Cross, while Alexandra Ephimownas Langareva served as an officer in a Don Cossack regiment. Yellow Martha, so-called because of her blonde hair, was a Cossack woman warrior who fought with honor in three major battles. Sophie

Haletchko, a twenty-four-year-old who before the war was working toward a doctorate in philology, was a cavalry sergeant major in the Galician-Ukrainian division, fighting with distinction in a number of battles.[30]

In the Austrian-Hungarian army, Corporal Marie Von Fery-Bognar fought with such courage that Emperor Franz Josef commissioned a special personal medal just to honor her. In November she fought in the Austrian front lines near Falze de Piava in a battle with Italian forces, giving a martial performance so inspiring that her grave became a shrine visited for years after by local women. The tombstone of an unknown Austrian woman warrior buried in the Italian town of Falze de Piava reads: "An Unknown Woman who cannot be better identified than with the words, Clothed as an Austrian Officer."[31]

By the early 1940s, Soviet women had entered all the military branches, even the Russian "naval infantry," an amphibious combat force.[32] The Komsomol schools turned out a quarter of a million mortarwomen, heavy machine-gunners, light machine gunners, snipers, and riflewomen. The Central Sniper Training Center for Women, originated May 1943, produced 150 sharpshooters a month, and its graduates killed 11,280 enemy troops. One of them, Nona Solovei, destroyed an entire German company after hunting them for twenty-five days.[33]

In 1941, when the Germans invaded Russia, teenager Liza Ivanovna Chaikina rallied the volunteer defense forces in the district of Peno. Trained in the use of rifle, machine gun, and hand grenade and desiring to aggressively engage the German army, she organized a sixty-eight-person guerrilla force, which she joined with the main guerrilla regiment led by a local resistance leader named Filimonov.

Liza and Filimonov's jointly commanded guerrilla force destroyed trains and railroad lines, raided German garrisons, killed couriers, and generally harassed the German army. Liza was betrayed by a villager, Timofey Kolosov, and arrested by the Germans in the village of Krasnoye Pokatishtshe. After torturing her, they stood her against a wall and shot her, with Liza shouting her defiance at them to the last.

Her comrades in arms, in retaliation for Liza's death, burned eleven German-occupied villages, and her betrayer was captured and executed by two of her guerrillas. Liza Ivanovna Chaikina was an inspiration for thousands of Russian women who fought as guerrillas, and her grave has become a national shrine.[34]

One of the most extraordinary martial records of a Russian woman fighter belonged to a young schoolteacher named Vera Krylova, the daughter of a factory worker. In the summer of 1941, after hearing Molotov's speech announcing war between Germany and Russia, she enlisted in the medical corps, having experience as a student nurse.

She quickly demonstrated competence and courage by working within eighty to a hundred feet of the German lines as she dressed the wounds of the injured Russian soldiers. Vera was credited with carrying and dragging hundreds of wounded men to safety as bullets from German sharpshooters meant for her exploded the earth around her. At twenty-one, she became a regimental medical inspector with the rank of captain—and Vera had not yet begun to fight.

In August 1941, the German army pushed toward Moscow as the Russian army rallied its resistance. In the confusion, Vera's company was separated from the main force while she, injured in an earlier skirmish, was riding in a wagon for the wounded. For days the remnant company, led by its commanding officer and the company's political commissar, meandered in deep swamp and forest to avoid capture. As they approached a seemingly deserted village, the Germans sprung an ambush. The Russian commander received a bullet through his head, and the political commissar panicked and shouted, "Every man for himself," immediately after which a German bullet found him. The exhausted and leaderless Russians stood numb in the face of German fire.

Quickly mounting a riderless horse that trotted beside the wagon, Vera fired into the air several times and ordered the company to follow her. She led them to shelter; however, the German plan became clear to her: using the village as a center, they had dispatched soldiers into the forest to encircle the weary Russians.

She thought to move quickly to the middle of the enveloping German offense before its units could link up. She commandeered some retreating Russian artillery and ordered it to fire on the village to soften the German position for her soldiers.

True to her nature, Vera led the first cavalry assault on the village, but as she approached a house on the edge of town, a German officer and five men rushed from hiding and pulled her from her horse. Vera fought them until a German rifle butt smashed into her face, knocking out three of her teeth. In a fury she cursed and spit blood on her attackers as she kicked and punched. Even her now weakened resistance proved effective because she bought time for her comrades to come to her rescue.

Dazed and bleeding, Vera rallied her troops once more and led them deep into the dense forest. The German army was unprepared for forest warfare, but Vera had a talent for it. Laffin writes that the Germans ". . . learned some of their costliest lessons in the forest of Bialowieza where Vera Krylova was in action."[35]

After running and fighting for two weeks, Vera's soldiers reached the last German barrier before the safe village of Serpukhov, a Russian guerrilla stronghold. A twenty-three-hour battle ensued at a river crossing as a German force fought to prevent Vera's company from joining the main Russian guerrilla force while also stalling for another unit to attack her from the rear.

Understanding the enemy's strategy, Vera waited for the right moment, mounted her horse, and led a charge across the river. The German defenders scattered, and she continued on to Serpukhov. At the outskirts of the town, she ordered her men to clean themselves and arrange their equipment in good order while she rode into Serpukhov to report to General Zakharkin.

The sentries first and then a junior officer prevented her access to the general, claiming that he was too busy to speak to a young woman. Vera, her hair and clothing plastered with mud and blood, limped up to the officer and cursed at him with such force that General Zakharkin appeared at his office door to check on the disturbance.

She announced herself formally to the general, described the actions of the past two weeks, and requested supplies so that her unit could enter the town in proper military fashion. The general gave her what she wished, but it was two days before Vera felt her soldiers were acceptable to be officially presented to him.

If her martial career had encompassed only her command of the lost Russian guerrilla unit, she would have earned her credentials as a warrior with objections from no one. However, when General Zakharkin saw her enter Serpukhov at the head of her unit, he was watching only the beginning of her dazzling warrior life.

In the winter of 1941 and 1942, Vera joined a battalion of Russian ski troopers under a war hero named Colonel Bynin. During the initial skirmish with Germans at a railway station, Bynin was wounded as his soldiers sought cover. He was lying in the no-man's-land between the station and the tree line where the guerrillas gathered. Ignoring the protests of her fellow soldiers, Vera donned her white camouflage overalls and crawled toward him, bullets throwing up puffs of snow as they zipped around her. Amazingly enough, she dressed his three bullet wounds and dragged him by his coat to safety.

On September 18, 1942, Vera was fighting near the Terek River in the southern Caucasus. A duel between German and Russian tank and infantry divisions had gone badly for the Russians, and they were forced to leave many wounded behind as they withdrew from the superior German force. Vera, aware that the wounded Russian soldiers would in all probability be killed as the Germans advanced, turned toward the front lines as her company backed away. She crawled from man to man, dressing their wounds as best she could and promising that she would not desert them. Moving from soldier to soldier, she collected loose hand grenades and stuffed them into her jacket pockets. The Germans paid little attention to her as their tanks slowly rolled toward the retreating Russians.

Vera rushed the closest tank and pelted it with grenades. The sudden sounds of battle drew the attention of the retreating Russians, who saw Vera attack a second German tank. Her heroics had surprised the Germans, which gave the Russians time to rescue the wounded and destroy several more tanks before they returned to the matter of escaping the German advance.

Vera Krylova survived the war and returned to teaching, one of the most honored of Russia's modern women warriors.[36]

As the havoc caused by the surprise Nazi blitzkrieg on Russia in 1941 resulted in massive destruction of the Russian armed forces, the Soviet high command instituted stark measures to rebuild the military. One such plan created three all-female air force regiments: the 586th Interceptor Air Regiment, the 587th Bomber Air Regiment, and the 588th Night Bomber Air Regiment.

The 586th Interceptors flew Yakolev fighters, or Yaks, aircraft modeled on the British Spitfire and the German Messerschmidt 109. These women battled with German Stuka bombers, Messerschmidts, Junker Ju-88 bombers, and Dornier Do-215 bombers and Neinkell 111s over a vast air front. The 587th specialized as a short-range bomber regiment, strafing and bombing German targets from Stalingrad to East Prussia, while the 588th night bomber group flew the antique Polikarpov Po-2s, fragile wood and canvas open-cockpit biplanes, attacking targets from the northern Caucasus to Poland.

Insight into the warrior exploits of the Russian women of the 586th Interceptor Regiment is offered by an interview conducted by American pilot Mary Lou Colbert Neale, the first female pilot to enter wartime cadet flight training, in September 1942. In 1990, she and thirty-nine other former WASPs (Women's Air Force Service Pilots) traveled to Moscow to meet with former Soviet women pilots.

The interview, published in *Military History* in December 1993, revealed the details of a famous fight in which Tamara Pamyatnikh of the 586th attacked forty-two German bombers over the city of Kastornaya and shot down two of them before her craft was crippled.

> NEALE: Tell me about shooting down those German bombers. Forty-two surrounded you, and you attacked!
> PAMYATNIKH: We, Raya Surnachevskaya and I, were not surrounded—we surrounded them! It was in March 1943, and we two were assigned as duty fighters to patrol the area over Kastornaya while the rest of the regiment took off to repel an air raid against Liski. . . . We were going toward the assigned grid square at an altitude of four thousand meters. I saw some black dots to the southeast. I thought they were birds. But no—they were flying too high and too evenly. I had orders to attack. I waggled my wings at Raya to say 'Follow me' and flew toward them. . . . We knew the rest of the regiment was fighting in another area. We

were alone. I saw one large group of enemy bombers and further back, another group of heavy bombers.

NEALE: But there were only two of you! I heard there were forty-two Junkers and Dornier bombers. . . . You could not have been expected to fight so many?

PAMYATNIKH: We had an opportunity to break up the formation with a surprise attack—they might think there were more of us if we boldly flew down at them. We had to try to prevent the bomb drop! So we both went into a steep dive and opened fire at the bombers flying in the center of the group. We pulled up into a chandelle (a simultaneous quick climb and turn) and saw two burning aircraft falling. The explosions went up from the ground. The bomber group scattered. Then we went toward the next group, which was approaching in tight formation.

NEALE: You said they were heavy bombers which were more heavily armed?

PAMYATNIKH: Yes, they were bristling with machine guns. We attacked from behind and from the sides. The enemy directed concentrated fire at us. I saw the machine guns and the gunner's head. I could even discern the features of his face. Suddenly my aircraft shuddered and then sharply turned over and started falling. I tried to open the cockpit, but a powerful force pressed me into the seat. I could not lift my arms, and the ground kept coming closer with each second. Then the canopy broke off with a crack. I undid my safety harness with difficulty and ejected. My right hand instinctively pulled the rip-cord ring. I felt the jolt from the opening parachute, and in an instant my feet touched the ground, my aircraft burning beside me. My neck and face were bloody. I looked up at the sky. The enemy was turned and was going in a westerly direction with Raya still attacking. That meant we had saved the station!

NEALE: Did Surnachevskaya survive?

PAMYATNIKH: Yes. She was more fortunate than I, although she did not know it at the time. She saw my airplane burning and falling. She told me that she was in despair at losing me and became so careless that she forgot all the air-combat rules and fired point-blank into the nearest Junker. It went down abruptly, covered with black smoke. But so close by that her plane was damaged and she made a forced landing in a farmer's field.

NEALE: Can you describe your injuries?

PAMYATNIKH: I had some burns. And my arm was broken. My leg? Oh, that was another time. Many, many of us in the 586th had wounds, most far worse than mine.

I want to tell you about our good regiment, the 586th. We were sent to Engels, many kilometers southwest of Moscow for training. We crammed a three-year course into a few months. We were equipped with Yak-1s, Yak-7Bs, and Yak-9s.

Operations started over Saratov, then to Stalingrad for the great battle from September to November 1942. And after that came the air battle over Kastornaya in early 1943.

NEALE: Which is where you and Surnachevskaya shot down two bombers each.

PAMYATNIKH: Yes. But the 586th did have many other missions. We covered important centers from east and west. We made about five thousand sorties, were in one hundred and twenty-five air battles, damaged forty-two enemy planes and destroyed thirty-eight.[37]

Twenty-one-year-old Lydia Litvak, one of the most famous of the pilots of the 586th, was known as "the White Rose of Stalingrad." Her Yak-9 fighter featured a large white rose on its fuselage, and small white roses under the cockpit indicated her kills. "Achtung! Litvak" would crackle over the German pilots' radios when she appeared in the sky, a salute to her deadly skills. Her talent as a fighter pilot was foreshadowed when she beat her male instructor in a practice dogfight during her combat flight training.

Lydia and her comrades in the 586th were transferred to the front in May 1942 just as Hitler ordered the second summer offensive. The German onslaught decimated the male fighter regiments, and the best women fighter pilots were conscripted to augment the dwindling ranks of the Soviet air force. Lydia's reputation precipitated her assignment to the formerly all-male elite Soviet 73d Right Air Regiment, whose pilots followed the Okhotniki, or "free hunter" style of combat. Whereas most other fighter regiments acted as interceptors scrambling to attack known enemy formations, the skillful and courageous free hunters searched in pairs or small groups for targets of opportunity.

Lydia experienced frustration during the early days with the 73d because the base commander allowed her no flying time. Finally, her friend Alexei Salomaten, a young male pilot, argued that she deserved an opportunity to demonstrate her skills. The commander permitted her one chance to accompany Alexei as his "wingman," but she was warned that if she erred whatsoever she would be sent home. Alexei instructed Lydia that she was not to protect him, as was the usual duty of the wingman, but rather she was simply to shadow his every move.

Eight thousand feet over Stalingrad, Alexei spotted a fellow pilot dueling with a German Me-109 and flew to his aid. The two Russian pilots combined to knock the Messerschmidt out of the sky, and through it all Lydia stuck to Alexei's tail. In fact, she was so concentrated on flying as he had ordered that she did not discover until they had landed that Alexei had been in a dogfight.

Alexei's report to the base commander extolled Lydia, who thereafter flew as his regular wingman. Their deep bond created a deadly aerial combat team, and in time they fell in love. By late December 1942 Lydia had personally shot down three fighters and three transports and had earned the name "the White Rose of Stalingrad," which became a household word throughout Russia.

In March, the 73d advanced to Donbass, where the Germans were preparing another summer offensive. Lydia scored two more kills flying out of Donbass with Alexei as her wingman but was downed as she executed her ninth kill. Fortunately, though bleeding profusely with a leg wound and her engine dead, she landed her wheelless Yak in a plowed field.

On return to her regiment, Lydia was elevated to the rank of flight commander, a crucial position. Often, the flight commander possessed the only radio, map, or precise notion of the mission, and if this officer was shot down, the other pilots were rendered ineffective in coordinating attacks. The flight commander became, therefore, a prime target for German fighter pilots.

Lydia's warrior fervor was heightened after Alexei was killed. In her first flight after his death, she challenged a German fighter pilot ace with twenty kill symbols displayed on his fuselage. After a fifteen-minute dogfight, she dispatched him—her tenth kill.

Several weeks later, acting as flight commander, she was attacked by three Messerschmidts and crash-landed. The next day she piloted another Yak, only to be shot down once again. The following day, August 1, 1943, her hand wrapped from a bullet injury sustained the day before, Lydia was again airborne, leading her squadron to intercept a group of German bombers. In an ambush, eight Messerschmidts descended from a cloud bank and attacked Lydia. Her plane was last seen billowing smoke, and the eight German fighters were closing on her. The wreckage of her Yak-9 was never found.

Lydia Litvak, the greatest Russian woman fighter ace, was credited with twelve kills and an undetermined number of assists in approximately a year of combat. As a flight commander, she led male pilots to numerous victories.[38] A memorial to her stands in the town of Krasny Luch near the site of her disappearance.

Ekaterina Budanova, like Lydia Litvak, served as a "free hunter." The second-ranking female ace, she was shot down after accomplishing her eleventh kill.

Olga Yamschikova of the 586th received distinction as the first woman to destroy an enemy aircraft at night. She performed the feat over Stalingrad on the night of September 24, 1942. The 586th's Irina Sibrova topped the record of many male fighter pilots by flying 1,008 sorties.

The 587th Bomber Regiment, waging battle from the Volga to the eastern front and from Budapest to Berlin, produced many heroines. Polina Gelman flew eighteen missions and was cited for heroism in battle five times. Major Tamara Aleksandrovna participated in four thousand sorties and engaged 125 enemy planes in combat.

Marina Raskova captained an all-woman crew, which included Valentina Grizodubov and Polina Osipenko, who flew nonstop from Moscow to the Far East in 1938. She convinced Stalin to create the all-female air regiments, and when she called for women pilots, thousands applied.

Her courage was legendary. One night, her aircraft lost altitude over a trackless Russian forest. To save her crew, she lightened the load by parachuting into the freezing night and ten days later found her way to a farmer's cabin. When she and her crew were shot down on January 4, 1943, the 587th was renamed the 125th Raskova Guardians in her honor.

Antonia "Tanya" Bondareva of the 588th learned to fly when she was in the seventh grade in 1936. Between 1938 and 1943, she trained 150 male military pilots. She joined the 587th at the age of nineteen. She once wrote to an American friend:

> We had to carry 2,400-pound bombs in a fast, complicated airplane. My crew consisted of myself as pilot; Galia Beltzova as navigator, and Raya Molashenko as bombardier. I was commander of our group.
>
> It is difficult to evaluate those times. We were all young—serious and funny, brave and timid, from almost every region of Russia. In those terrible times we went to war voluntarily to protect our land, which was endangered. You would do the same thing. . . .[39]

The 588th Night Bomber Regiment, dubbed the "Night Witches" by the Germans, was the most decorated Russian female regiment in World War II. Twenty-three of the thirty Gold Medals of a Hero of the Soviet Union awarded to women went to them. Flying primitive, unarmed biplanes, they averaged fifteen to eighteen sorties a night, but on some nights they achieved as many as three hundred. Evgenia Zeguelenko flew 980 missions, Major E. Niklunia flew six hundred, and Maria Smirnova made 3,260 combat flights, during which time she personally dropped one hundred thousand kilograms of bombs on German motorized units.

The Night Witches suffered heavy losses in their crude unarmed aircraft. One summer night in 1943 they were caught in searchlights and attacked by Messerschmidts. Eight of the Polikarpov Po-2s were downed and sixteen Night Witches lost their lives. The 588th totaled twenty-four thousand missions against the Germans.

In addition, hundreds of thousands of Russian women operated anti-aircraft installations. A German fighter pilot, a veteran of the African campaign, had this to say about the Russian AA batteries: "I would rather fly ten times over the skies of Tobruk than to pass once through the fire of Russian flak sent up by female gunners."[40]

The peak strength of the regular female combat forces in the Russian Army was attained in 1943, at which time between eight hundred thousand and a million women, or eight percent of total Russian military personnel, involved themselves in the war effort. Alexandra Beiko and her husband, Ivan, not wishing to be separated by war, bought a tank and fought together—she was the officer and tank commander, and Ivan was her driver/mechanic. They took part in several tank battles. She won the Order of the Patriotic War and Ivan won the Order of the Red Banner. Mariya Oktyabrskaya, after her husband was killed in battle, purchased her own tank, named it "Front-Line Female Comrade," and went into battle. She died in a firefight near Vitebsk in 1944. In the same year, a brave and robust country girl named Nina Kluyeva, without assistance, carried 615 wounded men from a battlefield, and Ludmilla Pavlichenko, a sniper, was cited for killing 309 Nazi soldiers.

In German-occupied Belorussia, seven thousand, or sixteen percent, of the partisans fighting the Nazis were women. Elena Kovalchuk commanded an infantry assault after the male squad leader was shot; Zoya "Tanya" Kosmodemyanskaya became famous for her abilities in assassination and sabotage; and Elena Mazanik killed the brutal Nazi governor of German-occupied Belorussia by placing a bomb under his bed.

Russian female medics carried weapons and performed numerous feats of valor. Sofya Klitinova hauled twenty wounded Red Army soldiers to safety in the face of blistering machine-gun fire. Twenty-three-year-old nurse's aide Usnolobova Marchenko proved equally courageous and lost both arms and legs for her heroic efforts.

And finally, Crimean scout Maria Baide was one of the first women to win what was at that time the highest Russian military honor, Hero of the Soviet Union. In the action for which her medal was awarded, Maria single-handedly took on twenty German submachine-gunners in a moving fight in which her group was scattered. They were too far away to help, but they did not have to worry. In the resulting engagement, Maria killed fifteen Germans, wounded several others, and dispersed those that were left standing.[41]

Throughout history, women have rallied in defense of their hometowns. Here, European villagers arm themselves with spears to repel an attack.

CHAPTER 11

Western Europe: For Duty, All

Rome, one of the greatest civilizations that ever flourished, began as a loose confederation of tribes that constantly skirmished with their local competitors, the Volsci and Etruscans. By the first century B.C., Rome controlled all shores of the Mediterranean and substantial inland territories in Europe, Africa, and the Near East, establishing an empire that would endure for centuries.

A very dramatic example of female valor was displayed in a battle of the Second Punic War. Carthage, in the fourth century B.C., sending its ships out from its harbors in North Africa, had succeeded in conquering the Spanish coast and most of Sicily. When in 264 B.C. the Carthaginians were poised to control the Strait of Messina, a narrow body of water separating Italy and Sicily, Rome's war against the *Punici*, as they called the Carthaginians, erupted into what is now known as the First Punic War.

In the Second Punic War in 221 B.C., the Carthaginian commander Hannibal came at Rome from bases in Spain, conquering Rome's allied cities en route. The town of Salmatis in Spain, however, proved a difficulty to the invaders.

Initially, no problems existed with the townspeople. Seeing Hannibal's army displayed before them, they surrendered and agreed to pay Hannibal three hundred talents of silver and three hundred hostages for their ransom. For some reason, the payment to Hannibal was not forthcoming, so he sent his soldiers to plunder the town. The citizens asked that they be permitted to leave, understanding that they could take nothing with them but their lives.

As the citizens of Salmatis filed from their city gates, the soldiers of Hannibal fell to pillaging. None noticed the women of Salmatis remove daggers and swords from the folds of their shawls and dresses. Arming both the men and themselves, the women returned with the men to their town and drove the soldiers out. Hannibal, particularly impressed with the fighting women of Salmatis, in tribute returned the hostages and the silver and turned his army away from Salmatis and toward the Alps.[1]

In 42 B.C. Hortensia and 1,400 women invaded the Roman Forum, where she delivered a speech protesting taxes newly levied against widows. Her speech and the implied threat conveyed by the "army" behind her convinced the forum to act on her demands. The following year Fulvia, armed with a sword and accoutred in armor, led her heavy cavalry against Octavius and later helped Mark Antony during his war with the triumvirate.

In the latter part of the first century B.C., Agrippa, wife of Roman Emperor Germanicus, often joined her husband in battle. According to the Roman historian Tacitus, she posed "a greater power in the army than legates and commanders."[2] Agrippa the Younger, daughter of Agrippa and Germanicus and wife of Emperor Claudius, proved so ambitious and violent that her son Nero arranged her murder in A.D. 59. Some years before her death, an event transpired that offers an interesting insight into the perceptions of military leadership among Celtic peoples of the era. When defeated Celtic war leaders from Britain—a group comprising men and women fighters, incidentally—were marched before Claudius, they ignored the emperor and instead lined up before Agrippa, assuming that she commanded the military of the nation. A later empress, Triaria, wife of Emperor Lucius Vitellius, accompanied her husband in battle as an armed knight. Her valor in battle was displayed in an encounter with the enemy Vosciian.

In 186 B.C. the Romans opposed the Gauls in northern Italy. After hours of fighting, the Gaulish men backed away from the Roman army, but a woman warrior, Chiomaca, stood her ground and killed several Roman soldiers before she was captured. Bound and helpless, she was raped by a Roman centurion. Later she escaped, found the officer, cut his head off, and presented it to her husband.[3] The Romans often found themselves defending against women warriors in their battles with the Teutons, Ambrones, Cimbrians, Gauls, and other European tribes who raided the Roman Empire over many centuries, culminating in the sack of Rome by King Alaric of the Visigoths in A.D. 410.

The Cimbrians fell on the northern borders of the Roman Empire in the first century B.C. Caius Marius, a Roman general who was recalled from North Africa to fight the barbarians, recorded many details of his campaign, including information about Cimbrian methods of warfare.

The most impressive weapon of the Cimbrians was called the "wagon castle," a large wooden enclosure riding cartlike on two immense wheels. Inside, the Cimbrian women and children huddled as they advanced with the men into battle. The women would shoot arrows from the top of the war wagons and occasionally sortie from their "castles" and fight with swords.

In a battle in 101 B.C., General Marius recounts that as the Roman forces pushed the Cimbrian men in retreat on the battlefield at Vercellae, the Cimbrian women emerged from the wagon castles with swords and swore to attack their own men if they did not put up a strong fight. When the army of Catulus joined that of Marius, the Cimbrian men were destroyed, but the women continued to fight, moving in and out of their mobile fortresses. When they realized that all was lost, they killed their children and then themselves "either by the hands of friends or by nooses twisted of their own hair."[4]

The Romans faced European tribal women warriors as they drove the Teutonic Ambrones from the field and back into their staging areas. Plutarch states:

> The Teuton women met them with swords and axes, and making a terrible outcry, drove the fugitives as well as the pursuers back, the first as traitors, the others as enemies, and mixing among the warriors, with their bare arms pulling away the shields of the Romans and laying hold on their swords, endured the wounds and slashing of their bodies—invincible unto death—with undaunted resolution.[5]

Teutonic woman warrior Thusnelda served as a key military adviser to Herman of Germany. In ancient times, Teutonic women warriors fought among the men in full armor, and an important part of the dowry of an upper-class Teutonic woman included a full suit of plate and mail armor, shield, lance, and sword. Archaeologists have unearthed Teutonic women's graves in which weapons, armor, and military insignia were present. Many Roman accounts of battles with this northern European tribe describe finding the corpses of numerous Teutonic women warriors on the battlefields.

Goth women warriors are recorded in A.D. 273 in descriptions of the triumphal parade in Rome of Emperor Aurelian after he returned from his campaigns in the east. Thirty Goth women military captives dressed as male warriors marched with signs around their necks reading "Amazons." This was the same parade in which Queen Bat Zabbai was forced to march. Historian Edward Gibbon, in his *Decline and Fall of the Roman Empire*, mentions the Gothic women warriors in Aurelian's procession and comments: "Among barbarous nations, women have often combated by the side of their husbands."[6] For example, during the Mithriadic Wars in 66 B.C., the Romans under Pompey won a victory at the Cyrtus River. Appian, a chronicler of the time wrote, "Among the hostages and prisoners, many women were found who had suffered wounds no less than the men."[7]

*   *   *

Women gladiators, professional "sports" warriors, were common from the inception of the games until the edict of Alexander Severus in A.D. 200, which banned them from the gladiatorial combats. They competed in the first games of the Colosseum opened by Emperor Titus in A.D. 80, and killed wild animals for the amusement of spectators. Juvenal writes that female gladiators owned the finest weapons and trained diligently at martial arts. Some came from the lower classes; some were slaves hoping to win their freedom; and some, like Eppia, who ran off with a fellow gladiator, leaving her husband and children, were married to Roman senators.[8]

An interesting account of a Roman woman possessed of great physical strength comes from the fifteenth year of the Second Punic War. Claudia Quinta watched with a group of Roman citizens as a boat carrying an image of the mother of the gods made its way along the Tiber into Rome. What happened next is told with various shadings, but the result is always the same. The boat ran aground, and the sailors could not move it. Claudia, out of sheer physical exuberance or, as one story states, to prove her virtue, said a prayer, waded into the Tiber, attached her belt to the boat, and single-handedly pulled it to shore.[9]

The martial prowess of women was witnessed not only in the gladiatorial games, but also at the very highest levels of Roman society. In the third century A.D., Victorina ruled with her son Victorinus. She was so intimately involved in military activities that the Roman army called her "the Mother of the Camps" and requested her to devise a new plan of rank succession. She rode on behalf of her son at the head of her armies during her wars against Emperor Gallienus.

In A.D. 217, Macrinus seized the throne from Julia Maesa, who at the time was acting as queen regent after the death of Caracalla. Julia escaped to Syria, where she quickly raised an army. When the great battle between Macrinus and Julia was joined outside Rome and it appeared as if Macrinus's forces would take the day, Julia and her daughters left the relative safety of their war chariots to inspire the fighters by their daring and spirit.

In the early fifth century, Galla Placidia held power in the western Roman Empire through several different men. At the age of fifteen, she governed as a regent for her brother until his death in 423. Her regency continued on behalf of her young son, Emperor Valentinian III. Galla's niece, Pulcheria, ruled in the eastern Roman Empire as regent for her brother Theodosius II. When he died in 450, she held complete control until her death several years later.

*   *   *

The midfifth century saw Attila the Hun, "the Scourge of God," sweep out of the Asiatic steppes with his nomadic hordes and aim for the heart of Europe. Genevieve, a warrior nun of Paris, led a force to drive the Hun from her city in 451, and in a later action when the king of the Franks besieged Paris, she led a foraging band outside the walls and successfully returned with provisions for the starving people.

A Teutonic princess, Ildico, was forced to marry the detested Attila. Jordanes, the historian, borrowing the account from Priscus, states that on their wedding night, while Attila lay intoxicated beside her, Ildico strangled him with her long hair in revenge for her father's murder.

Attila's invasion of Europe in the midfifth century disrupted tribes in his westerly advance. The Huns destroyed the Ostrogoths in southern Russia about 374 and forced the Visigoths, who lived west of the Ostrogoths, to apply to Emperor Valens for permission to move into Roman territory to escape. The ill treatment the Visigoths subsequently received at the hands of their Roman protectors stirred them to rebel and destroy Valens and most of his Roman army at the Battle of Adrianople in 378.

The new emperor Theodosius gave the Visigoths territory in the Balkans, but they soon wanted Austria too. When Rome refused, the Visigoth king Alaric sacked Rome in 410. The Visigoths finally settled in southwestern Gaul.

Several generations later, in 565, Brunehaut (also known as Brunhilde), daughter of the Visigoth king Athanagilde, married King Siegbert, the Frankish ruler of Austria.[10] Queen Brunehaut's sister Galsuinda was married to Siegbert's brother Chilperic. When Galsuinda was murdered by Chilperic's mistress Fredegonde, warrior queen of Neustria (part of modern France), Brunehaut swore revenge. She persuaded her husband to attack Chilperic, and for a while her military aims were satisfied. Then, in 575, assassins hired by Fredegonde killed Brunehaut's husband and pursued her to Paris.

Fortunately, Chilperic's son Childebert fell in love with Brunehaut, which compelled Chilperic to banish him and imprison Brunehaut. Through Childebert's leverage with the duke of Normandy, he freed Brunehaut, who immediately returned to her prime obsession, the destruction of Fredegonde and her family and supporters.

As Brunehaut played the violent court politics of her time, she accrued many enemies. The nobles found her threatening after she maneuvered herself several times into power up to the level of queen regent, while successfully blocking their various attempts to augment their own power. Exasperation with Queen Brunehaut can be heard in a speech hurled at her before the opening of a battle where the queen's army was aligned against a large force of rebellious nobles. When Brunehaut saw herself at a disadvantage, she rode between the two armies calling for the fighters to separate. One irritated duke shouted at her.

> Woman retire! You reigned long enough under the names of your husbands; let that suffice you. Your son is now our king; Austria is under our guardianship, not yours. Retire directly or our horses' feet shall trample you to the earth.[11]

Brunehaut, however, succeeded, and the armies did pull apart before she lost her retainers to the nobles. Though weakened briefly, she once more regained her power and summarily executed every nonsupportive noble she could capture. She dispatched an army against Fredegonde's son Clotaire, a young man who reportedly experienced his first battle in his mother's arms as she led her troops.

Brunehaut's son died in 596, and the Frankish kingdom was divided between her grandsons, Theodebert and Theodoric. The queen remained with Theodoric, who had taken Austria. At the death of Fredegonde in 597, she attempted to regain all that her rival had taken from her and to kill Fredegonde's relatives.

When she ordered the duke of Champagne murdered, the outraged nobles seized her and abandoned her deep in the wilderness to starve to death. Her incredible luck saved her again. A wandering forester found her and escorted her to Theodoric. Once there she again endeavored to maneuver her way to the highest levels of power in the kingdom and to destroy those who had influence over the king. In rapid succession she drove away St. Didier, bishop of Vienne; arranged the death of the mayor of the palace; and pitted her grandsons Theodebert and Theodoric against one another, resulting in the death of Theodebert.

Queen Brunehaut died a brutal death, betrayed by her subjects into the hands of Clotaire. He accused her of complicity in the deaths of a number of Frankish kings, specifically listing Siegbert, Merovech, his father, Chilperic, Theudebert, Theudebert's son Chlotar, Chlotar's son and the other Merovech, Theuderic, and Theuderic's three sons. Though Brunehaut was eighty years old at the time, Clotaire ordered her tortured for three days and carried naked on a litter through the countryside. Finally, she was tied to the tail of an unbroken horse by one arm and a leg. After the horse had dragged her over the rocky ground, rendering her barely recognizable, her grisly remains were burned and then buried.

Fredegonde, Brunehaut's longtime nemesis, was a very able enemy. Not only did she arrange for the deaths of her mistress, Queen Audovera, wife of King Chilperic; Queen Brunehaut's sister and Chilperic's second wife, Galsuinda; and numerous nobles, including Brunehaut's husband, King Siegbert, she also led and inspired her armies. In one famous action, she convinced the nobles to give her full command of their combined forces to perpetrate a ruse she had conceived. She informed them that as an added inducement for her men to fight bravely she would march at the head of the troops carrying her infant son, Clotaire, the future king. The various warlords agreed to her terms.

After a day's march, Fredegonde led the soldiers into a forest that bordered her enemy's camp. She instructed the captains to order their men to cover themselves and their horses with branches and to tie bells to the necks of some horses to imitate pastured horses wandering aimlessly as they grazed. When all was ready, Fredegonde turned toward the enemy camp with her baby in her arms, and the men followed. The ruse worked perfectly. Fredegonde's men were upon the enemy before they could mount a successful defense.

In 590 the Frankish king Childebert, Brunehaut's one-time lover, militarily engaged a warrior nun Chrodielde of the convent of Poitiers. Chrodielde had attempted to displace Leubevre, the abbess of Cheribert, and warfare ensued between the women of the two convents. When Chrodielde was driven from Leubevre's land, she spirited her followers into a fortified cathedral nearby and set about raising an army from the local population. King Childebert was called upon to end the war between the convents. He succeeded, but it was with the greatest of difficulty that he managed to bring Chrodielde and her army of nuns and street people under control.

The powers that abbesses historically commanded would surprise most modern observers. For example, in Saxony in the tenth and eleventh centuries, the abbesses of Quedlinburg and Gandersheim ruled like barons, commanding huge tracts of land with their knights and even striking their own coins.

In 1265, Abbess Odette de Pougy, a leader of the Abbey of Notre-Dame-Aux-Nonnains, challenged a project that was championed by Pope Urban IV. He wanted to build a church on the site where his father's shoemaker's shop once stood. The abbess forbade him to do so, saying the property belonged to her abbey. Pope Urban IV proceeded with the project despite the abbess's objections, and she responded with an armed party that drove the pope's work crews from the site. Two years later, he tried again, and once more Odette led armed men to remove the pope's men from her land. Enraged that the abbess would block him, the pope excommunicated the entire abbey. The sentence remained in effect for fourteen years, but Abbess Odette was resolute and the pope's church was not built until after her death.

The power of these women's institutions was reflected in the wealth displayed in the abbeys. Christine de Pisan described a visit to her daughter at the Dominican Abbey of Poissy in 1400. Two hundred nuns, every one of noble birth, were led by Prioress Marie de Bourbon, aunt of King Charles VI. Rich tapestries hung everywhere, and meals were served in vessels forged of gold and silver on tables covered in fine linen. Paintings and golden ornaments could be found throughout the abbey. Further, the abbey possessed glass windows, a highly unusual luxury for the times. When she left, the nuns presented de Pisan with a belt and purse embroidered with silver and gold thread.[12]

Some students of women's history, however, have a very low regard for the religious institutions of the time. Gerritsen, for example, writes:

> Monasteries and nunneries were distinguished from brothels by the greater lasciviousness of the life carried on within their walls, and by the ease with which the numerous crimes committed there were concealed by judges who themselves stood at the head of this system of corruption.[13]

In late fifteenth-century France, Abbess Renée de Bourbon had set about cleaning up and "reforming" the religious institutions of her domains when she confronted the monastery of Fontevrault, a fortress occupied by warrior monks and nuns. Abbess Renée spent almost twelve years attempting to wrest control of Fontevrault and finally resorted to overwhelming force. She raised a large army in Paris in 1477 and attacked the renegade monastery. She prevailed. The defenders quickly abandoned their fight, and she forced each monk and nun who wished to remain at Fontevrault to sign a personal oath of loyalty to her.

Warrior nuns posed such a problem in the fifteenth century that a law in Bologna forbade citizens to loiter around convents, not for the protection of the nuns but for the safety of the citizenry. In 1470 a Franciscan investigation decried the "irreligious and unbridled lives" of the sisters. The convents became so powerful that various popes established decrees against women engaging in martial combat in an attempt to weaken the power of the sisterhood. The papal ban against women wearing armor proved to be the technicality on which Joan of Arc was sentenced to be burned to death at Rouen.[14]

The shift in the perception of women as legitimate sources of power in Europe in the fifteenth and sixteenth centuries bears comment. A key is found in the struggle between powerful male and female leaders of religious communities. The power that abbesses had accrued over time, based on their positions as managers and tax collectors over vast tracts of land and dozens of villages, had put them in a position to thwart male church leaders from priests to bishops to, in some cases, the pope. The powers of these women were rationalized on the basis of ancient Christian ideas about religious organization and the prominence of the veneration of Mary, the mother of Jesus, in the Christian religion. With the return to the patriarchal orientations of the Greco-Roman world, which were being rediscovered during the Reformation and the Renaissance, some male leaders in all walks of life balked at being commanded by women.

Women seem to have exerted prominent positions of leadership in early Christian communities. Morris writes:

> New Testament accounts show that women naturally assumed administrative duties in the apostolic period, for it is a noteworthy fact that all assemblies of Christian communities mentioned in the Acts of the Apostles and in the Epistles of Saint Paul are said to be in the house of women: the church in the house of Chloe, in the house of Lydia, in the house of the mother of Mark, in the house of Mympha, in the house of Priscilla and Aquila. Note that the name of Priscilla is put first.[15]

Morris notes that John in his second epistle addresses his comments to an "Elect Lady," obviously singled out as the administrator of the group and her community, and ends his letter with greetings from her "Sister Elect."[16] The homage that men gave to women in early times was seen as a spiritual act in its emulation of Christ's obedience to Mary. The monks and knights who bowed before powerful women did not feel demeaned by so doing. They would "learn" that in the fifteenth and sixteenth centuries.

The women leaders of the great convents and abbeys of Europe often had the power of queens, though male bishops held sacerdotal powers: ordaining priests, dedicating and consecrating altars, and blessing sacramental oils. The bishops, in attempting to find a niche in which they could reap profit through taxation and tithing of parishioners, found themselves in conflict with the women leaders of the convents who claimed and were often acknowledged as having the more senior rights to these monies and kind.

Perhaps because typically more noblewomen than noblemen were literate, the abbesses kept excellent records and could bring them forth in litigations brought by bishops. When a bishop threatened to excommunicate Abbess Audisia of Brindisi and her entire community unless she relented to his demands for expanded powers to tax villagers, she appealed to Pope Gregory IX and presented him with the bulls, or papal decrees, of Pope Paschal II (1099–1118), Pope Callixtus II (1119–1124), Pope Honorius II (1124–1130), Pope Alexander III (1159–1181), and Pope Celestine III (1191–1198) to support her claims. Gregory IX in a decree issued March 15, 1233, supported the abbess against the bishop and included in his statement the prohibition against bishops excommunicating abbesses and their followers.

The official unraveling of the abbess's powers can be found in the Council of Trent, a convocation for ecclesiastical reform that lasted eighteen years, from 1545 to 1564. The call for the reformation of religious orders and the empowering of bishops as representatives of the pope, thus rendering them superior to women, came in the twenty-fifth session, which was held on December 3, 1563. The majority of male clerics concluded that the bishops' duty was to see that the nuns were enclosed, that their movements be restricted by the bishops, and that if they resisted, they could be dealt with militarily. This series of opinions was by no means unanimously supported. The bishop of Bracen, the bishop of Opinum in Calabria, the bishop of Zara in Dalmatia, and the bishop of Umbriatico in Calabria rejected the idea that bishops have the right to punish or discipline nuns.

* * *

In the eighth century Queen Bertha, wife of King Pepin of the Franks, was at his insistence crowned coruler of the empire in a ceremony identical to the one that had invested him. She accompanied him on military campaigns and joined him in all negotiations as an equal monarch. This custom continued among the Franks during the next century with Queen Judith, second wife of Louis the Pious, and later with Queen Richilda, wife of Louis the Pious's successor, Charles the Bald. Queen Ergelberge, wife of Charlemagne's grandson King Louis II, presided over the royal court at Ravenna and ruled jointly with the king, as did Roman Empress Adelaide of Burgundy in the later tenth century. When Otto II died in 983, his wife, Queen Theophano, accepted the title of Imperator Augustus and energetically defended her claim against jealous nobles as well as the Slavs and Danes. Beard writes:

> It was under a succession of five great feudal families that the anarchy of France which followed the dissolution of Rome was overcome. These great families were the Merovingians, the Carolingians, the Capetians, the Valois, and the Bourbons. From first to last, women were associated with men in this process of state and society building.[17]

Women defenders appear in the histories and epics of nearly every Western country, and every siege battle produced its exemplary women warriors. In France alone, the historians record the heroines of Marseilles, Saint Riquier, Perronne, Meta, Montelimar, Poitiers, La Rochelle, Sanceree, Livorn, Saint Lo, Aubigny, Cahors, Lille, Vitre, Autun, Montauban, Montpellier, Lamotte, Dole, and Saint-Jean-de-Losne.

Queen Carcas of Carcassone had several successful castle defenses to her credit. In the first case, no less a figure than Charlemagne laid siege to the queen. Her defense proved so resolute and heroic that he withdrew and allowed the lady to retain sovereignty and jurisdiction in the area.

In the second instance, the Moors surrounded her town. They laughed at her and shouted out that as a woman she should spend her time spinning, not fighting. In response the queen put on armor, took up her lance, and mounted her royal charger. On the end of her lance, as with a spinning distaff, she had attached a quantity of hemp, leaving the tip bare. Before she ordered the doors of the castle thrown open, she had the hemp ignited.

With lance aflame, the Queen of Carcassone rushed from her castle directly at the Moors, the spectral sight of which terrified them into flight. The shield and lance of Queen Carcas may still be seen at Carcassone, and over the gate of the city is a representation of her with this imperious inscription: *Carcas Sum*, i.e., "I am Carcas."[18]

Polish history in the eighth century proclaims the contributions of King Creche, founder of the modern city of Cracow. However, the great king's legacy may not have survived if not for his successor, his daughter Queen Wanda, who several times shielded the city against invaders. In like manner, Denmark owes a debt to Queen Thyra, who in the late ninth century commanded her troops against Germanic invasions, particularly in the Jutland and Slesrig areas. Thyra constructed a wall, the *Danneverke*, which impeded her southern enemies and was used in the defense of Denmark for centuries to come. Parts of Queen Thyra's wall stand today.

Saxo Grammaticus, ancient Danish historian, wrote:

> There were once women among the Danes who dressed as men and devoted every waking moment to the pursuit of war. Those who had force of character or were tall and comely were especially apt to enter into such a life.[19]

Such martially trained women often functioned as "shield maidens" and accompanied both male and female warriors in battle. They entered legend as "the Valkyries." The Irish, who were often terrorized by Viking attacks, remember through their oral tradition one Viking captain, Ingean Ruadh, "the Red Maiden." Called Rusla in her home country of Norway, the Red Maiden commenced her career with the overthrow of her brother, the king of Norway. She with her constant companion, the shield maiden Stikla, warred against Iceland, the British Isles, Telemark, and Denmark.

The Danes found a formidable adversary in Alhild, daughter of King Siward of the Goths. Together with her shield maiden Groa, Alhild led a band of Viking women in raids along the coasts of several nations.

The Swedes can boast Princess Torborg, daughter of King Erik. She, preferring the title "King" Torborg, ruled her own province and fought in numerous battles to hold her domains. Both rich and beautiful, Torborg received many suitors, and, to evaluate them, she challenged each to single combat. She was most interested in the men she could not defeat, finally marrying one of the strongest. Swedish history also tells of Alwilda, a pirate captain who raided shipping in the Baltic Sea. Another Scandinavian female pirate leader, Sela,[20] hunted the same waters.

In the tenth century the Swedes and the Danes fought one of their most bloody engagements The Battle of Bravalla. Saxo Grammaticus tells of the battle in his *History of the Danes* (Books VII, VIII, and IX), probably written sometime between 1208 and 1218. He claims as sources everything from ancient inscriptions to legendary oral histories, from songs to the materials of Icelandic scholars, local historians, and ancient manuscripts. Because Saxo was raised in the military class, we might assume his accounts of battles to be relatively accurate. Of course, Saxo also wrote of various Nordic heroes doing battle with dragons and giants, the presence of which he inferred from the megalithic ritual structures (huge standing stone constructions à la Stonehenge) that dotted the landscape.

Two hundred thousand warriors, five thousand ships, and kings of twelve nations with their armies were involved at Bravalla, the "most famous of legendary battles fought in northern lands," according to Saxo. Wisan, Webiorg, and Hetha, women sea captains, were active in the great battle, which pitted Harald Wartooth against his nephew Ring for control of Denmark. A more complex history of the Battle of Bravalla can be found in the Icelandic prose account, *Sogubrot af Fornkonungum*.[21]

Captain Wisan, leading a company of Wends (Slavs), fought in full armor with a long sword as King Ring's standard-bearer. A Slav warrior chieftain named Starkad chopped off Wisan's left hand in his attempt to capture the enemy king's banner, but even with the loss of her hand, she secured the battle flag. Hetha ably assisted her rescue with a hundred of her own elite warriors and a company of berserkers.

Captain Webiorg led her own troops, men and women of Denmark and Britannia, at Bravalla. In single combat she defeated the Swedish champion Seth but was finally killed by a crossbow bolt shot by Thorkil of Telemark, who realized that the only chance against the fearsome Webiorg was to strike from a distance.

Queen Hetha of Sle, later queen of Zeeland, rounds out the triumvirate of female captains at Bravalla. Her personal retinue of berserkers and squad of one hundred elite warriors, together with the forces of Wisan and Webiorg, stormed the beaches against the Swedes with their numerous small body shields rattling and their breasts exposed so that the enemy Swedes would know that they were killed by women.

To the south in 984, Verdun fell to the forces commanded by King Lothaire and his wife, Emma, Queen of France, daughter of Emperor Otto of Germany. When Lothaire left the prize of Verdun to Queen Emma's keeping the following year and moved with his troops to secure other vital cities, the enemy counterattacked. Fighting on the battlements, Emma thwarted the attackers until Lothaire returned, at which point she and her husband joined forces and dispersed the enemy.

King Lothaire's military partnership with his wife, Emma, reflected, perhaps, his relationship with his mother, Gerberge, wife of Louis IV, daughter of King Henry of Germany. At the death of Louis IV in 954, Queen Gerberge assumed regency on behalf of her young son, Lothaire. She used her own private army to preserve Lothaire's rights, as well as her capital at Reims. Lothaire's first taste for warfare came when his mother took him in her attack against Poitiers. In 960, Gerberge and her army recaptured the fortified town of Dijon, which had been seized by one of her own generals turned traitor. She ordered him beheaded in the presence of his family and supporters.[22]

Less than a century later in northern Italy, Matilda of Tuscany, like Lothaire, first experienced battle by her mother's side.[23] Born in 1046, Matilda inherited through her father, Margrave Boniface II, the plains of Lombardy and parts of Liguria and Umbria—an immense area of northern and central Italy that included the cities of Ferrara, Verona, Modena, Mantua, Parma, Brescia, Siena, Lucca, Pisa, Florence, Pistoia, Spoleto, and Camerino. Her education prepared her in German, Italian, French, and Latin—the languages required to rule her domains—as well as writing, an ability rare among rulers of her time. She excelled at embroidery and needlework and sent gifts of her work to such contemporary leaders as William the Conqueror, who defeated England in 1066.

The knight Arduino Della Paluda taught her riding as well as wielding a spear or lance while on horseback. He instructed her in the use of the sword, pike, and battle-ax while fighting on foot. Therefore, by the time she first appeared on the battlefield with her mother at the age of fifteen, she was accustomed to the weight of her weapons and armament.

Her dramatic initial appearance in battle prompted an account centuries later to enthuse: "Now there appeared in Lombardy at the head of her numerous squadrons the young maid Matilda, armed like a warrior, and with such bravery, that she made known to the world that courage and valor in mankind is not indeed a matter of sex, but of heart and spirit."[24]

In 1066 under the guidance of General Arduino, her martial arts instructor, Matilda directed four hundred archers at the Battle of Aquino, where her stepfather, Godfrey of Lorraine, defeated the Normans. Later that year, she and Sir Della Paluda jointly commanded archers, pikemen, and heavy cavalry in fighting around the Castel San Angelo in Rome. The charge she led against Sir Guibert of Ravenna drove the enemy forces from the city. During the next several years, she was reported at many battle sites, leading troops, commanding sieges, and devising battle plans.

The strong resolve of her fighting in Rome was incited by a deep devotion to the papacy, which first stirred when her family visited Rome in 1059 to witness the election of Pope Nicholas II. As a dedicated supporter of Rome, she was brought into conflict with German Emperor Henry IV, an enemy of the papacy. Their first encounter came in 1076.

Pope Gregory VII had excommunicated the emperor for his various transgressions. After deliberation with his counselors, Henry announced that he was traveling to Rome to seek forgiveness. Pope Gregory VII, harboring justified concerns about Henry's visit, staged the visit in Canossa, the strongest castle in northern Italy, under the protection of its owner, his most powerful protector, Countess Matilda.

For three days, January 25, 26, and 27 in 1077, Emperor Henry stood barefoot in the snow outside the walls of Canossa, clad only in rough woolen rags. On January 28, Pope Gregory allowed the German emperor to apologize. Three years later, Emperor Henry returned to Italy to punish the woman who had staged his humiliation.

This time, he surprised Matilda, seized Mantua, and conquered her army at the Battle of Volta in 1084. The countess withdrew into her stronghold at Canossa. In the subsequent months her major difficulty was not Henry's army but wayward vassals whom Henry threatened and cajoled to leave their countess. In July of 1084, for example, the rebellious bishops of Reggio and Parma attacked one of Matilda's castles, Sorbara, lying fifteen kilometers northeast of her city Modena.

Because the opposition outnumbered the small elite group of fighters Matilda had spurred to the relief of Castle Sorbara, she planned a nighttime raid. Swinging her father's sword, she charged, resulting in a bloody victory and the capture of both renegade bishops, six rebel nobles, one hundred knights, and five hundred horses.

One of Emperor Henry's major stumbling blocks in his Italian campaign was the thus far impregnable fortress at Canossa; in 1091, Henry himself directed his army against Matilda. Upon hearing of his approach, she responded, oddly enough, by dividing her army. Half she stationed at the outpost of Bianello, and the remainder went with her into Canossa.

Both sides commenced preparations for a long siege. Shortly, however, Matilda noticed that the weather conditions at that time of year produced a dense fog that rolled thickly each morning around her castle. She decided to take the fight to Henry.

One foggy morning, the countess led her men through a secret passage at the base of the fortress walls and surrounded Henry's encampment. With the war cries "St. Peter and Matilda," her men attacked while monks stood at the castle's turrets singing psalms for the souls of the soon-to-be dead.

Surprised, Emperor Henry's men fell back, pursued by the countess and her knights. A messenger she had dispatched prior to the attack had reached the other half of her army at Bianello. They now appeared, trapping Henry's retreating forces. Though Henry evaded capture, his army was decimated and his royal standard was captured.

Henry would not quit, and Matilda organized an alliance of Italian cities against further encroachments by the emperor, which lasted for twenty years. Her own realm, centered at Canossa, formed the barrier to any attempts by Henry to use an Alpine approach into Italy.

La Gran Contessa, as she was known, enjoyed the last years of her life in the peace of a Benedictine monastery founded by her grandfather. She died July 15, 1115, at the age of sixty-nine, one of the greatest women warriors who has ever lived. Five centuries later her remains were reinterred at St. Peter's in Rome in an elegant marble monument created in commemoration of her by Lorenzo Bernini, which honors her as a champion of the papacy and a great Italian heroine.[25]

At the time that La Gran Contessa of Tuscany was carving out her niche in martial history, Louis VIII of France married Blanche of Castile; Carolingian queens had traditionally held powerful positions because of their control of the royal treasurer and their position as paymaster to the knights of the king. The queens awarded the knights a yearly gift that was in effect their salary for the year. Further, women like Blanche had the duty to monitor treasury acquisitions as well as the activities of the royal manors.

Such a queen was more than ready when, in the mideleventh century, her husband died. She ordered her son's coronation at Reims on November 29 and summoned the various lords to give homage to the new king. Three powerful barons, the counts of Brittany, LaMarche, and Champagne, however, did not attend at Reims and soon were in open revolt against Queen Blanche and her son.

Blanche rallied her army and soon quelled the first glimmers of rebellion. However, some months later, rebel barons meeting at Corbell decided on a plan to kidnap the king. Being warned, the king sent for his mother, who in predictable fashion marched to the Castle of Monthery where her son waited at the head of her knights as well as the entire Paris militia.

Using her famed diplomatic skills, Queen Blanche won Baron Thibaut from the rebellion. When the barons he had betrayed attacked Thibaut, Blanche led her army from Paris and drove the invaders out of Champagne. She then turned her diplomatic charms on the rebel count of Boulogne and added him to her roster of noble supporters.

Queen Blanche was not afraid to defy ecclesiastical threats to her rights. In what would become a typical encounter, the bishops of Rouen and Beauvais placed an interdict on royal chapels and cemeteries and excommunicated royal officials when Blanche denied the church the right to tax citizens, a right she felt belonged to her as queen. She usurped the lands of the bishops until they promised to lift their interdicts and the excommunication order. They did.

In another challenge from the clerical side, the Chapter of Notre Dame Cathedral levied a tax on some serfs. They appealed to Queen Blanche, the person they considered their rightful lord, for relief. When some of the recalcitrant serfs were imprisoned in the dungeon of Notre Dame, the queen asked that they be released, but the chapter refused, answering her request by adding the prisoners' wives and children to the cells of the great cathedral.

When Queen Blanche was informed that some of the serfs had died in the dungeons, she summoned the castellan of the Louvre and the provost of Paris, placed herself at the head of a troop of armed men, and invaded the cloister on the north side of the cathedral. The clerics withdrew into the cathedral and closed, but did not bar, the doors, reminding the queen that a forced, or even an unannounced entry, into the cathedral was a clear violation of jurisdiction. Queen Blanche responded by having her men tear the doors from their hinges, after which she rescued the imprisoned serfs. Frances and Joseph Geis in *Women of the Middle Ages* write: ". . . to all intents and purposes, she may be counted among the kings of France. Among the greatest kings, one might amend."[26]

In the eleventh century Hermangarde, the great-granddaughter of Charlemagne, fulfilling the familiar function of the woman warrior as defender of the castle, held the town of Vienne against the onslaught of the comte d'Autun for two years. Isabel of Conches oversaw her husband's army, and Sichelgaita, a princess of the Lombards, fought in company with her husband, mercenary soldier Robert Guiscard. Large and muscular, Sichelgaita presented a "fearsome sight" when dressed in full armor. Queen Richilde of Flanders allied herself with Philip I of France and supervised troops in battle against her husband, Bandonin VI. Florine, fiancée of the king of Denmark, died fighting by his side in the First Crusade.

During the various crusades as kings, princes, knights, and nobles sought their fortunes in the holy wars, noblewomen were generally left in control of castle, army, and state. When Roger II of Normandy marched on crusade in the late eleventh century, Adelaide of Monserrat, his mother, ruled in his stead, making policy and protecting her son's domains. When King Philip Augustus of France fought with his troops in the Third Crusade, his mother, Adele of Champagne, controlled the country.

In 1066 William the Conqueror, in one of the most famous battles in history, attacked England and established Norman rule. While William was campaigning in the British Isles, his wife, Matilda, was entrusted with his estates in Normandy. After William's death, his son-in-law technically inherited the duchy of Normandy, but William's daughter Adela actually ruled.

Ermengarde, countess of Narbonne, in the twelfth century married several monarchs who showed indifference to the work of government by abandoning the management of their empires to her. She controlled southern France for fifty years, leading the French Royalists in battles with the English. She gained wide renown for her expertise in feudal law, so much so that she was often petitioned to arbitrate disputes between lords and vassals.

Also in the twelfth century, Urraca of Aragon controlled a vast territory in Spain, while her half sister Teresa held Portugal. At the age of twenty-seven, Queen Urraca inherited from her father the kingdom of Leon-Castile, over which she reigned for seventeen years, thirteen of which she warred with her estranged second husband, Alfonso "the Battler," king of Aragon. Urraca of Aragon died in battle in 1111.[27]

Twenty-six years later in northern France, one of the richest women of the times, Eleanor of Aquitaine, married Louis VII of France, forming with their combined domains one of the largest kingdoms in twelfth-century Europe.[28] Eleanor's kingdom alone—which even after marriage she continued to rule—equaled about one-third of modern France. Eleanor maintained this rich prize through diplomacy, cunning, and, when required, warfare.

Her martial nature was most dramatically demonstrated on Easter Day 1146 at Vezelay. The mesmerizing monk, Abbé Bernard of Clairvaux, was preaching the Second Crusade, appealing to all good Christians to fight the infidels and save the sacred places of the Holy Land. Entranced by his message, Eleanor knelt at his feet and promised thousands of her vassals to the crusade. She dressed in armor, wore gold-colored boots, and carried a sword because she too would go. A group of noblewomen, similarly armed and mounted on chargers, gathered around her as she spoke. Many of their names were recorded: Sybelle, countess of Flanders; Mamile of Roucy; Florine of Bourgogne; Torqueri of Bouilon; Faydide of Toulouse.

The Greeks saw Eleanor and her band pass through on their way to the Holy Land. The historian Nicetas of Greece wrote that the women warriors of the Second Crusade rode chargers, wore armor, and were armed with sword and battle-ax. He particularly spoke of their leader, "the lady of the golden boot."[29]

Queen Eleanor and her band met the Byzantine emperor Komnenos and traveled to Syria, where she rendezvoused with her uncle, the knight and ruler of Syria, Raymond of Poitiers. They continued to Jerusalem, where she joined a kindred spirit, Queen Melisende, ruler of the Christians of Jerusalem. Queen Melisende had warred against the Muslims and against her own son when he challenged her refusal to relinquish rule of the city to him as he came of age.

After returning from the crusade, Eleanor divorced Louis VII and married his archenemy, King Henry II of England. She later rebelled against Henry II but was defeated. Though Henry II forgave his sons for their part in the attempted coup, he imprisoned Eleanor for fifteen years. Years later when her son John became king of England, though in her eighties she commanded military actions in his name. Her spirit is summed up effectively in the last signature she applied to a royal proclamation: "Eleanor, by the Wrath of God, Queen of England."

Several twelfth-century women warriors engaged in warfare against their own relatives. Richilde, who allied herself with Philip I of France, fought against her husband because his political views differed from hers. Julenne Breteuil, daughter of King Henry I of England, fought for her husband, Eustache de Breteuil, against her father. After her failed attempt to personally assassinate him, she was forced to surrender. King Henry threw her from the walls of her city into the moat.

In Italy in the latter part of the twelfth century, Alrude, countess of Bertinoro, rode with her army to the relief of her allies in the besieged city of Ancona. Arriving late in the day, she made camp with William Adelardi of Ferrara and his forces in the hills overlooking the city. That evening, William brought the soldiers together to be addressed by Alrude, who spoke from the back of a wagon.

> Fortified and encouraged by the favor of Heaven, I have, contrary to the customs of my sex, determined to address you. I solemnly

swear to you, that, on the present occasion, no views of interest, no dreams of ambition, have impelled me to succor the besieged. Since the death of my husband, I have found myself, though plunged in sorrow, the unresisted mistress of his domains. The preservation of my numerous possessions, to which my wishes are limited, affords an occupation sufficiently arduous for my sex and capacity. But the perils which encompass the wretched Anconians, the prayers and tears of their women, justly dreading to fall into the hands of any enemy, who, governed by brutal rapacity, spare neither sex nor age, have animated me to hasten to their aid.

It is by those who are truly great that virtue is esteemed more than riches or honors. An enterprise, so full of glory, has already nearly succeeded; already have you passed through the defiles occupied by the enemy, and pitched your tents in hostile country. It is not time that the seed which was scattered, should bring forth its fruit; it is time to make trial of your strength, and of that valor for which you are distinguished. Courage is relaxed by delay. Let the dawn of day find you under arms, that the sun may illumine the victory promised by the Most High to your pity for the unfortunate.[30]

Her speech so enthused the armies that the ensuing clamor of applause convinced the enemy that a large opposition force had approached during the night. They doused their fires and slipped away in the darkness. The chronicles report that on her return home Alrude encountered numerous small groups of the retreating enemy and defeated each in turn.

Less than twenty years later, another woman warrior of twelfth-century Italy, Berengaria, the daughter of the king of Naples, married the famous Richard the Lionhearted of England. She accompanied him in battle in the crusade against Saladin and after his death founded an abbey with large adjacent land holdings, which she ruled until her death.

Twelfth-century historian Saxo Grammaticus related the account of the Gothic princess Alvilda of Sweden. When her father, King Sypardus, promised her in marriage to Prince Alf of Denmark against her will, she escaped to the seas as a pirate captain. Linda Grant DePauw, in *Seafaring Women*, observed that Alvilda and her all-female crew ". . . must have been a tough, muscular bunch. Gothic ships relied more on oars than on sails for propulsion; and they fought without guns, having only hand weapons."[31]

A pirate vessel that had recently lost its captain became her first prize. Now, with two ships in her fleet, Alvilda harassed shipping in the Baltic with such success that merchants clamored for local authorities to quell the pirate threat. Prince Alf, Alvilda's hapless suitor, unaware of the identity of the pirate captain, set out to destroy the sea robbers.

Alvilda and Alf joined battle off the coast of Denmark. After several hours, Alf's Danes boarded the pirate vessel and escorted the captain, accoutred in helmet and armor, to Alf. When the prince ordered the pirate leader to remove "his" helmet, he was stunned speechless at the sight of his beloved Alvilda standing before him. However, Grammaticus reports that he quickly regained his tongue and asked the princess to marry him. She accepted his proposal and retired from the sea.

European noblewomen of the thirteenth century not only waged war, they also responded in warrior fashion to infringements on their personal honor. Although selecting a champion to defend their reputation was acceptable for cripples, clergy, and women, some women chose to duel themselves. German law of the time detailed the procedure for a woman formally challenging a man to joust. Such a fight took place in Berne in 1228. The woman won.

One form of duel between a man and woman found the man armed with a club standing waist deep in a pit three feet wide with his left hand tied behind his back. Circling him, the woman swung a stone weighing from three to five pounds wrapped in the end of her shawl. If the woman lost, her adversary would bury her alive.

In Freisingen this type of duel was reserved for rape cases. If the woman lost the duel, she lost a hand; if the man succumbed, he lost his head. In Bohemia both the man in the hole and the woman were armed with swords, but the woman was kept at a reasonable distance by a circle drawn around the pit.[32]

In the early thirteenth century, expertise at castle defense earned Lady Guirande de Lavaur a bizarre death.[33] She safeguarded her castle from the armies of bishops from Toulouse, Lisieux, and Bayeux, as well as the renowned knight Simon de Montfort. Her efficient rejection of his assault force so outraged de Montfort that when he finally captured her, he dropped her down a well and ordered it filled with stones.

Twenty-six years later in Italy, another woman warrior, Blanche de Rossi, died under the weight of rock, but it was a fate of her choosing. Blanche accompanied her husband Battista de la Porta, commander of an army sent to defend the city of Bassano against the tyrant Ezzelino. She fought by his side in cavalry skirmishes and dueled on the ramparts of the city.

When the forces of Ezzelino ultimately prevailed, they killed General Battista de la Porta and presented Blanche de Rossi to the tyrant. Ezzelino was so captivated by her beauty that he offered her freedom if she would be his mistress. She jumped out the nearest window. Battered but alive, she was returned to Ezzelino. This time she agreed to his terms but asked to visit her husband's grave once more. Blanche was taken to the grave, and the large stone that covered the tomb was tilted back. She stepped into the tomb, and before anyone could react, she pulled the heavy stone down, crushing herself to death.

The crusades of the thirteenth century, as did those preceding, found many women warriors in the Holy Land. Margaret of Provence, who married the king of France in 1254, accompanied him on his wars in the Holy Land. When he was captured, their stronghold of Damietta was attacked by his enemies, but Margaret lent her strength to its successful defense. In like manner, Eleanor of Castile, wife of Edward I of England, marched with her husband and the English army to the wars of the Seventh Crusade. A historian of the time wrote, "French women warriors in this period were either duelists who made themselves locally famous in France or hard-fighting crusader soldiers who usually died unidentified."[34]

Madame de Chauteau-Gay exemplified the former. She was, as one commentator expressed, ". . . both gallant and handsome; she was generally to be seen on horseback, wearing huge top-boots, kilted skirts and a man's wide-brimmed hat with steel trimmings and feathers to crown all, sword by side and pistols at saddle bow."[35]

Though married, she challenged the captain of her lover's cavalry regiment to a duel after the officer had, in her opinion, mistreated her friend. Aware of Madame de Chauteau-Gay's fame with sword and pistol, the cowardly officer appeared at the duel with two swordsmen by his side.

Madame de Chauteau-Gay's squire asked her to withdraw because of the unfairness. She responded, "It shall never be said that I encountered them without attacking them." She engaged all three swordsmen at once and after offering an excellent account of her sword skills, she was, in the end, overcome and killed by her adversaries.

A little over thirty years later, a Castilian woman warrior, Maria de Molina, queen of Castile, carried on warfare from 1295 to 1301 as regent for her son Ferdinand IV. Other pretenders to the throne of Castile attacked Maria's city, even at times drawing in soldiers from Granada, Navarre, France, and Aragon, but the queen of Castile stood them all off. She lived not only to influence the direction of Castilian history under her son, but also under her grandson, Alfonso XI.

The exploits of the women warriors of Genoa, Italy, in their battles with the Turks in 1301 are recorded. The crusades of the latter part of the fourteenth century drew numbers of Genoese women warriors. Pope Boniface VIII wrote about the women crusaders of 1383 and their "warlike infatuation."[36]

In the same era that Navarre lent its soldiers to the enemies of Maria de Molina, Jeanne of Navarre, heiress of King Henry I of Navarre and count of Champagne, wife of Philip the Fair of France, pressed her army against the count of Bar. He was advancing upon Champagne, a city that Jeanne claimed, as she did Brie and Navarre. She prevailed and imprisoned the count. Her power so impressed her husband that, though a king, he never sought through his marriage with Jeanne to usurp her territories.

Women's historian Bebel Gerritsen writes, concerning the women of fourteenth- and fifteenth-century Europe:

> Troops of women wandered through the countryside as mounte-banks, singers, musicians, in company with traveling scholars and clerks, inundating the fairs and markets and all other places in which assemblies and fairs took place. In the army of mercenaries, they formed special divisions with their own sergeants.[37]

With respect to the labors of the women soldiers of the time, other than combat, Gerritsen notes:

> In the camps they had to help the soldier boys in carrying hay, straw and wood to fill up ditches, dikes, and pits and in cleaning the tents. At sieges they had to fill the moats with branches, fagots and brushwood to facilitate the attack. They assisted in bringing the artillery into position, and when the cannon wheels stuck in the mud, in lifting them out again.[38]

In 1357 Lady Cia Degli Ubaldini, in the absence of her husband, Francesco d'Ordelaffi, prince of Romania, defended the city of Cesena. Outnumbered ten to one, she stood in full armor with two hundred knights and two hundred foot soldiers against the attackers. The battle was so bloody that her father interceded with her to abandon her castle and sue for terms of surrender. Her response: "For death and all else but my duty, I care but little."[39]

Lady Cia Degli Ubaldini's effective defense made the cost of taking Cesena so high that she finally forced a settlement with her enemy, which allowed all her supporters, with their weapons, to leave the area in peace. She gave herself and her children up for ransom as part of her settlement.[40]

The 1300s claimed Caterina Benincasa, the patron saint of Italy. She, like Joan of Arc, who appeared a century after her, listened to the voices in her visions and directed warfare, in her case, against the Muslims.

*　　*　　*

A famous quarrel in the midfourteenth century over the Duchy of Brittany (west coast of France) provides an opportunity to observe the roles of women warriors. On one side in this epic struggle stood Charles de Blois, supported by his uncle, King Philip of France; opposing the French claim, Count John of Montfort, backed by King Edward of England.

A nun, Julia Duguesclin, sister of the knight Bertrand Duguesclin, played a key role in the successful defense of the fortress of Pontorson by the French. As the English armies advanced in Brittany, Julia and the nuns of a nearby convent sought safety at Pontorson. Unfortunately, however, Julia had moved from a place of safety into one of the military objectives of the English, who soon appeared at the walls demanding the surrender of the garrison.

The soldiers of Pontorson realized they were outnumbered, but before they could signal their surrender, Julia, in one of her brother's coats of chain mail, appeared on the battlements. She shouted her defiance to the English and rallied the garrison to resist.

As the English threw their scaling ladders against the walls, Julia was seen rushing amid the storm of arrows and repulsing the English scaling ladders. She was reported to have personally thrown three English soldiers from the walls. When Julia noticed that the English were falling back to regroup for a second onslaught, she quickly ordered the gates of Pontorson thrown open, and she threw her outnumbered troops at the raggedly retreating English.

At that moment Julia's brother Bertrand returned, and they trapped the English between them. The brother and sister team destroyed the attacking force and captured its general.[41] One of Marshal Bertand's knights, incidentally, was the noblewoman Janine-Marie de Foix, who fought in the French forces between 1377 and 1380.

The French side under Charles de Blois won a major victory when, through sheer force of numbers, they defeated the count of Montfort and imprisoned him in the Louvre. But if King Philip and de Blois felt the issue was settled, they had not reckoned on the wife of the captured count, Jane of Montfort.

The countess of Montfort carried her infant son from town to town and roused the people to continue their fight against the French for the sake of the imprisoned count and his heir. She reported that she had petitioned English King Edward for assistance and asked her supporters to hold out until the English reinforcements came.

The countess created defensive strategies for each town that joined her side and supplied them with the wherewithal to fight from her own castle stores. With her preparations completed, Jane, dressed in full armor, withdrew into Hennebonne, the most imposing fortress in Brittany, and waited for Charles de Blois.

Froissart, an eyewitness, recounted that the countess of Montfort:

> . . . wore a harness on her body and rode on a great courser from street to street, desiring her people to make a good defense. She caused damsels and other women to cut short their kirtles, and to carry stones and pots full of chalk to the walls to be cast down to their enemies.[42]

De Blois laid siege to Rennes, the site of Jane's personal estates, probably expecting to take her there. Instead, Jane had left William de Cadoudal in charge, promising him, as she had promised all others, that he must endure until the English came. The people, however, rose against him and the town was lost to the French. With Rennes under control, Charles turned toward Hennebonne.

Jane commanded her soldiers from the battlements, often leaping into breaches in the walls resulting from French cannon fire and fighting in hand-to-hand combat with the French soldiers who tried to flood the broken defense. In one characteristic action Jane found, as many commanders have done before and after her, that very often the best defense is a good offense. As the walls of Hennebonne weakened, the attackers spent their energy close to the fortress and, to Jane's discerning gaze, lapsed in their attention to their base camp and supply wagons.

She rapidly assembled five hundred of her best fighters and, in the midst of a furious attack by the French, swept from the castle with her men. She charged through the enemy's lines straight for the largely abandoned camp, setting fire to baggage wagons and weapons stores. The French pursued her, but they were too late. She and her knights kept riding, not toward her fortress, but to the nearby friendly town of Auray. After a five-day rest, she brought her forces back to Hennebonne, surprising the French by attacking their rear, and reentered her fort to command its defense.

In time, the artillery of the French forces turned the walls of Hennebonne to rubble, and the bishop of Leon held a conference with Charles de Blois concerning surrender terms. Jane would have nothing to do with the meeting but rather climbed to a high tower and looked out to sea, still hoping the English would appear. They did. Jane ran from the tower shouting, "The English have come! No capitulation! No capitulation!"

Charles fled toward his lines as Jane gathered the garrison to attack the confused enemy. The English relief, heavy cavalry and six thousand archers under Sir Walter Mauny, joined Jane's troops, and together they destroyed the French forces. Charles de Blois retreated with his remaining troops into the fortress of Roche de Rien, but Jane, augmented with the

English reinforcements, devised a night attack. This time Charles was captured and his army once more was seriously mauled by the forces of the countess of Montfort and the English.

As the capture of the count of Montfort had spurred Jane into valorous action, so too did the capture of Charles de Blois produce for her a formidable foe. Jeanne de Penthierre, Charles's wife, led his forces against the supporters of the count of Montfort.

Jane traveled to England shortly after her victory at Hennebonne and Roche de Rien and obtained from King Edward new forces under the leadership of Robert of Artois. She sailed back to France with a fleet of twenty-five ships, but the French attacked off the coast of Guernsey. Jane, sword in hand, joined the English soldiers in repelling the French sailors as they attempted to board the English ships. Froissart writes, "The Countess that day was worth a man; she had the heart of a lion, and had in her hand a sharp sword wherewith she fought fiercely."[43]

Once in France, Jane and Robert captured the city of Vannes, but Robert was killed in the latter phases of the fight.

The countess joined with Sir Thomas Dagworth and defeated the newly released Charles de Blois, exacting a truce in return. De Blois immediately broke the agreement and was again attacked by the Montfort forces and their English allies. De Blois and his son died at the Battle of Auray on September 29, 1364. Jane of Montfort lived to see her son acknowledged as the rightful heir of Brittany, the goal for which she had fought.

A year after the count of Montfort's capture and the commencement of Jane of Montfort's warrior ventures, Jane of Belleville saw her husband, Oliver III, lord of Clisson, beheaded by the French on August 2, 1343, for conspiring with the English in their designs on Brittany. Her sorrow quickly turning to anger, she gathered around her a band of loyal knights and made war on the supporters of Charles de Blois and French King Philip VI of Valois.

Early in her campaign Jane easily accessed enemy towns as a lady traveling with an escort. Once within the walls, her band killed without mercy, burning the town as they left. Jane is depicted in several sources as dressed in armor and brandishing a sword in one hand and a torch in the other.

Always near when she needed protection were the forces of the count of Montfort. Further, supporters in numerous castles and chateaus in the area offered her refuge, allowing her to reappear in some distant place to strike at targets tainted by their connection to de Blois and the French king.

When her notoriety brought too many French soldiers into the hunt for her band, Jane continued her one-woman war on the sea. In England, she convinced King Edward III, another Montfort supporter, to lend her three warships on the condition that she would outfit them. A further agreement stipulated that she would command the small fleet, whose captains and pilots would concur with her wishes.

Jane's ships hunted the French in both the English Channel and the Atlantic, and she never gave quarter. All French vessels she took were pillaged and sent to the bottom. In her later naval days along the coast of Normandy, Jane raided villages sympathetic to de Blois and the king, terrorizing them as she approached at the head of her raiders, sword and torch at the ready.[44]

The Italian setting produced in the fifteenth century the house of Sforza, a source of many famous women warriors. Actually, the Sforza line might never have been created if not for the valor of Margaret de Attenduli in the latter fourteenth century. While leading her soldiers at Tricarico, she heard of her brother's capture by the prince of Naples. She immediately marched on Naples and laid siege to the palace of the prince, who shortly released her brother in exchange for Margaret's withdrawal.[45]

Ten years after Margaret saved her brother in Naples, a young woman named Jadwiga was crowned queen of Poland. Though only sixteen, she demonstrated her strength by controlling the volatile Order of the Teutonic Knights and leading her army in several skirmishes in defense of Poland's national borders. Not only did she secure Poland's sovereignty against internal and external threats, she founded the University of Cracow—all before her death in childbirth at the age of twenty-eight.

At the time Queen Jadwiga controlled Poland, Margaret, third daughter of King Waldemar of Denmark, maneuvered her armies in the ultimately successful effort to unite the countries of Scandinavia under her sway. First she acquired Norway with a combination of bribery, diplomacy, and military force. She appointed her sister's grandson as a puppet ruler under her direction and then turned her attention on Sweden. The Swedes, suffering under the brutality of their King Albert, promised Margaret the crown if she would relieve them of Albert. The war lasted seven years, but in 1388 she defeated the Swedish king and united Denmark, Norway, and Sweden under her absolute authority.

Queen Margaret displayed her confidence and regal mien to a gathering of nobles from the various countries of Scandinavia, who reminded her of the many promises she had made in return for their political and military assistance. When they mentioned the documents containing her various promises, she replied, "I advise you to keep them carefully; as I shall keep the castles and cities of my kingdom and all the rights belonging to my dignity."[46]

On the southern borders of Margaret's kingdom five years after her death in 1412, Jacqueline, daughter of Count William of Hainault, inherited the title countess of Hainault, Holland, and Zeeland. Her father had called her "Dame Jacob" because of her rough-and-tumble nature as a child. The Hainault castle housed three lions as living symbols of the Hainault crest, and Jacqueline reportedly played with the beasts as she would her pet dogs.

As soon as she was confirmed in her position, Jacqueline was challenged by Lord Arkell, a man who could not tolerate female rule, perhaps because he had been defeated in battle by his own mother when he had contended for the family castle. At any rate, he rebelled against the new countess and lay siege to Gorku, one of her towns.

Countess Jacqueline sent three hundred ships and six thousand knights to remove Arkell, who had taken Gorku. He appeared to be winning the battle when Countess Jacqueline attacked the fortress at the head of reserve forces. She personally pursued him through the castle of Gorku and killed him in hand-to-hand combat.[47]

The one woman warrior in the Western tradition known by all is Joan of Arc.[48] Her exploits in the early fifteenth century paved the way for the birth of the modern nation of France. In the time of Joan, Armagnacs, Burgundians, English, and citizens of a variety of feudal domains populated France, but no French state was owned or ruled by a population that identified itself as "French." Their success at the Battle of Agincourt in 1415 had won for the English most of northern France, and they sought control of southern France by their siege of Orleans.

A seventeen-year-old peasant girl, Joan, lived at Dom-Remy, a French village on the Maese River, the dividing line between Champagne and Lorraine. At twelve, she had begun to communicate with the archangel Michael, Saint Catherine, and Saint Margaret. At first, she said, they spoke to her of ordinary things, but in 1429 Saint Michael told her to go to the aid of France.

> In the fifteenth century almost everybody talked with the angels or knew somebody who talked with them. . . . Angels and men could mingle and talk together as naturally as two next-door neighbors meeting on the street. To hear an angel call you from above was no more surprising than to hear your mother call you from the kitchen. There was no miracle in this. On the contrary, Joan would have regarded it as a miracle if you had told her that the angels did not speak to God's children on earth.[49]

When Joan expressed doubts to the archangel Michael that she, a farmer's daughter from a poor village, could save France, he instructed her to visit Robert de Baudricourt, lord of the village of Dom-Remy. Sir

Robert thought Joan was insane and sent her away. Six months later, she approached him again with her outlandish request based on her conversation with an angel. He considered having an exorcism performed for her, but the people of the countryside saw her as an authentic savior. Sir Robert became convinced of her powers after Joan accurately prophesied the results of a battle at Herrings, information conveyed to her by her angel. He provided her with a war-horse, sword, armor, and an escort to her interview with King Charles, the dauphin, at Chinon.

Joan again impressed Sir Robert de Baudricourt with her powers when she refused the sword he offered and requested one that would be found lying on a tomb behind the great altar at the church of Saint Catherine de Fierbois. Sir Robert dispatched a guard to Fierbois to test her prophecy, and when the soldier returned with the weapon, Sir Robert turned it over to Joan. When she reached Chinon, she convinced King Charles that she should lead his faltering armies.

> In those days it was not unusual for women to fight side by side with the men. There were thirty women wounded in the battle of Amiens. A number of women soldiers fought among the followers of Johannes Huss in Bohemia. There was hardly a medieval siege in which some woman was not conspicuous for heroism. It was therefore quite natural for Charles to accept the military services of Joan of Arc.[50]

Another historian concurs: "She evidently did not seem as unusual to her countrymen as she does to the twentieth century, which suggests that more of a woman warrior tradition than we know of was extant in her time."[51]

Joan rode forth from Chinon with Marshal de Boussac, Marshal La Hire, and a convoy of six thousand troops. They arrived at Orleans on April 29 and found a series of small English forts around the walls of the city. Joan understood that with this arrangement the English could not efficiently communicate or assist each other in repelling attacks, situations they apparently considered highly unlikely from the besieged population of Orleans.

On May 4 under Joan's command, Charles's troops attacked the first English fort. In a four-hour battle, four hundred English soldiers were killed. Though Joan argued against excessive killing, she could be quite ruthless if necessary to ensure victory. Her style of warfare was described by a nineteenth-century observer as follows: "To concentrate quickly, to strike swiftly, to strike hard, to strike at vital points, and, despising vain, noisy skirmishes and valances, to fight with invincible tenacity of purpose."[52]

Joan's power was strengthened by the impression she made on the imaginations of the warriors that surrounded her, both French and English. The demoralized French soldiers, fighting for a weakling king they barely knew, were transformed when Joan persuaded them that they were fighting not for Charles but for God and France. They believed that the angels were flying with them into battle. The English, on the other hand, saw Joan as a witch empowered by Satan.

On the Friday after capturing the first English fort, Joan's army occupied two more. She rode before her troops, dressed in armor, carrying a sword and battle-ax in her belt, and holding her standard, a flag depicting the fleur-de-lis on a white background. She was wounded several times but quickly returned to battle, for her men lost their fighting spirit and sense of purpose without her presence.

Joan raised the siege of Orleans on May 8 after the final English fort of Tourelles fell and proceeded toward Reims, where Charles was to be crowned king of France. The English mounted resistance along her route. She besieged the earl of Suffolk at Jargeau and in a ten-day battle killed six hundred English soldiers and captured the earl and his brother.

On June 18, four thousand English troops under Sir John Fastolfe joined with the army of Lord Talbot against Joan at Patay. Her fame had grown to such dimensions that when she approached, most of the English army, including Commander Sir John Fastolfe, fled. Afterward, he was stripped of his Order of the Garter for his cowardice.

Lord Talbot stood his ground but to no avail. He with a hundred English noblemen was captured, and 1,800 English soldiers were killed. The English tried to stop Joan at Sully and Troyes, but her army was invincible. With Joan riding in the lead, they arrived at Reims on July 15, 1429, and two days later Charles VII was crowned king of France. Two years later, Joan of Arc was tried and burned as a witch in the marketplace of Rouen, betrayed by French nobles who feared her power over Charles VII.

*　*　*

A contemporary of Joan's, Isabella of Lorraine, eldest daughter of Charles II of Lorraine, married René, duke of Anjou, in 1420 at the age of thirteen. Nine years later, Duke René was taken prisoner by the duke of Burgundy. Raising an army with the nobles of Lorraine, Isabella led them in a successful battle to free her husband from the Burgundians.

When René inherited Sicily after the death of Charles I, and perhaps remembering his wife's military and political expertise, he dispatched Isabella to claim his inheritance in the Mediterranean. She not only secured the island for René but also stayed to rule. Her just reign endeared her to the people of Sicily, and in 1437 René moved to live with her. Isabella of Lorraine died at the age of forty-four on February 28, 1452.

Another contemporary of Joan of Arc, Jeanne des Armoises, earned her warrior credentials fighting at Poitou and Guinee. Her skills at military diplomacy were established when she convinced the Spanish to provide a fleet of warships for her cause. Her martial prowess was rewarded in 1439 when the marechal de Rais placed her in command of a large army. Six years earlier in France, the duchess of Bar joined with Jean de Vergy to fight the English and reject their attempts to overcome Bar and Lorraine.[53]

During the era in which Isabella of Lorraine, Jeanne des Armoises, and the duchess of Bar commanded their troops in France, a young peasant girl from the Italian village of Sacco was introduced to Captain Brunoro, soldier of the duke of Milan in the wars against the duke of Venice. Brunoro, who had been left in command of territory newly taken from the Venetians, stopped one day during a hunting trip to enjoy a peasant festival and met Bona Lombardi. They were married within the year.

Fascinated with Brunoro's martial skills and horsemanship, Bona begged him to teach her the arts of a warrior so that she could accompany him in war, and, in a short time, she was always seen fighting beside him. She, in fact, saved him several times. In the first instance, Brunoro was captured by the king of Naples. Bona, with her soldiers, hurried to Naples and secured his release through a combination of flattery, bribery, and threat. In another case during the Milanese Wars, Brunoro led an attack against the Venetian castle of Povoze but was knocked off his horse and taken prisoner. Bona arrived shortly thereafter, rallied the soldiers, and stormed the castle to free her husband. She died of grief one year after his death in 1469.[54]

Bianca Maria Visconti warred with the Venetians in the midfifteenth century. Wife of Francesco Sforza, she displayed a variety of military skills. She defended her castle at Cremona against a Venetian attack and later directed a naval battle against them. In 1447 she overthrew the Ambrosian Republic and welded it into her other inheritances and conquests to create a new duchy in northern Italy. "The very noble" Luzia Stanga, the courtesans Malatesta and Margheritona, and a female salaried trooper in count de Gaiazzo's light horse squadron are among many other *cavalieress*, "equestrian women warriors," who left proof of their exploits in the Italian historical records.[55]

In the late fifteenth century, an alliance consisting of the king of England, the king of Aragon, the duke of Brittany, the duke of Guienne, and the duke of Burgundy was arrayed against King Louis XI of France. The dismemberment of his fragile empire was decided upon by the English-backed alliance, and each noble led his armies to secure his prizes.

When Charles the Bold and the duke of Burgundy joined forces against the French Royalist town of Beauvais, they expected little resistance from the town with no garrison. The citizens, however, decided to fight. After barricading the city gates, the men prepared their weapons and waited on the battlements. A young woman of the town, Jeanne Laine, organized the women to assist.

During the ensuing battle, the women brought arrows, food, and water to the male defenders and boiled water, oil, and grease to throw down on the attackers. When the Burgundians planted their scaling ladders, the citizens of Beauvais found themselves on the verge of being overwhelmed. A Burgundian fought his way to an abutment and planted his flag, but Jeanne threw the man over the wall. Then, pulling an ax from her belt, she chopped the standard pole in half and held the despoiled banner for the defenders to see. The men of Beauvais rallied for nine hours until reinforcements temporarily drove the Burgundians back.

Charles the Bold considered the defeat of Beauvais a matter of personal honor. He surrounded the town and laid siege with continual bombardment. A month passed, and Charles still did not control Beauvais. Finally, against the advice of his generals, he ordered an all-out assault on the battered city. Jeanne and the women stood on the ramparts with the men as the Burgundians came.

The troops of Charles the Bold seized a portion of the city wall and planted their banner, but it was soon chopped down and thrown back at them. A second time, they breached the wall and set their flag, and a second time it was hurled back. After the third failed assault, a four-hour battle, Charles the Bold ordered his troops to retreat.

On July 22 he withdrew from Beauvais and moved his army toward Brittany. The fierce resistance of the citizens of Beauvais against Charles the Bold granted Louis XI enough time to prepare a successful defense.

King Louis, in gratitude for the contributions of the city of Beauvais to his final victory, freed the people of all taxes and granted them the right to elect their own officials. Jeanne Laine, now known as Jeanne Hachette because of her efficient use of the ax in the battle against Charles, was raised to the status of nobility.

In Sardinia, Eleanora Di Arboreatook assumed control after her brother was assassinated and squelched a domestic uprising that threatened her ability to defend her country. She capped her warrior career with a victory in battle over the king of Aragon.

The fifteenth century witnessed the discovery of the New World, the Spanish Inquisition, the final expulsion of the Moors from European soil, and the attempted removal of all Jews from Spain—events based on decisions of Queen Isabella of Spain.[56] Christopher Columbus received permission to seek the Asian passage he envisioned from both Isabella and Ferdinand at Santa Fe, a military camp near the Moorish city of Granada, whose final fall weeks earlier was engineered by Isabella.

At the age of seventeen, Isabella of Castile selected Ferdinand of Aragon as her husband because joining their two kingdoms would advantage both of them. She never abandoned her authority to her husband; rather, she and Ferdinand coruled as independent monarchs. Both signed proclamations, and both images were stamped on coinage. They were, by midcareer, interchangeable. In 1475 when Ferdinand was absent, Isabella commanded the troops at Toledo, riding with them in full armor. Ferdinand exercised authority in Castile as Isabella exerted her power in his Aragon.

Her first taste of warfare came when she succeeded to the throne of Castile after her father's death. Juana la Beltraneja challenged Isabella's rights. Juana, through marriage, had allied herself with Portugal and warred with Isabella for years in her attempt to add Castile to Portugal.

Ferdinand directed the five-year war that ensued, and Isabella offered what aid she could. She discovered her talent for war and has since been described as "a great general but an even greater quartermaster-general."[57]

Isabella, as a lady of a large castle and therefore trained to manage food and supplies, found her experience useful when organizing for Ferdinand's always-moving army. She conscripted a labor force of thousands to build new and improved roads to expedite the movement of troops, supplies, and artillery. She hired professional Swiss soldiers and provided her artillerymen with a backup of military smiths and engineers.

At Toledo and later elsewhere, Isabella appeared with the army ready for combat. She had sought instruction in martial arts after she married Ferdinand and joined in his military ventures. She came to the Spanish siege of Baza in 1488 in battle regalia and rallied her troops to press the siege home. The Moors swarmed along the walls to catch a glimpse of the famous Castilian queen.

In their campaign against Granada, a city in southern Spain ruled for centuries by the Moors, Isabella argued against the Spanish nobles who told Ferdinand, after a period of siege, that he should retreat from the city's walls. She prevailed and Granada was taken, the final blow to the Spanish Moors. The same drive that convinced her that she was a crusader—the vision of an all-Catholic Spain—compelled her not only to war on the Moors but also to illegally expel 170,000 Jews from the country. She cleaned the highways of robbers to ensure safer travel, weakened the nobles, restored the currency, initiated a Spanish law code, introduced to her court polyphonic music newly created in Flanders, and supported Dutch painters who painted and taught in Spain.[58]

Isabella's accomplishments speak to her legendary physical strength and stamina. A comparison of the suits of armor of Ferdinand and Isabella indicates that she was slightly taller than her husband. She could live on horseback like a seasoned trooper when on the march. During the wars with Juana la Beltraneja, she rode many hundreds of miles, arranging the operations necessary for the support of Ferdinand's campaign. And she gave birth to five children between 1470 and 1485.

An historian notes that Isabella could spend the night issuing orders and then casually resume her embroidery. Her last orders called for her burial on the battlefield of Granada, the scene of her most glorious action, the victory that drove the Moors from Spanish soil forever. She once commented that she "knew only four fine sights: a soldier in the field, a priest at the altar, a beautiful woman in bed, and a thief on the gibbet."[59] Queen Isabella died in 1504.

Across the Pyrenees, in France, during Isabella's prime, King Louis XI had a daughter he named Anne. As a teenager, she married Pierre de Bourbon, a weakling whom Anne quickly dominated. Before her father died, he selected Anne as queen regent for her brother Charles VIII, who was only fourteen at the time.

When her regency was announced, two competitors, John, duke of Bourbon, and Louis, duke of Orleans, resisted. She placated John with a coveted high office, but Louis would not be bought. When Anne ordered his arrest, he fled to his castle, and she pursued with her army and routed him. He surrendered and was freed on the proviso that he leave the kingdom.

Louis went to Brittany under the protection of Francis II, a futile move because Anne envisioned the addition of Brittany to the kingdom of France. She drove her troops against the Bretons, who were captained by Louis of Orleans. He lost to Anne again, and this time she imprisoned him for two years.

Anne's brother, Charles VIII, died, ending her regency, and Louis, duke of Orleans, Anne's old nemesis, was named successor to the throne of France. She feared that King Louis would exact revenge for the stinging defeats she had dealt him. His words to her, however, proved that her one-time adversary, though perhaps not a brilliant general, was a gentleman. He wrote that she need not fear him in his new capacity as king and requested that she keep her seat on the council of nobles that advised him. He wrote, "It becomes not a king of France to revenge the quarrels of the Duke of Orleans."[60]

De Maulde La Clavière writes of Anne:

> The Lady of Beaujue was condemned to an attitude of knitted brow and drawn sword as a means of reassuring her good subjects and keeping the bad in awe; that haughty, ambitious, closed-fisted, masculine woman, as she was called by those whom she had re-

duced to a proper sense of the duty of prompt obedience—no one was in reality less like the cold statue she appeared in official life.[61]

*　*　*

Onorata Rodiani of Italy discovered her warrior talents through art. A midfifteenth-century artist, she was attacked by an impetuous nobleman while working on a mural that had been commissioned by the tyrant of Cremona. Onorata buried her dagger in her attacker's chest and vanished into the shadows, only to appear some months later as the captain of a *condottieri* (mercenary) band of professional fighters. "Captain" Onorata Rodiani died in the defense of Castelleone in 1472.[62]

In France during the same period, Royalist troops battled renegade nobles. In one such battle, Marguerite de Bressieux, princess of a Royalist castle, was captured by Louis de Chalon and along with her eleven ladies-in-waiting was raped by his men. Several months later, while Royalist troops under Raoul de Grancourt prepared to attack Louis de Chalon's castle, twelve knights appeared, dressed in black armor, wearing black crepe veils over their helmets, and carrying a black banner depicting an orange pierced with a spear. (Louis de Chalon was the prince of Orange.)

According to witnesses, they fought well. When they confronted one of the rapists, they raised their helmet visors before killing him to reveal the identity of his executioner. Marguerite, the group's captain, was badly wounded and died several hours after the battle. Her courage was honored by General de Grancourt when he buried her with full military honors.[63]

*　*　*

Claude Catherine de Clermont, wife of the duke of Metz, served in the early fifteenth century as governess to the children of the great Italian monarch Catherine de Medicis. Lady de Clermont's adept language skills prompted the de Medicis court to request her translations for foreign visitors. Her son, the marquis de Belleisle, in his father's absence sought control of the family estates and fomented rebellion among the other vassals of Henry IV.

Lady de Clermont gathered soldiers, defeated her son, and visited the vassals of the king to dissuade them from actions they would soon regret. Henry IV appreciated her courage and loyalty and plied her with wealth and honors until her death in the late 1500s.

*　*　*

The queen, not the king, is the most powerful piece in the game of chess, and the reason lies in the homage the chess masters of the fifteenth century sought to pay Italian woman warrior Caterina Sforza.[64] Born in 1462, Caterina was the illegitimate daughter of the duke of Milan. She married Girolamo Riaro, whose uncle, Sixtus IV, reigned as pope.

Caterina grew up with interests in martial arts, sports, and hunting, activities that honed skills she often used over the course of her turbulent life. Caterina's initiation into combat came in 1483 when she suited in armor to defend her husband's lands from the Venetians. When Pope Sixtus died, she held the fortress of Saint Angelo until the rightful heir could be determined.

Her entry into the Eternal City was pure pageantry. As she approached the Castle of Saint Angelo, the adoring citizens lined the streets shouting, "Duca! Duca!" Cerratini, an observer on the street that August 14, describes Caterina Sforza as she took control of the Castle of Saint Angelo:

> She was wise, brave, tall, well-knit and possessed of a handsome face. She spoke little. She wore a dress of green satin with a train two yards long, a large cloak of black velvet in the French style, a man's belt, with a purse of gold ducats. At her side was a curved Falchion (type of sword). She was much feared by the men, whether mounted or on foot, because, when she had a weapon in her hand, she was hard and cruel.[65]

Cerratini neglects to add that on that hot summer day in Rome, Caterina Sforza was seven months pregnant.

Her husband was killed by the Orsi in 1488, leaving Caterina as queen regent for their young son. She held the position for twelve years through attacks by the papacy, bullying local nobles, and finally the French army. The French, during their periods of military engagement with Lady Sforza, had formed an accurate impression of her. They called their largest piece of artillery "Madame de Forlì," Forlì being one of Caterina Sforza's cities.[66]

Caterina's insatiable taste for vengeance compelled her to destroy the Orsi family, her husband's killers. She arrested and publicly executed some, and others she had murdered. The patriarch of the family, Andrea Orsi, was forced to watch his palace pillaged and burned. Then he was stripped from the waist down, tied by his arm to a horse's tail, and dragged to death over the cobblestoned streets. Afterward, Caterina ordered his heart removed and his body dismembered.

Pope Alexander VI used such examples from Caterina's life to issue a Papal Bull, which called her "daughter of iniquity." He divested her hereditary holdings and delivered her central towns of Imola and Forlì to his illegitimate son, Cesare Borgia.

Caterina, realizing that Imola could not be defended against Borgia's army and wishing to remain in her domains to thwart the pope and Borgia, ordered her army into the fortress of Ravaldino and announced that she was about to give Cesare Borgia a demonstration of a woman's artillery skills. The citizens of the town fought Borgia's forces for days but surrendered against her wishes. She with her stalwart supporters repaired into the citadel to continue the fight. When Borgia's soldiers raped and pillaged despite the surrender, Caterina dispassionately commented that it was "a just punishment for a city which had surrendered like a whore."[67]

Caterina withstood for about a month before being captured by a French officer in the final assault on her position in January 1500. Cesare Borgia personally held her for a forty-eight-hour period during which time he repeatedly raped her, commenting later to his supporters that she defended her castles with more tenacity than she defended her honor.

The abuses of Borgia did not persuade Caterina to relinquish her rights to Imola and Forlì. She was imprisoned for several years while those who had stolen her possessions consolidated their hold. By the time she was released in 1501, Imola and Forlì had slipped from her grip forever.

In the final years of her life, she trained her son in the military and administrative arts required of a prince of the Sforza line. Admired by all of Italy, she became the close friend of Michelangelo and probably the only person he trusted toward the end of his life.[68]

She passed away in 1509, the same year another Italian noblewoman, Isabella of Este, commanded the defense of Mantua in the absence of her imprisoned husband. Isabella, daughter of the king of Naples, was educated in the manner of a prince of the house of Este rather than a princess. She combined both artistic and martial sensibilities, and her court drew such Renaissance luminaries as Raphael, Titian, the writer Castiglione, and Leonardo da Vinci, who painted her.

She not only defended Mantua when her husband was alive but held it for a decade after his death. She directed a vast spy network, one of her most effective military tools, from there. Emperor Maximilian declared that her actions were worthy of an "intelligent Prince of antiquity." He said she was the "most interesting" of all Italian women and he was "half in love with her."[69]

Some other Italian women warriors of note include Eleonora d'Arborea, who in the late fourteenth century occupied Sardinia and led a two-year war against the king of Aragon; Luzia Stanga, a woman cavalry fighter who "with sword in hand equals many brave men"[70]; the thirty women of the town of Mugello, who in 1352 kept knights at bay until reinforcements arrived; and the three women's battalions of Siena, who took to the walls to defend the city in 1554. Italian female soldiers fought at the siege of Pavia led by King Francis I of France and the siege of Padua laid by the troops of Maniago.

In 1517 Catherine Sigurana repulsed Barbarossa in his attack against the citadel of Nice, France. Two years later, Marie d'Estrada, wife of Hernando Cortes, joined the famed conquistador in his conquest of Mexico, "accomplishing extraordinary exploits of valor to the astonishment of all who beheld her."[71] A year after that, in 1520, Kristinia Gyllenstierna, newly widowed queen of Sweden, commanded the defense of Stockholm against the Danes.

Margaret of Valois, daughter of Henry II and wife of Henry IV of France, warred on her brother in the latter sixteenth century. She was captured and imprisoned in the stronghold of Usson. In a short time, however, she had engineered a takeover of the castle and became its mistress, a position she held for twenty years. She became the queen of France in 1594.

Sixteenth-century Spain produced Doña Maria de Padilla, wife of Don Juan de Padilla, the head of a confederacy centered in Castile during the youth of Charles V. Doña Maria's husband was captured by the enemy forces in 1521 and executed, thus throwing the Castilian alliance into turmoil.

Doña Maria persuaded the city of Toledo to remain loyal to her cause as she prepared to fight for the rights of Charles V and, in memory of her husband, the Castilian confederacy. She encouraged the French to attack Navarre, raised a loyal army, and tried unsuccessfully to persuade the nobles to join her.

The attack on Toledo came, and Doña Maria directed the resistance with such skill that the attackers could find no breach to enter. Although the enemies from without could not shake her grip on the city, the clergy within, angered at her trimming of their estates and powers, convinced the citizens that her charisma and martial mien resulted from witchcraft.

Doña Maria marched her loyal troops into the citadel as the townsmen surrendered the city. She held the citadel for four months but, understanding the impossibility of a sure victory, left the fortress in disguise and escaped to Portugal.[72]

A few years later in 1524, the constable of Bourbon laid siege to the French king's city of Marseilles. In time the constable's mortars broke breaches in the walls, and the Bourbon soldiers poured forward to penetrate the gaps. However, as the defenders were about to be overwhelmed, Ameliane de Puget, daughter of the governor of the city, appeared with a regiment of women soldiers to aid in driving the Bourbon troops from the city.

The constable of Bourbon next tried mining under the walls of Marseilles, but Ameliane and her regiment countermined and thwarted the

Bourbon plan. They left an immense gash in the earth, which was known for many years as the Tranche des Dames. Today, in honor of de Puget and the women of Marseilles, a road named Boulevard des Dames parallels the old site of the trench.

Two sisters, Gabriella and Claire de Laval, also fought in the defense of Marseilles. Each led an all-female contingent in the battle.

Louise Labé, a merchant's daughter born in Lyons in 1525, fought in male disguise. Her father reared her in the fashion of an aristocrat, stressing Latin, Greek, Spanish, and Italian, as well as music and martial arts in her education.

She became entranced by martial arts and warfare and at the age of sixteen disguised herself as a young man—giving herself the rank of captain—and fought with valor at the battle of Perpignan in the cause of the dauphin. Differing from many of the women warriors so far surveyed, Louise was satisfied with one taste of real battle. She married a rich rope seller and dedicated her life to literary arts. Her writings influenced such intellectual luminaries of the time as Erasmus and de La Fontaine. And, like the women led by Ameliane de Puget in the defense of Marseilles, she was honored by a street in Lyons named in her memory: Rue de La Belle Cordière.[73]

* * *

In 1543 Eleonore, daughter of the Pertor of Toledo, viceroy of Naples, married Cosmos I and found herself enmeshed in the ancient and bloody feud her husband's family waged with their hereditary enemies, the Strozzi. Eleonore, trained in riding and swordsmanship, battled the Strozzi with her husband and sharpened her fighting techniques. Her courage and skill with a sword resulted in the final victory of her husband's family.

One day, Eleonore was riding with fifteen of her husband's soldiers outside the family castle when she encountered the leader of the Strozzi family, Philip, who was scouting the castle's defenses with a force of forty-five horsemen. Eleonore, recovering from the surprise of the chance encounter faster than Philip Strozzi, drew her sword and ordered her troops to charge the shocked enemy. Eleonore personally took Philip Strozzi prisoner and proudly delivered him to her husband. She also fought alongside her husband in the wars between Charles V and Francis I, and her name appears among those conspicuous in the battle for Siena.[74]

In the midsixteenth century, Mary of Hungary, governess of the Netherlands, waged a destructive military duel with Henry II of France. From her girlhood she had relished hunting and martial arts; when her brother Charles requested her assistance in resisting the growing power of Henry II, she readily responded.

She often entered battle with Charles V, serving both as a military adviser with his generals and as a frontline fighter. Her most dramatic action came during the battle of Metz when Charles was laying siege. To prevent King Henry's arrival, Charles asked his sister to create a diversion. She dressed in mail and rampaged with her troops through Picardy, torching eight hundred villages and the royal palace of Folembrai.

Mary's raid so angered King Henry that he in turn burned some towns in the Netherlands, as well as the royal palace at Bains. Mary took great umbrage at King Henry's retaliation and "swore that all France should repent the outrage."[75] She destroyed many more French towns, and King Henry became obsessed with taking her prisoner.

Safe in her kingdom, Lady Mary gained renown for the elaborate pageants, feasts, and tournaments she sponsored. In her later life, she increasingly enjoyed scholarship and left her government in the Netherlands for her home in Spain, where she passed away in 1558.

Several years before Mary's death, the city of Vienna was attacked. Princess Belgioso of Bologna, as part of a larger army, led two hundred men, whom she had hired, against the Austrian invaders. Female captains Forteguerra, Piccolonimini, and Fausti, each of whom captained a thousand-woman regiment, successfully defended the city.

In 1535 the small town of Saint Riquier, with only a hundred soldiers manning its walls, prepared to battle two thousand Flemish soldiers under the command of a Belgian count. Marie Fourée de Poix marshaled a large force of women to fight with the relatively small number of men. The women thwarted the count's attempts, and he withdrew without his battle flag, which had been taken by Marie Fourée de Poix.

In a related exchange of letters between the count and his employer the archduchess concerning the episode at Saint Riquier, the lady wrote:

> I am astonished to see that you are so long in taking the place. It is, I understand, nothing more than a dove coup.

The count replied:

> It is true that the place is nothing more than a dove coup; but the doves within it are exceedingly difficult to take. The female doves are every bit as courageous and formidable as the males.[76]

Marguerite Delaye defended Montelimar in 1569 when the town was attacked by Admiral Coligny. In her gallant fight, Marguerite lost her arm, and the grateful townspeople later erected a one-armed statue in her honor. In the same conflict Marie de Brabançon, with fifty knights under her command, protected her castle at Benegon against almost two thousand soldiers of General Montare. She was finally forced to surrender and was held for ransom. King Charles IX honored her skill and courage by ordering General Montare to "escort the great-hearted lady, with full honor, back to her castle and give her liberty."[77] In nearby Flanders in the same period, the duke of Alva counted among his forces twelve hundred women warriors—eight hundred infantry and four hundred cavalry.

In 1581 the Netherlands again came under attack, this time by Spain. Again a woman warrior, Marie-Christine du Laing, princess of Espinoy, in full armor with a battle-ax tucked in her belt, mounted a charger and prepared her people for the Spanish assault on Tournai.

When the first wave came, Marie-Christine stood on the ramparts with her soldiers repulsing the Spaniards. Though wounded at that time, she maintained command for two months through twenty-three battles and a dozen sorties against the Spanish outside the walls of Tournai. When she at last surrendered the city, she left triumphantly, riding her war-horse at full gallop with her mounted and foot garrison behind her, banners flying. The Spanish soldiers cheered in a spontaneous show of admiration for her courage and style.[78]

The Spanish conquered the Dutch city of Ghent in this war but were soon confronted by a combined Dutch and English force set on recapturing it. Riding against the Spanish was cavalry officer Captain Mary Ambree.

At the Dutch city of Harlaam, three thousand fighting men and a unit of women warriors prepared to receive the fury of the Spanish army. The women, led by Kenau Hasselaar, a forty-seven-year-old widow, formed the elite corps at Harlaam. When the Spanish army was approaching, she proposed to the military governor that she raise a women's fighting unit and arm it at her own expense. Permission was quickly granted, and three hundred women instantly volunteered. Each woman, an expert with sword, dagger, and musket, wore light armor over her dress, disdaining to costume as a man.

Kenau Hasselaar's troops fought in all major actions, both within and without the walls of Harlaam. She also led them in countermining operations and in heavy construction to bolster damaged defenses. The grateful citizens of Harlaam granted Kenau a pension in the form of a permanent public position as tax collector. At this point, Kenau Hasselaar disappeared from the pages of history.[79]

In France during the sixteenth century, warfare between Catholics and Protestants flared sporadically. Protestant supporter Madeleine de Saint-Nectaire led her sixty knights in raids against Catholic armies that strayed too near her chateau. After a year of harassment, the Catholic governor of the area sent an overwhelming force of fifteen thousand infantry (a huge army for the times) and fifty heavy cavalry to crush her.

In a surprising move, Madeleine, rather than prepare for a siege, moved her small army out of the castle and attacked the Catholic forces. The stunned army withdrew into Lady de Saint-Nectaire's castle and locked the gate. Madeleine led her troops to nearby Turenne, where she strengthened her numbers, returned, and drove the occupying Catholic forces out of Miremont.

Madeleine de Saint-Nectaire's skill at small and effective military strikes prompted her enemy, King Henry IV, to say; "If I were not king, I would like to be Mlle. de Saint-Nectaire!"[80]

*　　*　　*

In the year that Spanish forces contended in the Netherlands with the likes of Princess Marie-Christine du Laing and Captain Mary Ambree, Catalina de Erauso, "the Nun-Lieutenant," was born in Sebastian, Spain. Her extraordinary martial career spanned both Old and New Worlds. At the age of four she was sent to a Dominican convent under the supervision of an aunt, where she stayed until, at fifteen and bored with convent life, she cut her hair short, dressed in male clothing, and set out to find adventure. She left a letter in which she asked her parents, "Why have you made me manly and strong like my brothers only to compel me now that I am fifteen to do nothing but mumble a lot of interminable prayers?"[81]

She found work as a page in one town, a clerk in another, and all the while strengthened herself and practiced sword fighting. When she felt ready, she joined one of the many expeditions to the New World.

Her natural warrior skills blossomed in South America with acts of bravery that soon ensured her promotion to lieutenant. Although she fought and traveled under many aliases, she was best known as Lieutenant Alonzo Dias. Her volatile temperament and her love for brawling, however, prevented further promotions. She apparently made little distinction between warfare and banditry and became implicated in a variety of violent crimes.

In one such encounter, she quarreled with a Chilean nobleman in a gambling house and fatally wounded him in a duel. She fled into the Andes and joined a band of three outlaw fugitives set on crossing the forbidding mountains to safety. The three men died in the snow, but Catalina made it to Tucumán. There she was again arrested on a murder charge, but her military record convinced the judge to release her.

Catalina, then thirty-five, moved to Peru, where she was again implicated in a murder. While in sanctuary at a church in Guamango and exhausted by her violent life, she confessed to the local bishop that she was a woman and wanted to go home.

She arrived at Cádiz in 1624 to a hero's welcome. Wherever she traveled in Spain and Italy, people flocked to hear of her adventures in South America. Pope Urban VIII granted her a private audience, and the famous Spanish artist Pacheco painted her in Seville.

Catalina soon became bored in Spain and returned to the New World, bought a team of mules, and became a well-known muleteer on the road between the port of Vera Cruz and Mexico City.[82] She passed her remaining years under the name Antonio de Erauso.

During Catalina de Erauso's first year in the Dominican convent, her countrymen were making war in France. Their assaults on the French fortress town of Leucate brought forth the heroic actions of Constance Cezelli, wife of the governor of the province where Leucate was located.

While leading a sortie against the encircling Spanish, Constance's husband, Barri de St. Annez, was captured, and she assumed command of the defenders. The Spanish general threatened the death of her husband if she did not surrender Leucate; however, her husband's last words to her had been that under no circumstance should she surrender the fort. She offered the general her jewels if he would return her husband, but he refused and left Constance her melancholy duty: abandon her husband and defend the fortress as ordered.

The Spanish attempted two assaults against Leucate, but Lady Cezelli's forces repelled them. In frustration, they murdered her husband and prepared another attack. Constance, though grief stricken, fulfilled her role as commander and repulsed the final Spanish assault before they lifted the siege. When King Henry IV heard of Lady Cezelli's feat of patriotic bravery, he awarded her the title "Governor of Leucate," a position she held and defended for twenty-seven years until her death.[83]

King Henry was compelled to deal with another woman warrior on less friendly terms. His wife, Margaret of Valois, queen of Navarre, grew estranged from Henry through time, raised her own army, and seized Agen, one of her husband's towns, in 1586.

The seventeenth century opened with the exploits of many female soldiers. Madame de Retz raised an army and led it against her own son. Madame de Longueville, sister of Louis II of Bourbon, prince of Conde, accompanied him fully armed into several battles, as did the duchess of Montpensier.

Barbara, lady of Saint-Balmont, a French swordswoman of great renown, was reported to have killed several hundred men in battle. She had studied swordplay and a variety of other martial arts from childhood. Fighting during the Thirty Years War, she commanded both offensive and defensive actions around Saint-Balmont and Verdun, while her husband, the lord of Balmont, rode with the duke of Lothrengein in campaigns in Germany. After the war, Barbara turned her attention to writing and never buckled on her sword again. Her first literary work, *Les Jumeaux Martyrs*, was published in 1651. She died nine years later at the age of fifty-one.[84]

In 1692, when the duke of Savoy moved against the dauphine, Mademoiselle de la Charce, at her own expense, armed the villagers of her domain. She placed herself at their head and harassed the duke's men in an endless series of rapid raids, striking out from her mountain stronghold. Louis XIV was so impressed with Mademoiselle de la Charce that he permitted her to display her armor and sword at the Royal Treasury of St. Denis, a rare honor for warriors of the time.

One of the more flamboyant woman warriors of the 1600s was Christina, queen of Sweden. Her youth was ordered for her, as was typical of royalty's lot. Because she would one day be a queen, she was educated in reading, writing, history, Greek, Latin, and the principal modern languages. She also was required to master horsemanship, sword fighting, and rifle and pistol shooting.

At sixteen, she presided over the Swedish Senate and at eighteen seized the reins of power and ruled as a personal sovereign. She would tolerate no prime minister interpreting the world for her; rather, she read the dispatches and dictated her responses. She insisted that her generals in the field keep her apprised of all actions, none of which could occur without her sanction.

In her early twenties, she abdicated the throne, cut her hair short, wore men's clothing, and always carried a sword slung from a wide leather belt. Accounts of her entrances into both Rome and Paris after her abdication describe Christina armed with sword and pistols mounted on a white charger at the head of an entourage of several hundred.[85]

Madame de Motteville, a contemporary of Christina's, writes:

> Her boots are like a man's and so are her voice and almost all her features. She affected to be a man in all her actions. She laughed immoderately when anything pleased her. She put her legs up on seats, and once she was spied by King Louis' mother with two hideously ugly women who wallowed in her bed.[86]

Queen Christina served as commander in chief in several campaigns of her Italian hosts against their archrivals in Naples. Her mother, Maria Eleanorea, wife of King Gustavus Adolphus, perhaps served as an early warrior model for her sword-carrying daughter. Queen Maria traveled with King Adolphus on his campaigns in northern Europe and in his wars with the Catholic nations to the south.

In 1652 Anne-Marie-Louise d'Orleans, duchess of Montpensier, commanded the defense of Paris when she found the duke hiding under his bed as the Austrian Royalist troops massed before the city. The duchess ran to the Bastille and commanded the battery to open fire on the Austrians. When Anne of Austria regained control, she sent the duchess of Montpensier, not the duke, into exile.

Historians note that officers fought duels over the prestige of being in the duchess of Montpensier's regiment. In the latter part of her life, however, a profound paranoia destroyed her once-proud and decisive personality. She wore a mask, ostensibly to cover the marring caused by smallpox, called herself Madame Dupré, and feared that anyone who came near her was an assassin.

Even so, Lord Conde wrote to her, "I place my fortresses and my army at your disposition, and de Lorraine and de Fuensaldagne do the same." She turned them down and repaired to the quiet of her estate at Saint-Farbeau.[87]

In 1670 "La Maupin," the legendary French opera singer and sword fighter, was born in Paris, the daughter of Gaston d'Aubigny, secretary to the count of Armagnac, one of the seven grand officers of the crown. Mademoiselle d'Aubigny's father directed her education. Studies in grammar, dancing, drawing, and writing were balanced with her training as a sword fighter under the watchful eye of her father, a devotee of the martial arts schools, or *salle d'armes*, of Paris. Aware of the thousands of professional duelists who haunted the streets of Paris, Monsieur d'Aubigny wished to train his daughter to defend herself. By the age of sixteen, she was seen as a prodigy of the sword and could defeat her father as well as the best swordsmen of the *salles d'armes*.

At the age of eighteen, she fled Paris with her lover Seranne, who killed a man in a duel. Her fencing demonstrations along their route to Marseilles paid their room and board.

Her boundless energy and artistry enhanced an excellent singing voice. She debuted at the Paris Opera in 1690 and over a period of fifteen years sang twenty-nine different parts.

She died at a convent in 1707 at the age of thirty-seven. Rogers writes:

> She was the first contralto to appear before a Parisian audience and in her time the most applauded performer in France. She was, if not the first swordsman of her day, very nearly the most effective and renowned and in her alternative part of a woman of many loves, not all of them, light, she was a famous and widely desired beauty.[88]

*   *   *

After the death of King Louis XVI of France, eighteen-year-old Mademoiselle de La Rochefoucauld led her army "for our God and our king." A staunch Royalist, the young woman always appeared at the forefront of battle leading cavalry charges, and at Chollet she was seen to rally her troops three times against the Republicans.[89]

The violence of the French Revolution in the eighteenth century spawned women warriors at every turn. Julienne David, for example, captained a ship as a privateer during the revolution.

The attitude toward female fighters at the time was reflected in *Mère Duchens*, published in 1791. The heroine says:

> I offer my services to the nation as a warrior. I am naturally inclined to fist fight, and I am used to boxing with my dear husband. At the first drumbeat I take up arms, I raise a squadron of Amazons, I put myself at their head, I thrust into the enemy battalions as if they were butter.[90]

In the same year that *Mère Duchens* was published, Pauline Leon petitioned the National Assembly that an all-women's battalion be formed. Dozens of women donned male attire and joined the revolutionary army, and even after the Revolutionary Convention issued a decree against female soldiers in April 1793, many women continued in disguise.

Madame de Larochejaquelein writes:

> I saw two sisters, fourteen and fifteen years old, who were very courageous. In the army of Dr Bonchamp, a young woman became a dragoon to avenge the death of her father, and performed prodigious feats of valor during the whole war, under the name *L'Angevine*. I one day saw a young woman, tall and beautiful, with pistols and a saber hung at her girdle, come to Chollet, accompanied by two other women armed with pikes. She told me that she was from the parish of Tout-Le-Monde, and that the women kept guard there when the men were absent in the army.[91]

A major figure during that violent time was Anne Joseph Theroigne de Maricourt. As a young girl, she had been cruelly seduced by a nobleman, yet ironically her entire life became involved with the nobility. She was the mistress of the prince of Wales and received letters of introduction to Paris society from the duke of Orleans. In the French Revolution, however, she led thousands of anti-Royalists in bloody attacks against the aristocratic society of France. Dressed in soldier's attire and wielding a sword, she exhorted mobs that pillaged the Hotel des Invalids, burned the Bastille, and slaughtered nobles at the Abbey, La Force, and Bicêtre. She recognized the noble who had seduced her in line at the Abbey awaiting execution. Drawing her sword, she ran him through on the spot.[92]

Anne had such control over the mobs that she could silence them with a wave of her hand. Months after the fall of the Bastille, she rallied thousands of women in a march on Versailles to protest food prices. When the horde approached, the panicked guards prepared to attack, but Theroigne persuaded the leader to hold fire by demonstrating her control over the mob. She later led three hundred fish vendors into the National Assembly in a boisterous protest against government pricing policy.

Also at this time, Mademoiselle de La Rochefoucauld earned a reputation as a warrior in her fights against the Republicans after the murder of Louis XVI. She was well-known for her fiery speeches to her troops before battle. "Follow me! Before the end of the day we either sing our victory on earth, or hymns with the saints in heaven!" The day before she died in battle she wrote to a friend in Paris: "God knows that I do not fear death. But I hear the trumpet sounding alarm, and I must bid my tender friend a long, I fear too long, adieu."[93]

On July 9, 1793, Charlotte Corday, a young woman living in Caen, France, told her aunt that she was making a journey to England. Instead, she secured a room in Paris within walking distance of the home of Marat, the most bloodthirsty leader of the Reign of Terror. When he announced that two hundred thousand more heads would roll before the revolution was complete, Charlotte decided that she must act. She wrote a letter offering him intelligence on his enemies in Caen, information that she must relate in person. Once in Marat's presence, as he reclined in his tub, some accounts relate, she stabbed him to death. Charlotte Corday was tried on the morning of July 17 and executed by guillotine the evening of the same day.

In the mideighteenth century, Maria Theresa, the Hapsburg queen of Hungary and Bohemia, fought many battles, and though defeated by the Prussians in the Silesian War, she won her share of engagements. History remembers Maria Theresa Valperga Amelia Christina; queen of Hungary and Bohemia; archduchess of Austria; sovereign of the Netherlands; duchess of Milan, Parma, and Placentia; and grand duchess of Tuscany as one of the greatest queens of her time.

In Germany in the latter eighteenth century, Anna Sophia Detzliffin disguised herself as a male and fought in Prince Frederick's regiment during the Seven Years War. She was wounded numerous times in sword duels on the front lines, and although captured by the Austrian army, she escaped and rejoined her regiment. She fought at the Battle of Kundersdorf, 1759, which the Prussian army won at the cost of twenty thousand lives, and she fought with the Battalion of Grenadiers at Strehlen and Torgau. In 1761 she fought with Le Noble's Volunteer Regiment under Colonel Colignon.

Active in the Napoleonic Era, cavalrywoman Theresa Figuer of Lyon had four horses shot from under her because of her impetuous charges into the enemy lines. Under General Dugommier, she fought at Toulon, Ulm, and Austerlitz.[94]

In the late eighteenth century, Madame de Beauglie in full armor led thirty knights in a defense of the coast near La Vendée, and in 1794 Madame Liberté Barrau fought at her husband's side in battles with Spanish forces.

From 1792 to 1799, Angelique Brulon fought in male disguise in the defense of Corsica. Her sex was finally discovered, but she had shown such courage and martial skill that her fellow soldiers requested that she continue to accompany them in battle. She fought in seven major campaigns, was cited for exceptional bravery at Calvi, and in the attack on Fort Gesco was noted for her skill in hand-to-hand combat. In one encounter, after her right arm had been injured by a saber wound, she fought with a dagger in her left hand, ultimately killing her adversary. Soldiers that she commanded voluntarily wrote the following testimony: "We, the garrison of Calvi, certify that Marie-Angelique Josephine Duchemin *veuve* Brulon, acting sergeant, commanding the attack of Fort Gesco, fought with us with the courage of a heroine."[95] She retired at the age of fifty-one with the rank of lieutenant, and Napoleon III presented her a French Legion of Honor ribbon in a special ceremony.

Other women of the early-modern era who won the French Legion of Honor included Marie Schellinck, who fought in twelve major battles and received wounds at Jemmappes, Austerlitz, and Jena. She was cited in the Order of the Day for gallantry in action at the battle of Arcola. In 1811 when Napoleon visited Ghent, Marie Schellinck's hometown, she was presented to the Empress Marie-Louise, who gave her a silk dress, a brooch, and a pair of earrings as a token of her respect for the young woman's military service.

French Legion of Honor recipient Virginie Ghesquiere entered the army disguised as her brother and was quickly involved in fighting. At Wagram she was promoted to the rank of sergeant for saving an officer's life, and in Portugal she was noted in the Order of the Day for distinguished service fighting under the command of General Junot.[96]

The Fernig sisters, Felicite, twenty-two, and Theophile, seventeen, were daughters of the local militia leader in the French Flanders village of Mortagne. Felicite was a champion archer, and both girls were crack shots. Intimately knowledgeable of the countryside, having tramped it for years with their father, they could set up ambushes and lead snipers to advantageous shooting positions. For a period, the girls fought in the local militia without their father's knowledge by joining night raids with blackened faces and dressed in men's clothing.

When their identity was discovered, their father presented them to General Dunouriez, and their story was told. The general was so impressed that he gave the girls uniforms and horses. They fought with General Beurnonville, who reported to a government review body that "the Fernig girls were very capable of killing their men." Another review board that was inspecting army units noted that they were "respected and honored in the midst of an army of young men."

Later, Felicite became known to King Louis Philippe when she rode beside him, then the duke of Chartres, in a cavalry charge at Jemmappes. In the same battle, she saved the life of a young Belgian officer named François van der Wallen who lay helpless before the drawn swords of two enemy soldiers. Felicite killed the two swordsmen and brought the officer to safety.

Felicite's sister Theophile was not idle during the fight. She captured a Hungarian major. The Fernig sisters have a joint monument that stands today at the site of the Battle of Jemmappes.[97]

At the aforementioned Battle of Jena, the queen of Prussia, prior to the attack, rode along the front lines where she could be plainly seen by the French. She wore a silver and gold tunic of brocade reaching to her feet and red boots with golden spurs. Over her tunic she wore light body armor and on her head a helmet of polished steel with a large plume. She was attended by four personal guards.

When the battle turned into a rout of the queen's forces, her escort was scattered by a group of French Hussars. The endless riding lessons required of the nobility paid off for the queen as she outran the Hussars and safely entered the gates of Weimar with the Hussars and a detachment of French dragoons hot behind her.

In 1807, French woman warrior Ducaud Laborde, better known as "Breton Double," was honored by one of the more memorable presentations of the French Legion of Honor medal. Napoleon removed his own Legion of Honor and presented it to her.

She fought in uniform as a hussar in the French army under Napoleon, though she did not try to impersonate a man. On February 8, 1807, at the Battle of Eylau, Breton Double killed a Russian captain in a sword duel and rescued a detachment of leaderless French troops. On June 14 of the same year, at the Battle of Friedland, she was shot in the right arm and slashed across the right thigh by a Russian saber but, in spite of her wounds, she succeeded in taking six prisoners. Breton Double was fighting at Waterloo where she saw her husband killed. Her leg was shattered by a cannon ball, and she was captured by the British, who she later acknowledged treated her with great respect.[98]

The historian Bulwer wrote of this time:

> French armies have never been engaged in the neighborhood of
> Paris without there being found many of these females, who one

sees in the salons of Paris, slain on the field of battle, to which they have been led, not so much by passion for her lover as by a desire for adventure, which they are willing to gratify, even in the camp.[99]

Sir Walter Scott, commenting on a trip to Paris, wrote:

One morning when passing through the Palais Royale at Paris I saw a woman dressed in military costume with boots, spurs and saber. No Frenchmen seemed to consider the sight a strange one.[100]

Between 1792 and 1795 Louise Houssaye de Baumes served in the French infantry and fought with distinction at Quiberon, while Louisa Scangatti served as an infantry lieutenant in the Prussian army.

In March of 1798, fighting against the French at the Battle for Frauenbrun, sixty-four-year-old Martha Glar led 280 women into battle with disastrous results. She, her daughters, and granddaughters and 160 other women perished, as did all the men of her family.

This eyewitness account of French woman warrior Louise Belletz was recounted to Madame de Staël by Marshall Massena, an officer in Napoleon's army:

I perceived a young soldier belonging to the light artillery, whose horse had just been wounded by a lance. The young man, who appeared quite a child, defended himself desperately, as several dead bodies of the enemy lying around him could testify. I immediately dispatched an officer with some men to his assistance but they arrived too late. This artilleryman had alone withstood the attack of a small troop of Cossacks and Bavarians. His body was covered with wounds, inflicted with shot, lances and swords. There were at least thirty. And do you know who this man was? A woman! She had followed her lover to the army. The latter was a Captain of artillery; she never left him, and when he was killed, defended like a lioness the remains of his body.[101]

*   *   *

A woman warrior of the early nineteenth century so captured the imagination of the poet Lord Byron that he wrote:

Her lover sinks—she sheds no ill-timed tear;
Her chief is slain—she fills in his fatal post;
Her fellows flee—she checks their base career;
The foe retires—she heads the sallying host.[102]

He was writing about Augustina, "the Maid of Saragossa," who in 1808 inspired the defenders of the Spanish town of Saragossa with a garrison of only 220 soldiers. She fought against the twelve-thousand-man French army of General La Fèvre in "one of the most heroic defenses of history."[103]

The city was not built to resist strong attack; historians of the battle agree that the ancient walls were crumbling. The French army's lackadaisical approach to the siege reflected the contempt they held for the defenses and populace: "monks and cowards."[104]

After a supposedly easy victory for the French evaporated in a bloody two-month struggle against the townsmen led by Captain Palafox, General La Fèvre turned to other means. He bribed one of the citizens to fire the beleaguered town's powder magazine, and on June 2, 1808, the roof-rattling explosion and the simultaneous charge of the French army stunned the weary citizens of Saragossa.

In that desperate moment, a young woman walked out of the church of Nostra Donna del Pillas, "habited in white raiment, a cross suspended from her neck, her dark hair dishevelled and her eyes sparkling with supernatural lustre"[105] and mounted the walls. She grabbed a flaming taper from a wounded cannoneer, raised it, and shouted to the exhausted defenders, "For so long as the French are near, Saragossa has one defender! Victory or death!" She touched the fuse, and the 620-pound cannon roared into the face of the attackers. When the Saragossan soldiers and citizens saw her struggling to reload the cannon, they erupted in cheers and rallied against the French soldiers who were pouring against their walls.

General La Fèvre was forced to retreat and prepare for a long siege. Frustrated and embarrassed by his unexpected difficulty, he moved his artillery into the surrounding hills and ordered a round-the-clock bombardment of the old city. In time the daily pounding took its toll, and the advancing French troops moved into the streets at the edge of Saragossa and fought house to house, gaining control of half the town.

The French commander, wishing to end the carnage and confident that his victory was inevitable, demanded the surrender of Saragossa. Captain Palafox read the message to the gathered survivors. He asked Augustina, who stood nearby smeared with blood and grime, for her response. She drew her sword and shouted, *"Guerra al cuchillo!"* ("War to the knife!"). The battered citizens cheered, and Palafox sent her words to General La Fèvre.

The French came again, and Augustina and Palafox led the defense, fighting within the crumbled walls of Saragossa. On August 17, three months after the appearance of Augustina in the defenders' ranks, the mortified and depleted French withdrew from the wall-less town. The next time they sought Saragossa, they arrived with thirty-five thousand soldiers. No city before or after has withstood an enemy for so long with its walls utterly destroyed.

Acting Governor Palafox offered Augustina anything she wished in gratitude for her heroism in saving the town and its tens of thousands of citizens. She asked to retain the rank of cannoneer and to be allowed to wear the coat of arms of Saragossa. She, of course, received both honors.

W. Jacob, who traveled in Spain in 1809 and 1810, met Augustina in Seville, attired in a blue artillery tunic. When Lord Wellesley entered Seville and was greeted by the Junta, Augustina was present as an honored guest. The famed English poet Lord Byron visited Seville and sought her out, and English traveler Sir John Carr writes of meeting her in his *Tour through Spain*:

> Upon the sleeve of one of her arms she wore three embroidered badges of distinction, commemorative of three distinguished acts of intrepidity. The day before I was introduced to this extraordinary female, she had been entertained at a dinner party by Admiral Purvis on board his flagship.[106]

Augustina's fame overshadows another woman warrior who fought in the Battle of Saragossa, Countess Burita. Whereas Augustina used her inspired energy to fire the warrior spirit of the citizens and garrison troops, the countess organized the women to fight the French side by side with the men.[107]

*   *   *

In 1805 a Frenchwoman, Jeanette Colin, not wishing to leave her husband, disguised herself as a man and sailed with the French fleet out of Cadiz. She fought on deck with pistol and sword against the British at the Battle of Trafalgar. In 1812 Elizabeth Hatzler fought beside her husband as a French dragoon (musket-carrying infantry trooper) in the front battle lines against the Cossacks. She saved her wounded husband's life by carrying him for miles during a French retreat. Four years later, Augusta Kruger, a lieutenant in the Ninth Prussian Regiment, battled against the French on numerous occasions and was awarded the Russian Order of St. George and the Iron Cross. During the Napoleonic Wars, Louisa Scangatti served as a lieutenant of infantry in the Austrian and Sardinian armies.

Josephine Trinquart, in the early nineteenth century, demonstrated outstanding heroics in a rescue attempt. Leading two other soldiers to a wounded officer, Josephine found herself alone when her companions were killed in an ambush, yet she pressed on to the injured man.

As she tried to move him to safety, she was attacked by two horsemen. In short measure, she had shot one of the riders and bayoneted the other. Now, with two horses, she helped the officer to mount one, and she, riding the other, led the wounded man to safety.[108]

In 1827, the marchioness of Chaves, holding the commission of captain in the Seventh Cazadores, led her troops of Portuguese insurgents in the defeat of two government regiments. She was given the captured colors of the defeated armies and promptly had them made into a gown, which she wore on festive occasions.[109]

The Italian patriot Garibaldi struggled for the cause of independence in the midnineteenth century. His Brazilian-born wife Anita, an expert horsewoman, rode with him into many battles and served as a captain in his cavalry. The king of Italy dedicated a monument to her in Rome in 1932. History also records that Marietta Guiliami and Herminia Manelli fought for Garibaldi in 1866 at the Battle of Spicheren.[110]

In the mid-1800s, Italian Louisa Battistati took a principal role in the five-day revolution in Milan. On the first day of the fighting, she confronted an enemy soldier carrying a carbine and disarmed and killed him. She then organized a band of young men and successfully defended the Poppietti bridge for three days. When the enemy stormed Milan, she directed the defense of a building in which 580 widows and orphans sought safety. Later she assisted in the defense of the nearby town of Bettabia.[111]

In the late nineteenth century Virginie Chesnières held the rank of sergeant in the French Seventeenth Infantry Regiment. She gained fame by managing a rearguard defense for Napoleon as he retreated over the Pyrenees before the advancing British forces. In the same era, Sylvia Mariotti fought with the Eleventh Battalion of Italian Bersaglier in numerous battles between 1866 and 1879.

Jeanne Bonnemere, fighting in the early and mid-1800s, received her first battle honor after taking a bayonet wound while rushing to the rescue of a French officer she had seen fall. By the time of her retirement in 1867, she was privileged to wear the Turkish Cross of the Medjidie, as well as Crimean and Italian battle medals.

In late middle age, she left retirement when called to fight at Metz. When Metz fell, she reported to Orleans, where, even in her advanced years, she served as a courier between Orleans and Paris. Though captured several times, she managed in each case to work her way out of the enemy's hands.[112]

Louise Clemence Michel distinguished herself as a war heroine of the first order by leading the uprising that prevented the Communards from capturing Paris. On April 5, 1871, Louise marched into battle at the head of a squad of women warriors. She later said of herself, "Barbarian that I am, I love cannon, the smell of powder, machine-gun bullets flying in the air, all the horrors of battle become poetry."[113]

In 1916, the French Academy awarded forty-seven of seventy prizes to women "as most distinguished examples of military courage."[114] For example, at the Battle of Loos in April of 1915, Emilienne Moreau killed two German snipers and fought in the front ranks to repel the invaders. For her various acts of valor she was awarded the French Croix de Guerre, the British Red Cross Medal, and the St. John Ambulance Society's Medal. Fighting again in 1940, she earned a second Croix de Guerre.

French women fighters found their way into the air wars. Belgium-born, Hélène Dutrieux, nicknamed "the Eagle," was the first woman to be acknowledged as a military fighter pilot by the French government. Her success moved the Union of Female French Flyers to ask the government for permission to form an all-female air regiment. They were refused.

The German war effort included Elsbeth Schragmuller, or "Fraulein Doktor," as she is known in the annals of espionage. She headed the French section of the supersecret military espionage section of the German Army's great general staff. In her job as "spymistress," she recruited and trained German secret agents, and between 1915 and 1916 her section dispatched ninety spies. She distinguished herself as the first woman in modern times to direct a top secret military anti-intelligence organization.

An early twentieth-century female fighter, Dolores Ibarruri, fought for the freedom of Spain, and, like Louise Clemence Michel, she left as part of her legacy words that captured her warrior nature. In the early phases of the Spanish Civil War in 1936, Dolores uttered on the Republican-controlled radio what would become the rallying cry of the revolution: "It is better to die on our feet than live on our knees." Dolores, known as *La Passionaria*, "the Passion Flower," headed an all-women's brigade and directed a number of battles against fascist troops. Many women fought the fascists in the Spanish Civil War, including women from other countries who joined the International Brigade.

Stanislawa Ordynska was one of over two hundred women fighting in the Polish army in the early twentieth century. In World War II, thousands of Polish women joined the Polish Home Army against the Nazi invaders. Two thousand women, along with fifteen thousand male resistance fighters, were captured by the Germans and sent to concentration camps. The women could have discarded their patriotic insignia and melted into the population, but, still wearing their insurgents' armbands, they surrendered with the men. As they were marched through the streets of Warsaw by the Nazis, the civilians fell to their knees. An observer said, "This was an unforgettable, almost shocking scene, because in Poland one kneels in reverence only to the Holy Sacrament."[115]

French women warriors proliferated in World War II. One chronicler notes that "tens of thousands" of women participated in the French resistance.[116] Marie-Madeleine Fourçade headed "the Alliance," an intelligence network that placed over three thousand agents in the major cities of France and that obtained valuable information on German defense in Normandy that was used in planning the invasion of Europe.

In the liberation of Paris, women led partisan units and battled the Nazis in the streets along with male fighters.[117] Elaine Mordeaux commanded many raids of the French resistance forces, and her final action typifies her martial character and career. Leading a large guerrilla unit, she attacked the 101st Panzers and in a one-hour battle, though losing two hundred of her own soldiers, killed three thousand Germans and destroyed over one hundred trucks and tanks.

She died courageously in this fight. According to the reports of survivors, she emptied her machine gun and then threw dynamite at the Germans. When it was gone, she bent to take a weapon and ammunition from one of the bodies stacked around her but was killed by a Nazi sniper.[118]

The Nazis employed almost five hundred thousand women in uniform as support troops, with the German Air Force, the Luftwaffe, claiming the lion's share. One hundred thousand German women served as Flakwaffenhelferinnen, antiaircraft auxiliaries.[119] Toward the end of the war, in a last-ditch effort to defend Germany, Hitler agreed to the Werewolf Plan, a scheme that called for the formation of guerrilla units composed of men and women, as well as the establishment of women's battalions in the Volkstrum, the "People's Army." Gertrud Scholtz-Klink organized several women's battalions toward the end of the war. This inclusion of women in the military demonstrated an about-face from the Germans' initial position on women fighters. Early in the war, the Germans were horrified to find tens of thousands of female soldiers marching with captured Russian infantry units. The Nazis called these women *Flintenweib*, a pejorative appellation meaning "musketwomen."[120]

The only woman and probably the only civilian in World War II to be awarded the German Iron Cross First Class was Frau Hanna Reitsch. She served as test pilot on early versions of jet airplanes before the concept was even known outside the German war machine. In one of her many memorable actions, she flew into Berlin while it was under siege by the Russian army, landed on a rubble-strewn street, delivered the general who had come to replace Goering, and flew out again.[121]

A newspaperman for the Petersburg *Dijen* reported from Warsaw on a number of women fighting in German army uniforms who were captured and brought to the hospital at Ouyasdoff. The military doctors who examined them said that their wound patterns indicated that they had fought in the trenches and had been involved in a number of bayonet fights.

The Danish resistance claimed many women warriors. Alma Allen led male and female guerrilla units against the Nazis in dozens of raids, while sister Dane, Ruth Weber, was a crack machine-gunner on a merchantman that penetrated Nazi blockades.[122] Edith "Lotte" Bonnesen, an employee of the Danish Ministry of Transportation, worked with the underground hiding agents and planning sabotage raids. She held the responsibility for coding and transmitting secret radio transmissions from the Danish underground to London.

Twenty-year-old Eva Jorgensen Klovstad of Norway joined a resistance organization led by her fiancé. After the Germans scattered the group, forcing Eva's lover to flee to Sweden, she, under the code name "Jakob," rebuilt the unit and fought against the Germans until the end of the war.

Beatrix Terwindt, a Dutch airline employee, joined British military intelligence in London. In 1943, she parachuted into Holland to coordinate the "escape lines," networks of secret agents who specialized in helping downed airman, escaped prisoners of war, resistance fighters, and soldiers trapped behind enemy lines flee Nazi-occupied areas.[123]

The most massive of these lines was established and managed by Andree "Dedee" de Jongh, a twenty-four-year-old Belgian nurse. The "Comet Line," as it came to be called, was credited with the escape of over one thousand people in three years of operation. Dedee personally escorted one hundred escapees to freedom on thirty-two danger-filled trips through the Pyrenees.

In August 1941, Dedee appeared at the British consulate in Bilbao, Spain, with two Belgian resistance fighters and a British soldier who had been stranded in Belgium after Dunkirk. She told the vice-consul that she would return with another group of escapees, and four weeks later she made good her promise.

To assist her courageous activities, British Intelligence dispatched Michael Creswell to be her liaison. Because Dedee referred to her charges as "packages," Creswell first code-named Dedee "the Postman." However, when she transported an entire British bomber crew through Nazi lines from Belgium to Spain in one week, he renamed her operation "Comet."

A Royal Air Force pilot, John Hoskins, offers this statement about his escape through the Pyrenees on the Comet Line with Dedee and her partner Florentio:

> Florentio kept going at a murderous pace and we began to fall further and further behind. In the end, Dedee and Florentio were

carrying all our packs. She was very annoyed that we simply could not keep up. She was only a slip of a girl, but she had enormous strength and courage.[124]

The Nazis finally penetrated her organization in 1943, capturing three British airmen and her at a farm house in the Pyrenees foothills. She admitted her position as leader of the Comet Line, but her interrogators refused to believe that a mere young woman could have managed such a complex organization. Andree "Dedee" de Jongh spent the rest of World War II in the concentration camp at Ravensbruk.

Nancy Wade, a New Zealander, was living with her French husband, Henri Fiocca, in Marseilles when the war broke out in 1939. After he was called up, she became an ambulance driver, later moving on to serve with the French resistance. Her partisan group is estimated to have saved over a thousand downed airmen and lost soldiers from capture by the Germans.

Nancy became a thorn in the side of the Germans, and in November 1942 the Gestapo records indicate their concern with an enemy agent they called "the White Mouse." After being captured in 1943 and escaping with resistance help, she was flown to England, where she underwent grueling training for the Special Operations Executive by Colonel Buckmaster, a famous spy master. As the only woman in Special Operations, she was ranked as a marksman with a Sten gun and was taught various methods of silent killing.

On March 1, 1944, Nancy with a male agent dropped into France near Montluçon. Operating under the name Madame Andrée, she worked her way into the leadership of a seven-thousand-man guerrilla force, the Maquis d'Auvergne. In her first major action, Nancy's guerrillas were attacked at their base on the plateau above Chaudes-Aigues by twenty-two thousand German soldiers supported by aircraft and artillery.

Nancy and her men slipped out of the trap after dark, leaving fifteen hundred German soldiers dead. By July, she was operating out of the Allier district with a force of two thousand maquis, attacking German convoys that were rushing troops and supplies to the Normandy front.

The Americans came to know Nancy through a rescue of two American officers. She led twenty of her guerrillas and two Americans who had come to help. After the first flurry of battle, Nancy and the two Americans were the only guerrillas left standing. Instead of retreating from the German tanks and armored cars, Nancy and the Americans attacked the convoy with bazooka rockets and neutralized it before they withdrew to safety.

In a later action, Nancy, with Commander Tardivat, another maquis leader, and fourteen men, entered the town of Montluçon, a Gestapo headquarters where hundreds of German soldiers were garrisoned. Nancy, Tardivat, and their men killed thirty-eight German soldiers and escaped with no losses.

Britain honored her with the King George Medal. America awarded her the Medal of Freedom with Bronze Palm for her aid in rescuing the two American officers, and the French government award her two Croix de Guerre, a third Croix de Guerre with Star, and the Resistance Medal.

Concerning Nancy Wade, Commander Tardivat later told a historian:

> She is the most feminine woman I know—until the fight starts.
> Then she is like five men.[125]

Although their exact numbers are unknown, many women served in the American Civil War. Sometimes they fought disguised as men, sometimes they were spies, and in other cases, as in that of "Michigan Bridget," the wives and sisters of soldiers followed their men into battle and took up arms after their loved ones were felled.
Corbis-Bettmann

CHAPTER **12**

North America:
New World Warriors

Women warriors occupied the minds of the early Spanish explorers of the New World, due in large part to the popular literature of the fifteenth and sixteenth centuries, which celebrated treasure hunting, adventure, and Amazons. One such work, *Amadis* by Montalvo, left its legacy in the name of a state.

Montalvo wrote of the Amazon Queen Califa and described her domain, "California," as lying to the west of the Indies. Cortes believed that the realm of Califa would be in Colima on the west coast of Mexico. He used the name California for the Gulf of California and "Santa Cruz" for what is now known as Baja California. However, when Juan Rodriquez Cabrillo sailed north along the west coast of Mexico in 1542, he reported that he entered the domain of Queen Califa's California, and California it has remained. Fifty years later, Sir Walter Raleigh, colonizer of the Atlantic coast, in his *History of the World* and later in his *Voyages of Discovery to Guiana* published in 1596, attested to the presence of women warriors, Amazons, among the New World peoples.[1]

The European explorers brought with them the classical images of the Amazons derived from Greek mythic history, and what they found in the native cultures of the Americas only supported their preconceptions. Matrilineal Indian societies abounded—societies in which family affiliation was traced through the mother's line, not the father's, and where land, crops, and houses were inherited through the mother. These powers of kinship dominance and land gave the women a strong voice in government, including warfare. This suggested to the patriarchal and anthropologically naive Europeans that such a "strange" form of social organization could be explained only by the presence of classic Amazons at some point in Indian history.

In certain Indian cultures, a male's warrior status was crucial in courtship behavior. Among the Cheyenne, for example, success in courtship was almost entirely based on success in war. "A man could not even court a girl unless he had proved his courage," a Cheyenne warrior recalled. "A girl's mother was with her all the time, and if he walked up to her, the mother would talk about him and ask what he had done in battle." Cheyenne women would greet men who had shown weakness on the battlefield with a mocking chant: "If you had fought bravely," they gibed, "I would have sung for you." One old Cheyenne warrior recalled, "It was hard to go into a fight, but it was worse to turn back and face the women."[2]

South of the Cheyenne, the Comanche of Texas and Oklahoma also acknowledged the military support of women. Women who assisted in raising and motivating a war party through their inspirational songs and speeches received a share of the successful war party's booty, while in the villages of the Mandan that were scattered along the lower Missouri River basin, women fasted and prayed while their men were in battle.

The Apache women of New Mexico and Arizona likewise were expected to pray for their warrior husbands every morning for four days after the men left on a raid, and every time the wife removed a pot of stew from the home fire, she remembered her husband with a prayer for his safe return. In many of the Indian towns of the Pacific Northwest, women lent their support to a war party by creating life-size effigies of the enemy and attacking them each morning with ceremonial knives. In this way, they attempted to transmit their warrior spirits to their fighting men.[3]

From the last bastions of the traditional Native American lifeways in the Far West to the Atlantic seaboard in the time of the early English colonists and Spanish explorers, oral and written history has recorded many cases of Indian women warriors. In the West, the exploits of Sarah Winnemucca, a Paiute Indian, were widely recorded during the Bannock Indian Wars that erupted in Nevada in the summer of 1878. The capture of her father and brother by the Bannocks from their camp near Pyramid Lake stirred Sarah into action. She signed on as a scout and interpreter for General O. O. Howard.[4] He wanted to bring the Bannocks to heel, but he could not locate their mountain stronghold or find Indians who would lead him until Sarah appeared. She offered to guide him to the Bannocks if he would forestall his attack long enough for her to attempt rescue of her father and brother.

She rode from southern Idaho into eastern Oregon in search of her family's kidnappers, a trip that took three days and two nights. She had nothing to eat or drink and arrived at the Bannock stronghold in a late-night storm. Without stopping to rest, Sarah dressed as a Bannock woman and slipped past the sentries into the restless camp, finding her father and brother in the center of the three-hundred-tepee settlement. She guided them to safety and returned to General Howard with her information. For this feat of courage, strength, and bravery, Sarah was asked to ride with General Howard throughout the Bannock Wars to serve as his scout, adviser, and interpreter.

For most Americans, the buffalo-hunting horse nomads of the North American high plains, resplendent in their feathered war bonnets, epitomize the Indians. Everyone has heard of the Crow, Cheyenne, Blackfoot, Comanche, and Sioux. In this world the male warrior and buffalo hunter predominated, but women warriors are also remembered.

The Cheyenne tell the story of Ehyophsta ("Yellow Haired Woman"), who participated in a battle with the Shoshoni in 1869. The battle scenario was familiar in Plains Indian history. As the hunters left camp to take advantage of a nearby opportunity, the appearance of buffalo, for example, the women, children, elderly, and wounded would be left behind, offering a prime target for the enemy. In this case, however, the Cheyenne warriors had set an ambush for their hated adversaries, only feigning their departure.

They hid, with their Arapaho allies, to give the small village the appearance of defenselessness. When the Shoshoni attacked, the Cheyenne and Arapaho burst from their lodges, and a pitched battle ensued in which Yellow Haired Woman, mounted on her favorite horse, engaged in battle with the Shoshoni horsemen. She noticed a Cheyenne warrior struggling with a Shoshoni. Rushing to his side, she stabbed the Shoshoni several times, stopping only long enough to take his scalp.

In time the Cheyenne exhausted the Shoshoni, and the enemy abandoned the attack, leaving behind their wounded and dead. Several Shoshoni were found hiding in the rocks nearby. Yellow Haired Woman requested the right to interrogate one of the captives, and a Shoshoni warrior was turned over to her.

Without hesitation she lifted the man's arm and stabbed him through the armpit, then scalped him. On the basis of this action, the killing and scalping of an enemy, she was initiated into a secret society comprised of Cheyenne women warriors. Their meetings were closed to the public, and to this day little is known of these organizations. A similar group, the Izuwe, existed among the Plains Apache of Oklahoma. The group met at the request of a warrior seeking their potent blessing prior to battle.

North of the Cheyenne and the Plains Apache, the Crow wandered in northern Wyoming and southern Montana. In 1855, a Crow warrior named Woman Chief was considered by her people as the third-best warrior in the band. Beginning as a hunter in her youth, she turned to warfare in her late teens. The following account describes an encounter, witnessed from a nearby U.S. Army fort, in which Woman Chief defended herself against a number of mounted Blackfoot warriors.

Several Blackfoot came to meet her, rejoicing in the occasion of securing an easy prize. When within pistol shot, she called on them to stop, but they paid no attention. One of the enemies fired at her and the rest charged. She immediately shot down one with her gun, and shot arrows into two more without receiving a wound. The remaining two sped to murder the woman. They fired showers of balls and pursued her as near the fort as they could. She escaped unharmed and entered the gates amid the shouts and praises of the whites and her own people.[5]

In the deserts and arid mountains of the Southwest during the midnineteenth century, Victorio was chosen war chief of the Warm Springs Apache. With Geronimo, Cochise, Red Shirt, and Victorio, the Apache proved formidable foes. In most battles Victorio was accompanied by the second most-honored warrior of the Warm Springs Apache, his sister Lozen.[6]

She specialized in horse stealing, a highly prestigious form of Indian warfare, and was unsurpassed in cutting out enemy horses and stampeding herds. As a respected Apache warrior, Lozen always sat with the warriors when they devised battle plans. In 1886, the Apaches selected her to negotiate the surrender of Geronimo's band to the U.S. Army.

From the eighteenth through the midnineteenth centuries, the Blackfoot, a confederation of three Algonquin-speaking tribes, reigned as military lords of the northern high plains. Rich in guns and horses, they pushed against the Sioux to the east, the Crow to the south, the Nez Perce and Flatheads to the west, and the Cree to the north.

Modern anthropologists describe the existence among the Blackfoot of "Manly Hearted Women," women who hunted and raided with the men.[7] This group existed in a place and time that saw chronic warfare and where women held very weak social positions. The beating of wives occurred routinely and was considered a right of husbands, and a woman could be mutilated by her husband for the mere suspicion of adultery. Under these conditions, the Manly Hearted Women must be seen as exceptional.

Brown Weasel, a Blackfoot woman from Montana, had an understanding brother to teach her the skills of hunting and warfare. He first hunted with her when they were children. When as a teenager her archery and riding skills improved, he allowed her to accompany him on buffalo hunts and to ride with the men while the other women waited for the hunters' return. She finally joined the men on raids against the many enemies of the Blackfoot.

On her first raid, she stole horses and killed one enemy. As her party retreated under fire, she rescued her father, who had been shot from his horse. Moving toward the enemy to rescue a fallen comrade while one's party retreated was rated one of the most elevated warrior behaviors.

Brown Weasel's dazzling performance in her first fight would not have occurred had she heeded the wishes of the war chief. He had ordered her to return home, and when she refused, he threatened to cancel the raid. She responded that, as a man, he could do whatever he wished, but that she was going to raid the Crow.

Her second attack on the Crow netted the raiding party over six hundred horses, a major victory for the Blackfoot. The Crow pursued the Blackfoot horse thieves, and the first two Crow on the scene had the misfortune to encounter Brown Weasel. With no time to summon the men of her party, she engaged the enemy herself. Carrying the rifle inherited from her father, she ran into the herd and grabbed the halter of the lead horse so that the captured animals would not stampede. When the raiders saw a mere woman challenging them, they casually approached. She shot the one carrying a gun and, having expended her single shot, grabbed the fallen Crow's rifle and fired at his retreating comrade.

For her tremendous courage, Brown Weasel was bestowed the war name Running Eagle, an ancient appellation that had been borne by many warrior heroes in the Blackfoot past. She earned the right to recount her exploits with the warriors at public gatherings. This powerful male preoccupation of "coup counting" was the only way warriors, in the absence of writing, could imprint their performance on the public mind. Running Eagle became a raid leader, which acknowledged the esteem in which she was held by the male warriors. She died in a battle with the Flathead Indians around 1850.[8]

Hate Woman, another Blackfoot woman warrior, rather than being separated for one moment from her beloved husband, rode with him on raids armed with a six-shooter. She was allowed the rare opportunity to "count coup" and retell her adventures during the annual ceremonial of the sun dance. These tales, told and verified by eyewitnesses, confirm that she raided five times and that her favorite booty included a saddle, a beaded ammunition bag, and a war club. She "bragged" of a horse-stealing raid in which she, her husband, and another man stole fourteen horses from the Sioux. Her husband later recounted, "My wife said she loved me, and if I was to be killed on a war party, she wanted to be killed too. I took her with me in five war parties."[9]

Sioux Indian women warriors would often steal from a village after a raiding party left, joining it a distance from the camp. Revenge was often the motive. One such woman of the Sioux, Brave Woman, vowed that she would not marry until she had avenged the death of her brothers at the hands of the Crow. Taking up her father's old "coup stick" and weapons, she fulfilled her promise to her slain brothers. Many women acted so bravely in battle that they, like the Blackfoot Manly Hearted Women, were given the honor of recounting their deeds in warrior rituals and of acquiring a war name. A Sioux woman warrior named Moving Robe was said to have taken part in the Battle of the Little Big Horn.

Among the Mandan Indians, an unknown woman was credited with war honors for her actions against the enemy Assiniboin. Although many of the other women fled the attack, she lurked near the door of her lodge and felled with a stone mallet the first Assiniboin to attempt entry. She scalped him in true warrior fashion.

The Mohave, Klamath, Tewa, Cocopa, Kamia, Navaho, Zuni, and dozens of other American Indian societies record the exploits of women warriors in their histories. In the Yuma tribe they were called *kwe'rheme*, and they dressed like men.[10] In some cases, the women warriors formed the *berdache* class (men who dress and act like women, women who dress and act like men), while in others conventional women raided for the sake of adventure, as did Running Eagle, or love, as did Hate Woman.

Among the Pawnee of eastern Nebraska, the matrilineal custom awarded women control of houses and land; therefore, women would be roused to battle when enemies raided their village. In one instance, the Ponca Indians raided a Pawnee village, carrying hay to burn them out of their thick-walled earth lodges.

The village men, seeing that they were outnumbered, stayed in their earth-lodge fortresses while the Ponca pillaged. One old woman, however, would not concede her village without a fight. She stripped to a loincloth, tied her hair in a knot on top of her head, and rubbed soot on her face, black being the color of victory and defiance among many Plains and Prairie tribes. Taking up a war club, the old woman stepped from her door into the Ponca raiders and killed the first one she reached. Her victory cry stirred the men of her house to action, and, inspired by her example, they rushed from their lodges and drove the Ponca away. For her valor she was thereafter called "Old Lady Grieves the Enemy."[11]

Northeast from the Pawnee live the Ojibwa, a people with a long history of women warriors. One, Chief Earth Woman, began her military career for love but ended it raiding with the Ojibwa men simply because she enjoyed the excitement.

Her initial experience in warfare came when her lover joined a raiding party that was setting out to attack the Sioux. Traditionally, the Ojibwa women paddled along with their warriors for a short distance; however, this time, when the other women turned back, Chief Earth Woman kept pace with the warriors, not finding it within herself to abandon her sweetheart.

She convinced the war chief that in a dream she had received special powers to predict the movement of the enemy. Since such abilities were accepted by the Ojibwa, she was allowed to accompany the raid. When her predictions proved true, enabling the Ojibwa to surprise a Sioux party, she was welcomed into the warrior band. In the first skirmish her lover killed a Sioux warrior, and Chief Earth Woman scalped him. From that point on, she was granted all the rights and honors due victorious warriors.[12]

In the east, the Cherokee of North Carolina and Tennessee, farmers and warriors like the Pawnee, also had women warriors. In 1776 General Rutherford left a description of a skirmish with a war party of Cherokees in which he lost nineteen men before driving the Indians off. An Indian was found lurking in brush near the battlefield—a woman dressed as a warrior with tomahawk, musket, and bow and arrow. She had been wounded in the thigh and was unable to retreat with her party.

Legend tells of Cuhtahlatha, wife of a Cherokee chief, who rallied the retreating Cherokee after her husband was killed by rushing at the enemy with his tomahawk shouting, "Kill! Kill!" In the seventeenth century, Nanye-hi, known in history as Nancy Ward, performed a similar feat in a battle in which the Cherokee engaged their long-time enemies, the Creeks. Fighting with her husband, Kingfisher, Nancy chewed the tips of his bullets to render them ragged and therefore capable of inflicting more serious wounds. When he was shot, she fought with such courage that she was rewarded with a share of the war booty taken from the defeated Creeks, a right of warriors.

Her courage won Nancy the title of Beloved Woman, an honor reserved for women who performed exceptionally heroic deeds. She was selected by the women as their leader and was given a vote in the Council of Chiefs. Beloved Woman sat with the men during councils of war and advised on military strategy and the fate of captives and war prisoners.

In New England in 1620, the Pilgrims, fearing an uprising among the Indians of Massachusetts, traveled to a site just north of Boston to resolve their problems with Indian leaders. When they arrived, an Indian told them to leave quickly because the squaw sachem ("woman chief") of a local tribe had been attacking everyone who came into her people's territory.

The woman who provoked such fear was known as the "Massachusetts Queen" to the Pilgrims. She was married to Nanepasket or "New Moon," a sachem of several Massachusetts tribes residing near Mystic Pond, before he was assassinated in 1619. The squaw sachem succeeded well into old age in inspiring fear in her enemies and defending the confederation of Massachusetts tribes against several enemies who maintained a chronic state of warfare with her.[13]

Farther south about thirty years later, another Indian confederation, the Powhatan, controlled the area from the Potomac River south to the James River. The woman that the English called "Queen Anne" was married to Totopotomoi, the chief of the Pamunkey, the most powerful of the thirty or more tribes comprising the Powhatan confederacy.

After being widowed in 1656 when her husband and a hundred Pamunkey braves helped the colonials repel an invasion by several mountain tribes in a battle near Richmond, Queen Anne assumed leadership of the Pamunkey. In that capacity, she figured prominently in Virginia history for the next forty years.

The colonial government frequently petitioned her for assistance in various military ventures. When Nathaniel Bacon, a prosperous farmer from western Virginia, raised a force to challenge the colonial government, Queen Anne was called. This time, seeing the English leaders in obvious need of her warriors, Queen Anne told the governor that she would not help until she was paid compensation for the deaths of her husband and his warriors at the battle on the James River. The government paid, and her warriors assisted the militia to quell Bacon's rebellion. King Charles II, as a mark of his appreciation, sent Anne a silver crown inscribed with the legend "Queen of the Pamunkey."[14]

Several decades later, in New England, King Philip, chief of the Wampanoag, led a large confederation of independent tribes in an uprising against the English colonists. He envisioned a confederation of all East Coast tribes to resist European colonization of Indian lands.

Many tribal leaders were drawn into the battle, including a squaw sachem whom the English called Queen Wetamoo. Her followers referred to her as the squaw sachem of Pocasset (a village of the Wampanoag). Queen Wetamoo led one hundred of her own warriors in support of Philip's attacks against fifty-two of the ninety English towns, with twelve of them being completely destroyed. She was widely recognized as one of the most vocal in her insistence that Philip destroy all English settlements.[15]

An eyewitness, captive Mary Rowlandson, offered this description of Queen Wetamoo.

> She loved to be thought beautiful. She had a woolen coat covered with girdles of wampum from the loins upward. Her arms from her elbows to hands were covered with bracelets. There were handfuls of necklaces about her neck and several sorts of jewels in her ears. She had fine red stockings and white shoes, her hair powdered and her face painted red.[16]

By 1675 the tides of war turned against King Philip and his followers. In December 1675 during the Great Swamp Fight, the turning point of

King Philip's War when the Indians were driven into a swamp and encircled by the English militia, Queen Wetamoo fought in the rearguard. She directed the building of rafts that helped some of the warriors escape.

Wetamoo slipped away during the night and joined the remnants of the Narragansett. In August of 1676 the British surrounded her camp. Once again she escaped and launched a canoe into the fast-moving river that ran by the village. The colonists riddled her canoe with bullets, and she fell into the water and drowned. The English beheaded her and mounted the head on a pike for display in Plymouth. Six days later, King Philip was beheaded and his head was similarly mounted in Plymouth. It remained there for twenty years.

Wetamoo was not the only woman warrior to aid Philip. Awashonks, squaw sachem of the Sogkonate (now Seconset, Rhode Island), led her warriors as allies of the great Indian war leader. She first entered history in 1671 when the records of the Plymouth colony indicate that she signed a peace treaty in the Plymouth courthouse. Within the year forty-two male Indian leaders of the area agreed to support Awashonks's arrangement with the colony, including the highly unpalatable requirement that they relinquish their arms to the colonial officials.

For several years, Awashonks and her people lived peacefully with the settlers, but Philip's rhetoric and her irritation at the arrogance of the colonists in Plymouth stirred her to join his military efforts. She fought his war for a year and, unlike Queen Wetamoo, survived to govern her people in the difficult times that followed.[17]

Women warriors were encountered by French colonists in a battle with Indians near Victor in western New York in 1687. Accounts from the fight state that five Seneca women fought beside their warrior husbands and were considered by the French as formidable as their men.[18]

In the South, Coosaponakeesa, a Creek Indian woman with the equally wonderful English name Mary Musgrove Matthews Bosomworth, was born in the Creek town of Coweta, Alabama, in 1700. Because of her noble birth in a society that was traditionally partitioned into noble, warrior, and commoner castes, both settlers and Indians called her "Queen" and "Princess."

In the early 1700s Colonel John Musgrove was sent by the Carolina government to forge a peace treaty with the Creeks. Mary and the Colonel's son fell in love, married, and lived among the Creeks for several years. In the 1730s John Musgrove Jr. died, and Mary married another Englishman, Captain Jacob Matthews, commander of twenty colonial rangers stationed at Mount Venture.

As a colonial war with Spain loomed closer, Mary used her considerable influence to rally the Creek warriors to fight with the Georgians against the Spanish. When Jacob Matthews died during those campaigns,

Mary, then forty-nine, married Thomas Bosomworth. Shortly after, he was assigned the Creek agent for the government of South Carolina.

Perhaps prodded by her ambitious third husband, who desired a cattle empire on the Carolina sea islands, Mary, as queen of the Creek Nation, demanded a clear title to St. Catherines, Ossabaw, and Sapelo Islands from the English governor in Charleston. She reasoned that she was owed a large reimbursement for her past services, military and otherwise. In closing she wrote, "If my claims are not recognized, I will wipe out the colony when I arrive at Savannah with my warriors."[19]

Queen Mary's wish was granted but not because of the scare she put into the citizens of Charleston when she appeared at their gates with hundreds of Creek warriors. She won through the courts, which judged that her political position and services had earned her the island of St. Catherines and the right to sell Ossabaw and Sapelo Islands to the colonists.

A century after Queen Mary, the warrior spirit of southeastern Indian women was expressed among the Florida Seminole. In New Orleans, on February 1839, General Zachary Taylor had forcibly assembled 166 Seminole captives who were to be shipped to their new reservation in Arkansas. Peters, in *The Florida Wars*, writes:

> Among the prisoners were women who had fought so long that they were more defiant than the men. They boarded the transport taunting their husbands for cowardice in refusing to die upon their native soil.[20]

One Indian "queen" ended her career with the well-earned title "Fiend of Wyoming" (a Pennsylvania valley). Esther Montour, wife of Eghohowin, chief of the Munsee, controlled the tribe after her husband's death, when she moved her capital to a new location, which she called Queen Esther Town. In 1778 Colonel Thomas Harley's forces attacked the village.

Queen Esther won her bloody reputation at the Wyoming Fight. As sixteen captured white men were held by her warriors, Esther killed them in cold blood with her knife and tomahawk. Later, she slaughtered nine more whites in a similar fashion as they were pinned around a large circular boulder. It was estimated that her actions that day, after the dead were tallied, produced 150 widows and 600 orphans.

Indian leaders like Queen Esther made the frontier a dangerous place in the seventeenth and eighteenth centuries. In late March of 1622 after a massacre of colonists in an Indian raid, Virginia's Governor Wyatt ordered that all colonists abandon their farms and move into a central location for safety. The majority of the eighty families involved complied with the governor's orders. One Mrs. Proctor, however, refused and defended her farm against Indians' raids for two months until the governor sent agents to forcibly remove her to safety.[21] Every state in the union can draw from its chronicles numerous examples of frontier women who demonstrated great valor in defense of their families and homes.

In the summer of 1787, for example, in Nelson County, Kentucky, John and Alice Merrill were awakened after midnight by their dogs barking outside their mountain cabin. When John came down from the sleeping loft and opened the front door, the muskets of seven Indian raiders thundered, breaking his arm and leg. Falling backward, he pushed the door partially closed and called to his wife for help.

Alice jumped from the loft, grabbed an ax, and attacked the Indians who were pushing through the door, killing or badly wounding four of them. Her success in barring the door was countered by footsteps on the roof. While several Indians attempted to batter the door down, others were trying to come down the chimney. Alice ripped her feather bed open and dumped the feathers onto the smoldering coals of the night-banked fire. The feathers ignited in a flash of smoke and fire, and one of the Indians fell into the fireplace, where Alice killed him.

Two others pushed the door open. Alice killed one and badly wounded the other, who withdrew into the night. Later an escaped captive of the raiders' tribe recounted that the wounded man returned to tell with pride of his battle with the fierce and courageous "Long Knife Squaw."

In the late seventeenth century the Shawnee were raiding colonists in eastern Tennessee, and most communities built a blockhouse, which would serve the safety of settlers. One such place was Buchanan's Station in the Cumberland Valley of Tennessee. The actions of Sarah Buchanan, Susan Everett, and Nancy Mulherrin in defense of Buchanan's Station against Indian forces illustrate the varied facets of the women warriors.

The day prior to the attack, the three women, returning from a visit to a nearby farm, came upon hundreds of Shawnee warriors hidden in the forest about three hundred yards from the fort. Realizing that they could not run from the warriors, Sarah Buchanan made the decision for all of them, and she spurred her horse toward the Indians, shouting cavalry commands. The others, recognizing her strategy, quickly joined her. The Shawnee, their vision blocked by the undergrowth, momentarily thought that they were being attacked by a cavalry unit and fell back long enough for the women to reach the fort.

That night the defenders prepared to repel the Shawnee, but as morning broke and the odds became clear, some inside Buchanan's Station expressed the desire to surrender and take their chances as Shawnee prisoners. Sarah again seized the moment. "Let us fight and die together," she shouted. Her husband, fired by her gallant spirit, ordered the men to commence shooting, and the battle was on.

The assault raged for hours until the defenders, who were running out of bullets, slackened their fire, thereby heartening the Shawnee raiders who drew closer to the blockhouse. At that moment Sarah, Susan, and Nancy appeared with their aprons full of three hundred bullets that they had fashioned by melting down their pewter plates.

Sarah discovered an old blunderbuss and carried it to the wall. She loaded this cross between a shotgun and a small cannon and handed it to James O'Connor. Each time he shot it, he was knocked down. Sarah loaded the antique while exhorting O'Connor to get up and fight. Again he fired Sarah's blunderbuss, and again he went down. Sarah and Jimmy continued their teamwork until the Shawnee finally abandoned their attack. After the fight, Major Buchanan and the other defenders exclaimed that the fort would have been taken and everyone killed if not for the courage of Sarah Buchanan, Susan Everett, and Nancy Mulherrin.[22]

An even more dazzling defense of a frontier fort was engineered by fourteen-year-old Madeleine De Vercheres in 1692. The Canadian "Joan of Arc" single-handedly held Fort Vercheres against an Indian attack that occurred when Iroquois scouts discovered that the garrison of the fort had departed to assist threatened allies. Madeleine found that she was the only able-bodied person remaining in the fort with the wounded, old women, and children.

Understanding that she could not fight the Iroquois, she endeavored to trick them. Loading a number of muskets, she stashed them at various windows along the walls and placed hats and coats from the men's barracks with them. As she ran from musket to musket, she changed her hat and coat to give the appearance of many men in the fort. The ruse worked, and the Iroquois left Fort Vercheres in the hands of its one-woman army.[23]

In the autumn of 1777 the defenders of Fort Henry, located on Wheeling Creek in Ohio County, Virginia, found themselves outnumbered forty to one by an Indian force. The raiders attacked the fort continuously from sunrise until noon, forcing the defenders to expel the bulk of their shot and powder. At midday the Indians backed off to rest. The defenders knew the Indians would come again, and they also knew that they did not have enough powder to repulse the second wave.

Someone remembered a keg of powder, used for blowing stumps out of the ground, in a storehouse about thirty feet outside the gate of the fort. Many men volunteered for the almost suicidal mission to retrieve the powder, but Colonel Shephard refused to risk even one of his few men. A young woman named Elizabeth Zane spoke up, but the appreciative colonel also rejected her. Elizabeth responded by walking toward the gate.

Shephard nodded to the guard and the doors swung open, allowing her to enter the emptiness between the fort and the guns of the Indians.

She walked slowly, and the Indians, curious about her actions but not threatened by a lone young woman, held their fire and watched. When Elizabeth emerged from the storehouse with the powder keg under her arm, they opened fire. She raced for the gate as bullets zipped around her, and the men of the fort cheered her on. Elizabeth made it, her dress and sun bonnet pierced by numerous bullets, and the powder enabled the defenders to hold the Indians until they lifted the siege.

Countless acts of courage under fire are recorded for the women warriors of early North American history, and sometimes their martial acts were displayed on a grand scale. Frances Mary Jacqueline, born in France, arrived in Nova Scotia in 1625 and married Charles de la Tour, a frontier trader. She traveled with him throughout New England and honed her skills with musket and tomahawk. Frances and Charles lived a good life until an ambitious Jesuit priest named d'Aulnay Charnise contrived to have Fort La Tour for his own.

In Charnise's first attack, Madame de La Tour assumed command of three ships and a number of small craft and engaged Father Charnise and his forces on the bay, while her husband commanded the fort and its cannons. Charnise's marine support was driven from the bay.

Several more times in the 1640s, Madame de La Tour prominently fought on the battlements of Fort La Tour, throwing Charnise's soldiers from their scaling ladders. Charnise eventually used his political clout to brand Charles de La Tour an outlaw, forcing him into hiding. With Charles out of the way, Charnise again prepared to attack Fort La Tour, now defended by Madame de La Tour.

Knowing from experience the dangers and costs of an attack against Madame de La Tour but driven by his hatred for her, Charnise prepared his forces for four months. His planning paid off, and Madame de La Tour was captured after a fierce resistance. Father Charnise ordered her head locked in a metal collar from where she watched him hang each of her soldiers. He killed her shortly thereafter.[24]

A generation later, Mary Reed was born in Bristol, England. She was raised as a boy and served as a page to a French noblewoman. After her mistress died, Mary's skill with pistol and sword enabled her to join the mercenary fighters of the duke of Marlborough in his wars in Flanders. She started in the infantry, but her courage and intelligence soon earned her promotion to the more prestigious cavalry. She rapidly gained a reputation as a fierce and dangerous duelist with both pistol and sword.

After marrying a fellow soldier and settling down with him to manage an inn in Flanders called the Three Horse Shoes, Mary killed a nobleman in a duel, gaining what would soon prove to be a politically dangerous victory. When her husband died, she feared the vendetta that was being mounted against her by the deceased nobleman's family and felt that nothing was left for her in Flanders. She disguised herself as a boy and in 1718 shipped out of Holland for the Caribbean. During this time, pirate ships endangered any Caribbean voyage, and one of the most notorious outlaw commanders, Captain Anne Bonney, spotted the ship carrying Mary Reed and captured it after a brief battle.

During the skirmish for the ship, Anne observed Mary in a wild cutlass fight with a man almost twice her size. Both were badly wounded when Mary pulled her pistol and shot her adversary in the head. Anne approved and perceived the tough little fighter to be a woman. They soon become lovers, and "Pirate" Mary proved a strong second in command to Anne Bonney.

The details of their adventures from 1718 to 1720 are widely recorded; their names appear in any good source on the history of piracy. Still, historical "facts" sometimes depict Anne and Mary simply as good friends and credit Jack Ketchum with driving Anne to a life of crime. The actual records, however, point to a much more lively reading.[25]

Anne and Mary took refuge in New Providence from the hectic life on the high seas. During one of these respites Anne met the local dressmaker, a frustrated craftsman named Pierre. When he bemoaned the problems of providing dresses of quality without fine cloth. Anne described the bolts of silk and velvet often found on the ships she raided and invited Pierre to join her crew. He agreed on the condition that his boyfriend, Jack, could accompany him. Anne used Jack's size and strength to help control the crew.

Their first voyage together proved a success. Several days out, they overcame a merchant ship, and Pierre, henceforth known as Pierre the Pansy Pirate, found his woven treasures. He made Anne a pair of black velvet trousers with polished silver coins down the outside seams. These became her trademark. For his Jack he sewed a new coat out of calico, and thereby created his friend's pirate persona—Calico Jack.

The criminal imagination that produced Anne Bonney's notoriety is typified by an incident in which she took two prizes in rapid succession by a highly unusual tactic. After a battle that resulted in the capture of a merchant ship, Anne ordered extra rations of grog for her victorious crew, and a party ensued. Pierre the Pansy Pirate found in the cargo bay several trunks of gaudy French dresses destined for a bordello in Boston, and the men donned them and danced drunkenly on the deck while Anne remained relatively sober at the helm.

Several hours into the victory party, she spotted another merchantman on the horizon. She quickly read the wind and the direction and speed of drift and shouted orders to her drunken crew. The sails were loosened and trimmed to render the appearance of a ship adrift. The men were instructed to hide their weapons under their party dresses. Red paint was brought from the ship's stores and daubed over the crew, who artfully draped themselves in the rigging and over the sides to emulate a massacre. The ploy worked. Anne's ship drifted up to the merchantman with no resistance, and the pirates in their silk and taffeta gowns swarmed aboard.

After a few more ventures, Anne, Mary, Pierre, and Jack retired to an estate in Jamaica, but the bounty on pirates had grown so high that professional pirate hunters pursued them relentlessly. Anne and her crew were overcome in a well-designed ambush, and her fame prompted many eyewitness accounts of the capture.

Toward the end of the fight Anne shouted in disgust at her outnumbered men from the rigging, "Dogs! If instead of these weaklings I only had some women with me!" Onlookers reported Mary and Anne to be the most skilled warriors of the entire crew.

Mary died in prison of pneumonia, and Pierre and Jack were hanged. Anne Bonney escaped, but some reports indicate she was hanged years later with her gang, a group of "fanatical nuns."

Like Mary Reed, many women encountered pirates in the sixteenth and seventeenth centuries. American Anne Channing gained fame for her fighting skill and for a single noble gesture she made when buccaneers attacked the ship upon which she and her husband were traveling.

When the pirate vessel closed, women and children were ordered below decks, and all complied except Anne. She fought with the men of the crew, firing at the pirates as they came, carrying ammunition, helping the wounded, and shouting support to the defenders. In time the pirates prevailed, and Anne, fighting now for honor, threw her husband's side arms and sword into the ocean, rather than allowing the pirates to take them.

During the mid-1700s, the English and the French fought for control of the New World. The French fortified their chief depot, Louisbourg, located on the island of Cape Breton, until they felt it was impervious. The English disabused them of this notion in the summer of 1758, when they occupied the town after a month-long battle.

The French defenders had little chance of success. The English general Amherst brought fourteen thousand troops, and Admiral Boscaen commanded twenty ships of the line and eighteen frigates. The French had 2,800 troops under the command of Chevalier de Drucourt in Louisbourg and only five ships to defend the harbor.

When the townspeople petitioned General de Drucourt to surrender to such overwhelming forces, Madame de Drucourt inspired them to fight by joining the French defenders on the battlements. She relieved the artillerymen as they fell exhausted or wounded by their cannons. Her position fired with such rapidity and accuracy that the English officers used telescopes to identify the French cannoneer. They were so impressed with her courageous fight and martial skill that on July 26, when Louisbourg fell, General Amherst offered terms of an honorable surrender and treated both Chevalier and Madame de Drucourt with consideration.[26]

After France lost Canada, England ruled from the St. Lawrence River to Florida and eastward to the Mississippi River. The colonists, now freed of the danger of French invasion and more entrenched in their new home, resisted various unjust edicts from London. When the English navy commandeered American ships on the open seas in 1775 to retaliate for the colonists' boycott of English trade goods, the rebellion ignited.

Though the Sons of Liberty achieved fame during the American Revolution, few realize the existence of the Daughters of Liberty. The British arrested a group of colonists disguised as Indians who were terrorizing British sympathizers and discovered that five of them were women. Abigail Adams wrote to her husband, John, "If particular care and attention are not paid to the ladies, we are determined to instigate a rebellion, and will not hold ourselves bound by any laws in which we have no voice or representation."[27]

As the rebellion escalated, many women were moved to warrior effort. In Old Middlesex, Massachusetts, when Prescott moved out with his regiment of "Minute Men," Mrs. David Wright of Pepperell, Mrs. Job Shattuck of Groton, and a group of local women put on their husbands' clothing, armed themselves with muskets, axes, and pitchforks, and took possession of Jewett's Bridge, an important link between Pepperell and Groton. They elected Mrs. Wright their captain and vowed that no enemy would cross their bridge.

Captain Leonard Whiting, a heavily armed courier carrying British intelligence dispatches from Canada to Boston, failed to fight his way through Mrs. Wright's small army and was taken captive. The women discovered the letters and sent them to Colonel Prescott.[28]

A rebel sister in arms to the women of Groton was a southerner named Nancy Hart, who was reportedly six feet tall and cross-eyed. She lived with her "poor stick of a husband" in a one-room cabin near Webb's Ferry, Georgia. As the British sympathizers and the patriots separated themselves into rival groups, Nancy sided with the patriots. The Tories, therefore, used every opportunity to harass her.

One afternoon, five Tories appeared at her cabin while her husband was hunting. They had tracked an escaped rebel to her house, and she gleefully described exactly how she had helped him by sending the first Tory search party on the wrong trail.

Irritated and exhausted from their march, the Tories ordered Nancy to prepare them a noonday meal. Alone with her ten-year-old daughter, she was forced to do their bidding. Soon the men were passing a whiskey jug around the table and showing signs of drunkenness. Nancy encouraged them by presenting another bottle. She had noticed their muskets against the wall near the door, and she had a plan.

As a ruse she asked her daughter Sukey to draw a bucket of water from the well, but instead the girl, following her mother's whispered instructions, carefully picked the clay chinking from between two logs next to the front door. Nancy busied herself setting the table, each time walking between the men and their guns. At an opportune moment she slipped a musket through the hole in the wall to Sukey, who crouched on the front porch.

Nancy passed the first two guns without notice, but as Sukey reached for the third musket, an officer saw her. She grabbed the fourth musket and aimed it at the Tories. When one started toward her, she shot him and snatched the last musket before any of the men could move.

The gunshots hurried Nancy's husband and his companions as they returned from their hunt. When Sukey saw them at the edge of the yard, she yelled to her mother that help was coming. The Tories, hearing Sukey's news, rushed Nancy.

She fired point-blank, killing one of the men, as she called out for Sukey to pass a musket through the wall to her. By the time the remaining Tories had recovered from the smoke and noise of the rifle report in the small room, Nancy had the loaded gun aimed at them. She demanded that "they surrender their damned Tory carcasses to an upright Whig woman."

Nancy turned the Tories over to her husband and his friends with the suggestion that shooting was too good for them. Mr. Hart hanged the Tories. This incident happened along a small stream that the Indians called Wahatehe, "War Woman Creek."

In another instance, Nancy tied four logs together with wild grapevine and floated across the Savannah River to ferret out intelligence concerning British and Tory military activities, which she then passed on to the Georgia militia. Disguised as a man, she gathered intelligence for the patriots in British-occupied Augusta. And in one memorable incident, Nancy marched a Tory to a patriot fort at the end of the gun she had taken from him when he made the mistake of walking too close to her when they met on a stretch of deserted road. Nancy survived the war and lived to see her eight children grow to adulthood. Hart County, Georgia, was named in her memory.[29]

One of the most well-known woman warriors of the American Revolution, Mary Hays McCauley, fought for seven years in the Pennsylvania State Regiment of Artillery alongside her husband. She served as second in command at her husband's artillery post, swabbing the cannon's bore between shots, assisting in loading, and aiming and firing for her husband when he needed rest.

Mary's comrades first noted her courage and daring during the retreat of the American forces from Fort Clinton. As was the custom of the cannoneers when forced to abandon their weapons in a retreating action, the American gunners loaded their cannons for a parting shot as the British closed on their positions. However, in the excitement Mary's husband dropped the match when he saw that the British were almost upon him, and he ran with the retreating Americans. Mary turned toward the advancing British, grabbed the match, and set off her husband's gun in the face of the attackers. In the confusion she escaped the British bullets flying around her. This happened several months before she earned her famous nickname, "Molly Pitcher," at the Battle of Monmouth.

Sunday, June 28, 1778, was unusually hot. Molly divided her time between assisting her husband at his cannon and carrying water to the parched soldiers on the front lines. In the absence of a bucket, she carried the water in an old, chipped pitcher and became "Molly Pitcher" to the grateful soldiers.

As the battle raged, Mary saw her husband shot dead at her feet. Having assisted him on numerous occasions, she stepped up to the gun and took her husband's place, firing so rapidly and accurately that she drew the attention of General Greene, who introduced her to George Washington the following day. He was so impressed by her that he presented her with a commission of sergeant in the Continental Army.

She fought with the army for eight years and was so admired by the soldiers that whenever she passed they begged to fill her sergeant's cocked hat with coins. With her military pension and the assistance of the military wives at West Point, she lived until 1843 and was buried at West Point.

Molly is remembered in her hometown of Carlisle, Pennsylvania, by an impressive tombstone, engraved with the legend: "The Heroine of Monmouth." A cannon and a flag keep watch over her grave. She is also celebrated at Monmouth battlefield with a bronze relief depicting her standing at her cannon, a water pail at her feet.[30]

Molly Pitcher's courageous actions were repeated by Margaret Corbin at the Battle of Fort Washington the same year. When her husband fell, Margaret fired the cannon with such accuracy that her position drew heavy fire, and she was badly wounded. In July 1779, the following resolution was passed in Congress:

Resolved: that Margaret Corbin, wounded and disabled at the Battle of Fort Washington, while she heroically filled the post of her husband, who was killed by her side serving a piece of artillery, do receive during her natural life, or continuance of said disability, one-half the monthly pay drawn by a soldier in service of these States; and that she now receive out of public stores, one suit of clothing or value thereof in money.[31]

Margaret Corbin, "Captain Molly," as her friends called her, died in 1788. At Fort Washington is mounted a memorial tablet that reads: "The first woman to take a soldier's part in the war for liberty."[32]

General Greene encountered another woman warrior when he led his force against Fort 96, one of the strongest British positions in central South Carolina. The British sent Lord Rawdon to divert General Greene's rebels, and he forced the latter's temporary withdrawal north across the Saluda River. As Greene considered his next move, his scouts appeared with the news that Rawdon, for some reason, had split his forces. Greene realized that if he could contact General Sumter, who was fifty miles away in territory mostly controlled by the British and their sympathizers, they could overcome Rawdon's troops. Between Greene and Sumter, however, lay swamps, trackless forests, and deep rivers.

When Greene's call for volunteers proved futile, an eighteen-year-old area native, an excellent horsewoman named Emily Geiger, argued to undertake the mission. Greene had no choice and sent her with a letter for General Sumter.

Traveling at night, Emily crossed the Saluda River but was stopped by three British scouts outside Columbia. Feeling that the lone female rider might be more than just a young woman out for an evening ride, as she claimed, they locked her in a guardhouse and sent for a nearby Tory matron to search her. Emily quickly memorized Greene's note to General Sumter, and then ate it. Finding no incriminating evidence, the British scouts released her, and she continued on to deliver her message to Sumter.

General Greene presented her with a pair of earrings and a brooch as a token of his esteem for her courage, and General Lafayette visited her in 1825 and recognized her valor with a beautiful silk shawl. The South Carolina Daughters of the American Revolution in 1900 erected a marble memorial to Emily Geiger in the State Capitol at Columbia with a simple inscription reading: "In memory of Emily Geiger's Ride, 1781."[33]

Many valiant horsewomen risked their lives for the revolution. In the first years of the war, sixteen-year-old Betsy Dowdy, a native of the North Carolina coast, obtained information from a talkative British soldier that Virginia's Governor John Dunsmore was planning a raid on patriot houses and properties along the eastern shore. Betsy saddled her pony and rode into the dense forests and swamps of the tidewater lands.

She survived the British scouts, the alligators, and the swamp and delivered the information that allowed the Virginia Continentals to trounce Governor Dunsmore and his nine hundred loyalist troops, paving the way for the capture of Norfolk by the patriots. Betsy Dowdy's information was credited by the officers of the victorious forces as the key to the victories against Dunsmore and the taking of the port of Norfolk.

In another instance, key intelligence destined for General Washington was entrusted to twenty-year-old Deborah Champion. She made the long and dangerous ride from New London to Boston and delivered to Washington the materials that allowed him to prepare his next move against the British.

The year after Deborah Champion's ride, the British attacked Danbury, Connecticut. The patriot militia of New York under the command of Henry Ludington of Carmel, New York, was scattered at various isolated farms when a rider from Danbury came to urge the militiamen to attack the British as they returned to the sea. Ludington had to remain at his home to coordinate the military response of the militia, leaving no one to ride into the night to give the call to arms. The chore was taken on by Ludington's sixteen-year-old daughter, Sybil. The young woman successfully covered over forty miles of dark and dangerous backroads, and the New York militia came to punish the British for their attack on Danbury.

During the eighteenth and nineteenth centuries, North American women were routinely involved with armies in the field. Indeed, with the constant manpower shortages, sustaining Washington's army in the field or in garrison would have been impossible without them.

Martha Washington, wife of General George Washington, camped with her husband and his troops even during the cruel winter of 1777–1778 at Valley Forge. She liked to say in later years that she had been blessed with the good fortune to have heard the first cannon volley as well as the last in the closing campaigns of the Revolutionary War.[34]

Valley Forge also saw the heroism of Mary Knight. Living on a farm near Washington's camp, she braved the British pickets every few days to deliver medicines and supplies to the American soldiers struggling to survive.

William Fowler, an eyewitness, recounts another woman's contribution at Valley Forge:

> Suddenly a great shout was heard from the sentinels who paced the outer lines, and at the same time a cavalcade came slowly through the snow up the valley. Ten women in carts, each cart drawn by ten pair of oxen and bearing tons of meal and other supplies, passed through the lines amid cheers that rent the air. Those devoted women had preserved the army, and Independence from that day was assured.[35]

In 1780 Sir John Johnson marched from Niagara with half a thousand British, Tory, and Hessian troops. Only the upper fort at Schoharie commanded by Captain Hager stood in his way. As the enormity of the force moving against him became clear, Hager ordered all women and children to retreat into the cellars and bar the doors.

A young woman named Mary Hagidorn stepped forward with a heavy spear in her hand, announcing that she would not hide in a hole in the ground. Waving her weapon, she told him in a loud voice that she was the best spear fighter in the fort. When none of the men countered her, Captain Hager said, "Then take your spear, Mary, and stand ready at the pickets."[36] Captain Hager's confidence was not misplaced. Mary fought well through the battle and was roundly praised as one of the sturdiest fighters in the engagement.

A year later in the upper Mohawk Valley, John Shell, his wife, and sons were attacked by a band of thirty-six Tories and Indians under Captain Donald MacDonald. From midday until dusk, MacDonald's men maintained a heavy fire against the fortress home of the Shell family. Mrs. Shell prepared bullets and loaded guns during the first hours of the fight.

Toward dusk, MacDonald tried to force the door with a crowbar, but John Shell suddenly opened it and drew him inside, wrestling him to the floor. When the Tory forces saw their leader disappear into the little fort, they rushed to the walls, thrust their rifles through the gun slots, and fired blindly into the room. As her sons cringed against the walls, Mrs. Shell hammered at the gun barrels with an ax, bending them enough to render them useless.

When MacDonald fought his way free of Shell and ran out the front door, Mrs. Shell shouted from a second-floor window, apparently with great authority, that help was on its way from Fort Dayton. MacDonald and his men, many of them with bent gun barrels, ran from the phantom troopers.

In the same era, Anne Trotter, wife of soldier Richard Trotter, was drawn into warfare with Indians after her husband was killed in battle at Point Pleasant. In her grief she was transformed, hence "Mad" Anne Trotter as she was subsequently known. She stopped wearing female attire and working with the women of the camp. Vengeance ruled her thoughts as she strode through the camp dressed in a hunting shirt, trousers, and moccasins armed with a knife, a tomahawk, and a gun.

She joined a group of armed men who marched to garrison a fort at what is now Charleston. Accounts from this place and time portray Anne as a crack shot who often won shooting contests with the men. Her courage, intelligence, and stamina made her a trusted messenger. On one occasion, the garrison at Charleston had been under siege for an extended period and their ammunition was close to exhausted. The nearest source of ammunition was at Camp Union near Lewisburg, a distance of a hundred miles through dense forest.

Anne not only succeeded in reaching Camp Union, but she also returned to Charleston laden with ammunition and supplies, a heroic feat acknowledged by the garrison commander as the sole reason that any of them survived. In her later years she lived with her son in Gallipolis and happily spent her time hunting, fishing, and wandering the countryside.[37]

During the siege of Augusta and again in the battle for Cambridge, two brothers from South Carolina fought on the side of the rebellion while their wives, Elizabeth and Grace, remained at home to care for their husbands' mother. Often women, because the British saw them as no threat, could glean important intelligence from the drunken bragging of British soldiers, from casual conversations overheard in shops, and from the gossip of servants.

Elizabeth and Grace Martin learned in this fashion that two British officers carrying important dispatches were passing through the area that night. The women knew the countryside well and decided on an ambush site where thick brush grew near the trail. They dressed in their husbands' clothing, armed themselves, and waited in the darkness. They easily robbed the British officers.

The women took the intelligence dispatches to General Greene and returned home in time to dress and receive the two British officers, who begged a drink, telling the sympathetic women of their near-fatal encounter with two local highwaymen.

In the winter of 1792, the American patriot John Hancock put his famous signature to the following document:

> On the petition of Deborah Gannet (born: Sampson), paying compensation for service performed in the late Army of the United States.
>
> Whereas it appears to this Court that the said Deborah Gannet enlisted, under the name of Robert Shirtliff, in Captain Webb's company, in the 4th Massachusetts Regiment on May 20, 1782, and did actually perform the duty of a soldier in the late Army of the United States to the 23rd day of October 1783, for which she has received no compensation:
>
> And whereas it further appears that the said Deborah exhibited an extraordinary instance of female heroism by discharging the duties of a faithful and gallant soldier, and at the same time preserving the virtue and chastity of her sex unsuspected and unblemished, and was discharged from the service with a fair and honorable character.

Therefore—RESOLVED, that the Treasurer of this Common-
wealth be and he is hereby directed to issue his note to the said
Deborah for the sum of thirty-five pounds, bearing interest from
October 23, 1783.

Sent up for Concurrence . . . . . . D. Cobb, Speaker.

In Senate, January 20, 1792. Read and concurred.
    by Samuel Phillips, President.
APPROVED: John Hancock.[38]

Deborah Sampson was born in Plympton, Plymouth County, on
December 17, 1760. She once confided that her main motive for disguis-
ing herself as a man and joining the rebellion stemmed from a desire to see
the world beyond her little village, a world that school books had opened
to her.

After a few false starts, she enlisted at Bellingham, Massachusetts,
under the name of Robert Shirtliff and with a group of fifty recruits was
quickly marched to West Point for training. She was assigned an infantry
position with Colonel Henry Jackson's Fourth Massachusetts Regiment.
Her first action occurred when a scouting unit with whom she was traveling surprised a contingent of enemy cavalry near Tarrytown, and a three-
hour running battle ensued. Deborah fought bravely and later found a
bullet hole in her hat and two in her coat.

In her next battle, the Massachusetts Regiment was joined by French
soldiers under the command of General Lafayette on the outskirts of
Yorktown. Deborah engaged and killed a British soldier. She received a
saber wound, which she treated herself rather than risk revealing her true
sex in a doctor's examination.

After wintering at West Point, Deborah and two men requested their
captain's permission to lead a raid into New York. He concurred, and
twenty volunteered. In the fight resulting from their ambush of an enemy
caravan, Deborah received wounds in her thigh and head that, though
only superficial, produced great quantities of blood. Surprisingly, Deborah's identity was not discovered.

She rejoined her unit but was so weak that she asked to stay behind
with a wounded soldier. She hid in an empty house, which she later found
belonged to Tory sympathizers. Deborah pulled the wounded soldier,
Richard Snow, into the attic and listened through the ceiling to the British
supporters discussing plans.

She later expressed in her biography that the true horror of that night
came when Snow died, and dozens of cats swarmed into the attic and at-

tempted to eat the corpse. She had to fend the cats off with her cutlass while she lay silently in the dark. The next day Deborah escaped and brought men from her unit to capture the Tories and recover Snow's body.

Her secret identity was finally discovered, not in the carnage of the battlefield as she had feared, but in a Philadelphia hospital by a surgeon named Dr. Binney. In 1783 while working for General Patterson as an aide, she caught a "malignant fever."

> I was soon seized with it. I scarcely felt its symptoms before I was carried to the hospital. All I distinctly remember was the prospect of death, which seemed not far distant. I was thrown into a loathsome bunk out of which had just been removed a corpse for burial; soon after which, I became utterly insensible.[39]

Deborah was honorably discharged from the army by General George Washington, who made no mention of her sex when he thanked her for her service. She returned home and on April 7, 1784, married a farmer named Benjamin Gannett from Sharon, Massachusetts. She had one son and two daughters and died at her home in Sharon on April 29, 1827.

*   *   *

During the American Revolution, Fanny Campbell of Lynn, Massachusetts, was one of the first "licensed privateers" in America's cause against the British. Her decision to fight on the high seas began with adventure and romance. A few months before the revolution began, Fanny, disguised as a "Mr. Channing," enlisted as second officer on the British merchant brig *Constance*. She planned to rescue her hometown sweetheart, William Lovell, who languished in a Cuban jail, falsely accused of piracy.

Once on board the *Constance*, Fanny stirred the crew to mutiny by falsely claiming that the captain was transporting the American crew to England to impress them into the British navy. The successful mutineers installed Fanny as the new captain.

Several days later, the British bark *George* approached the *Constance*. The captain of the *George* quickly realized that the *Constance* was controlled by mutineers and, trusting in his superior firepower, attacked. Fanny led the mutineers and defeated the *George*.

With her two-ship fleet she headed for Cuba, where she freed not only Lovell, but ten other jailed Americans. Back at sea again, Fanny's pirates took another British ship, which carried the news of the American Revolution. She realized that the war presented her with a chance to escape the label of pirate by joining the revolution as a privateer, and she made for Marblehead, Massachusetts, to legitimate her new status.

While her crew waited in Marblehead harbor for the legal papers to be drawn up, she and William Lovell returned to Lynn, where they were married. The return to her hometown affected Captain Fanny powerfully, and when William returned to the new privateer fleet at Marblehead, Fanny stayed home. In time, she became the mother of a large family.

Fanny Campbell was not the only woman privateer to harass the British during the American Revolution. In the West Indies, British shipping was attacked by the female commander of the French privateer *La Baugourt*.[40]

In the War of 1812, Lucy Brewer of Plymouth County, Massachusetts, served aboard the U.S.S. *Constitution* under the name George Baker. Her skill with firearms earned her a battle station ninety feet above the deck in the main fighting top, where she was assigned to hit enemy officers and key personnel. Lucy was there when Old Ironsides went against the British warship *Guerriere* on August 19 in a two-hour battle and again several months later off the north coast of Brazil when the U.S.S. *Constitution* forced the British man-of-war H.M.S. *Java* to strike her colors. Acknowledged by the U.S. Marine Corps as the first woman Marine, Lucy Brewer fought until the war's end and was, along with all the crew of the U.S.S. *Constitution*, awarded prize money by Congress for the taking of the *Java*.

A few years later, the Mexican War in Texas presented a new generation of women warriors with opportunities for adventure. When the family of Eliza Allen of Eastport, Maine, refused her permission to marry the man she loved, she disguised herself in men's clothing and joined the war against Mexico. She fought in a number of battles and was twice wounded.

In 1836 Sarah Borginis fought with the defenders of Fort Brown, Texas, and later served with General Zachary Taylor and his army of four thousand in his campaigns against the eighteen-thousand-man Mexican army of General Santa Anna. Sarah achieved the rank of brevet colonel and was given a full military burial at her death in 1866.

While Sarah Borginis rode with General Taylor's army, a woman named Caroline Mayhew was thrust into the role of captain aboard the stricken vessel *Powhatan*. After smallpox incapacitated her husband, the ship's captain, Caroline Mayhew, with the full support of the all-male crew, captained the ship to safety. The crew credited Caroline with saving their lives, and in gratitude they showered her with the only gifts they had—scrimshaw carvings and an ivory box incised with her initials.[41]

Ten years after Caroline Mayhew's adventure on the *Powhatan*, another captain's wife, Mary Patten, brought her husband's ship home safely when he fell ill. She captained the clipper ship *Neptune's Car*, one of the largest, fastest sailing ships in existence. In a race with two other clippers from New York to San Francisco, Mary was faced with constant disruptions by Chief Mate Keller, a saboteur hired by the owners of one of the rival ships. At the time Mary was a pregnant nineteen-year-old with a dying husband.

Under these extraordinary conditions, she guided *Neptune's Car* through the notorious waters of Cape Horn. For fifty nights, she slept in her clothes on constant call to make command decisions that would affect the fate of her ship and crew. During one forty-eight-hour period as the clipper fought its way through the treacherous waters of Cape Horn, Mary remained on deck day and night, ordering the sails raised and lowered as the gale-force winds capriciously shifted direction and force.

After Mary successfully navigated the Cape Horn passage, Keller attacked her as she nursed her husband. The crew heard the shouts and ran to her defense, where they found Keller unconscious on the floor in the cabin doorway with a large lump on his forehead.

A ten-day lull in the winds off the coast of South America slowed *Neptune's Car*, which came in second in the three-ship race. The insurance company that had underwritten the clipper, however, was thrilled with Mary's performance. They awarded her a $1,000 bonus enclosed with the following letter.

> We know of no instance where the love and devotion of a wife have been more impressively portrayed than in your watchfulness and care of your husband during his long, painful illness. Nor do we know of an instance on record where a woman has been called upon to assume command of a large and valuable vessel, and exercised a proper control over a large number of seamen, and by her own skill and energy impressing them with a confidence and reliance making all subordinate and obedient to that command.[42]

Mary Patten died of tuberculosis at the age of twenty-three. The hospital at the Merchant Marine Academy at Kings Point, New York, was named in her honor.

Remarkably, in the same year another clipper ship captain's wife performed a similar feat. Hannah Burgess was the wife of William Burgess, captain of the *Whirlwind*. On voyages with her husband, she relished learning about navigation and the operations of the ship. In 1856, when Captain Burgess was given command of an even larger ship, the *Challenger*, Hannah accompanied him.

On November 22, 1856, William fell ill. The first mate, well aware of Hannah's skill and leadership qualities from sailing with her aboard the *Whirlwind*, asked her to take command. Hannah captained the *Challenger* for three weeks and brought it safely to port at Valparaiso.[43]

Five years after the clipper ship commands of Mary Patten and Hannah Burgess, early on the morning of April 12, Confederate General Pierre Beauregard requested the surrender of Fort Sumter from its commander, Major Robert Anderson. When Anderson refused, the citizens of Charleston, South Carolina, awoke to cannon fire and the beginning of the American Civil War.

The role of women in this war was impressive. Hundreds fought in the Union Army disguised as men. The number was higher for women of the Confederacy because many of them were reared in a rural setting with firearms, and the war was literally happening in their own backyards.

When a Confederate company advanced into a hail of Yankee bullets in the streets of Gainesville, Florida, the women of the town took to the streets, supplying the Confederate soldiers with water, helping the wounded, and loudly repeating the battle commands as the captain shouted them.[44]

In Virginia near Hanover Junction, Confederate General Wickham and his men were being driven back by the Union Army to his own farm when he noticed his mother and two grandchildren standing on the front porch watching him as the bullets ripped through the air. He ordered an officer to tell his mother to go inside the house. Her response to the young officer was, "Go and tell General Wickham that he can command the men of the South, but he does not command the women of the South, and we will stand here and die with you until you whip those Yankees. Go and do it."[45]

On March 15, 1863, in Salisbury, North Carolina, seventy-five women armed themselves with axes and hatchets and went in search of food hoarded by speculators. They broke into the local railroad station as well as government warehouses. A few weeks later, on April 2, about one thousand women and boys converged on the Confederate Capitol Building in Richmond to protest food shortages, rocketing prices, and the food speculators and hoarders, breaking windows as they moved through the city streets. Finally, they commandeered wagons and carts and commenced looting the downtown district, first filling their carts with food, clothing, and meal and later with anything they wished. Richmond's mayor was so intimidated by the mob that he threatened to order his soldiers to fire on the women if they did not disperse. Only a personal appeal from President Jefferson Davis could diffuse the impending massacre.[46]

Many women helped both North and South as intelligence gatherers. Antoinette Polk observed Union soldiers massing and correctly understood they were preparing to attack a group of Forrest's rangers encamped at her father's home at Ashwood. Her wild night ride saved them. Miss Porterfield of Loudon County, Virginia, sighted a large army of Union soldiers preparing to cross the Potomac. Late that night, she walked five miles through a forest thick with Union scouts and pickets to deliver her intelligence, an act that saved a large segment of the Confederate army from an ambush.

When New Bern, North Carolina, was captured by Union soldiers, a number of local women assisted General Robert E. Lee to acquire the information he would need to liberate the town. Elizabeth Carraway Harland sketched the specifics of the inner fortifications at New Bern and smuggled the map out of the town in a ham that her daughter told the Union guards she was delivering to a sick relative. Mrs. A. M. Meekins disguised herself as a poor country woman and moved freely through the town deriving accurate troop estimates for General Lee. Emmeline Piggott carried military intelligence between New Bern and Beaufort in the folds of her dress. When she was finally captured by the Federals, she destroyed the papers in classic fashion—she ate them.

In the Virginia mountains a woman named Nancy Hart became so well known as a guide for the Confederate attacks on the Federal outposts that the Union Army offered a reward for her capture. Colonel Starr captured her at Summerville in July 1862 but did not hold her for long. Two weeks later, she somehow shot her guards and escaped on Colonel Starr's horse. In two days, she returned to Summerville with several hundred Confederate soldiers and captured Colonel Starr and his West Virginia Regiment.

Confederate General "Jeb" Stuart credited two Virginia women for intelligence gathering that assured his victories. Also, the capture by Confederate Colonel John Mosby of Union Colonel Stoughton at Fairfax Courthouse, Virginia, was made possible by the information provided by a woman spy.[47]

One of the most effective spies, Rose Greenhow, worked for the Confederacy. Born in a wealthy family in Washington, D.C., in 1817, she became conversant with Washington political society and utilized those contacts through her long career spying for the South. The Confederacy's first victory at Bull Run is attributed to intelligence reports concerning Union troop movement around Washington acquired and transmitted by "Wild Rose" and her assistant, Betty Duvall.

Greenhow established a network of fifty spies, forty-eight of them women, that reached from Texas to Washington. Her notoriety prompted the Union Army to hire the legendary detective Allan Pinkerton to find her. Her spy ring operated while she was imprisoned, and after her release she continued intelligence gathering for the Confederacy. "Wild Rose" Greenhow was drowned in September 1864 while running a Union blockade off Wilmington, North Carolina, in the *Condor*.[48]

Inspired by the exploits of "Wild Rose" Greenhow and encouraged by Turner Ashby, Stonewall Jackson's chief of scouts, a young woman of the

Shenandoah Valley town of Martinsburg named Belle Boyd became a Confederate spy and courier. She moved through the battle zones with messages for Jackson, Beauregard, Stuart, and others.

After her second arrest in Martinsburg for suspicion of spying, she moved to Front Royal to live with her aunt, only to find that the Union Army's General Shields had commandeered the old woman's house. Belle and her aunt were allowed to remain with the servant staff.

One evening Belle listened through a knothole she had enlarged in the ceiling over the dining room table where General Shields and his officers discussed strategy. She crept from the house after midnight and rode fifteen miles to deliver the intelligence to Ashby and returned to her bed before sunrise.

Belle's most dazzling act of courage and determination came on May 23, 1862. Her hero, Stonewall Jackson, was marching toward Front Royal in his pursuit of General Banks. Banks's men were preparing to destroy several bridges to thwart Jackson's pursuit, but Belle knew that if Jackson advanced quickly enough he could prevent it. When she could find no man to carry her message through the field between the slowly advancing Confederates and the Union soldiers at Front Royal, she went into action.

She ran down the main street, through a group of Union officers, past the northern pickets, and into the breach between the two armies. Eyewitnesses describe her in a pale blue dress with a white sunbonnet, running toward the Confederate lines as the Union soldiers fired at her. When she could see the Confederate lines, she climbed on a fence railing and waved her sunbonnet for the Rebels to advance quickly. Turner Ashby, recognizing the young woman who stood in the torrent of Union musket balls, ordered the charge. The Confederates, because of Belle's courage, saved the bridges at Front Royal. "Miss Belle Boyd," said General Jackson in a note to her, "I thank you, for myself and for the army, for the immense service you have rendered your country today."[49]

The most complete account of a woman warrior from the Civil War period was written by Loreta Velazquez several years after her military career ended. Born in Havana, Cuba, June 26, 1842, Loreta was sent to New Orleans in 1849 to live with her mother's sister to complete her formal education. In her late teens, she married a Louisiana planter named Roach and had two children, both of whom died in infancy.

When the Civil War broke out, Loreta insisted that her husband, an officer in the U.S. Army, resign his commission and join the Confederate cause.

> I was perfectly wild on the subject of war; and although I did not tell my husband so, I was resolved to forsake him if he raised his

sword against the South. . . . Having decided to enter the Confederate service as a soldier, I desired, if possible, to obtain my husband's consent, but he would not listen to anything I had to say on the subject; and all I could do was to wait his departure for the seat of war, in order to put my plans into execution without his knowledge. I was obstinately bent upon realizing the dream of my life, whether he approved of my course or not.[50]

Loreta's interest in warfare had deep roots. She wrote:

From my earliest recollections my mind has been filled with aspirations of the most ardent kind to fill some great sphere. I expended all my pocket money, not in candies and cakes, as most girls are in the habit of doing, but in the purchase of books which related the events of the lives of kings, princes, and soldiers. The story of the siege of Orleans, in particular, I remember, thrilled my young heart, fired my imagination, and set my blood bounding through my veins with excitement. Joan of Arc became my heroine, and I longed for an opportunity to become such another as she. I was fond of imagining myself as the hero of most stupendous adventures.[51]

Within three days of her husband's departure, Loreta had a uniform sewn with special padding to disguise her female form. She took the name H. T. Buford and awarded herself the rank of lieutenant. A week later in Hurlburt Station, Arkansas, she recruited 236 men for her private battalion. She planned to deliver the battalion, which she equipped at her own expense, to her husband, thereby earning her way into the war, but before she could carry out this project, her husband was killed.

Loreta, her children and husband now gone, relinquished her command, bought several horses at Clifton, and embarked alone for the fiercest fight she could find. On July 15, she introduced herself at the Confederate army headquarters and was assigned to General Bonham's command. Three days later, she was in the first fight of her life.

The Union launched a sharp attack against General Longstreet's brigade at Blackburn's Ford, and after a back-and-forth battle that raged through the afternoon, the Union forces were repelled. Loreta was unimpressed by her first real battle.

During the great part of this fight, the men belonging to the two armies who engaged in it were often not more than a few feet from each other, and it seemed more like a series of duels than anything much as I had imagined a battle would be. It served however to initiate me and to make me impatient to see an engagement of real importance in which I should have an opportunity to make a first-rate display of my fighting qualities.[52]

Two days later, she joined the Fourth Alabama Regiment under General Bernard E. Bee in time for the battle that would ensue on the twenty-first at Bull Run. Loreta's accounts of her mood at this time show her almost intoxicated with the thrill of forthcoming battle.

> The morning was a beautiful one . . . and the scene presented to my eyes, as I surveyed the field, was one of marvelous beauty and grandeur. I cannot pretend to express in words what I felt as I found myself one among thousands of combatants, who were about to engage in a deadly and desperate struggle. The supreme moment of my life had arrived. . . . I was elated beyond measure, although cool-headed enough, and watched the preparations going on around me with eager interest. . . . As the hot July sun mounted upwards through the almost cloudless sky, and the mists of the morning dispersed by his ardent beams, the approach of the enemy could be distinctly traced by the clouds of dust raised by the tramping of thousands of feet, and, once in a great while, the gleam of the bayonets was discerned among the heavy clumps of timber that covered the undulating plain which the commanders of the armies of the South and the North had selected for their first trial of strategy and strength. The desultory firing with which the battle opened soon was followed by rapid volleys, and ere the morning was far advanced, the sharp rattling of musketry, the roar of the artillery, and the yelling of the soldiers, developed into an incessant tumult; while along the entire line, for miles, arose clouds of yellow dust and blue smoke, as the desperateness of the conflict increased, and the men on either side became excited with the work they had in hand. . . . At noon, the battle was at its fiercest, and the scene was grand beyond description.[53]

As time passed, Loreta's unbounded joy in war diminished. In one action where she captured a sergeant and some of his men, she killed a Union officer who was trying to escape.

> I fired my revolver at another officer—a major, I believe—who was in the act of jumping into the river. I saw him spring into the air, and fall; and then turned my head away, shuddering at what I had

done, although I believed that it was only my duty. An officer near me exclaimed, "Lieutenant, your ball took him,"—words that sent a thrill of horror through me.[54]

After surviving the Confederate defeat at Fort Donelson in the bitter cold February 1862, her mood was bleak.

If repentance for my rashness in resolving to play a soldier's part in the war was ever to overcome me, however, now was the time; and I confess that, as the sleet stung my face, and the biting winds cut me to the bones, I wished myself well out of it, and longed for the siege to be over in some shape, even if relief came only through defeat. The idea of defeat, however, was too intolerable to be thought of, and I banished it from my mind whenever it occurred to me, and argued with myself that I was no better than the thousands of brave men around, who were suffering these wintry blasts as much as I. . . . The agonized cries of the wounded, and their piteous calls for water, really affected me more than my own discomfort; and had it not been for the heart-rending sounds that greeted my ear every moment, I could, perhaps, have succeeded better than I did in bearing up under the horrors of the night with some degree of equanimity. Every now and then a shriek would be uttered that would strike terror to my soul, and make my blood run cold, as the fiercest fighting I had ever seen had not been able to do. I could face the cannon better than I could this bitter weather, and I could suffer myself better than I could bear to hear the cries and groans of these wounded men, lying out on the frozen ground, exposed to the beating of the pitiless storm. Several times I felt as if I could stand it no longer, and was tempted to give the whole thing up, and lie down upon the ground and die.[55]

On April 5, 1862, Loreta was seriously wounded by mortar shrapnel while fighting with General Hardee near Shiloh Church, and her sex was discovered during the treatment of her various wounds. Though never again to take the field, she spent the next several years as an intelligence gatherer for the Confederate forces, surviving many dangerous missions in enemy territory. She penetrated the staff of Colonel Lafayette C. Baker, chief of the U.S. Secret Service.

Her career ended in 1864 when her part in the "Northwest Conspiracy," an unsuccessful Confederate plot to free the ten thousand Rebel officers and soldiers imprisoned on Johnson's Island in Sandusky Bay, was revealed. Before she died years later, however, the irrepressible Loreta

Velazquez had added world travel, gold prospecting, and wild west adventure to her long list of accomplishments.

Women soldiers are occasionally mentioned in journals and travel accounts from the midnineteenth century. Lieutenant Colonel Freemantle, an English traveler, wrote that on a train trip from Chattanooga to Atlanta, he met a young woman soldier who had fought in the battles of Perryville and Murfreesboro. Englishman Fitzgerald Ross wrote of meeting on a trip between Augusta and Atlanta a woman who held a captain's rank.[56]

Very little is known about the identities of the unknown numbers of women who, disguised as men, fought in the Civil War. Names, regiment assignments, and engagements fought stand as their only memorials.

In May of 1862, Mrs. L. M. Blalock joined the 29th North Carolina Regiment disguised as her husband's brother and fought in three major battles. Mrs. Amy Clarke fought at her husband's side at the bloody Battle of Shiloh and later followed Bragg into Kentucky, where she took several wounds before she was captured.[57]

Mary Ellen Wise fought with the 34th Regiment Indiana Volunteers, Mary Hancock with the Illinois Regiment, and six-foot-two Mary Dennis as a regular soldier in the Minnesota Regiment, while Sarah Emma Edmonds, in men's attire, fought in a number of critical Civil War battles. In the late 1800s, she became the first female regular in the Grand Army of the Republic. Born in 1841 in New Brunswick, Canada, she fled an abusive father and, disguised as "Frank Thompson," earned her living selling Bibles first in Hartford, Connecticut, and later in Flint, Michigan, where she was living when the Civil War broke out.

"Frank Thompson" joined Company F of the 2nd Michigan Regiment of Volunteer Infantry and fought with her regiment at Bull Run, the Battle of Blackburn's Ford, and in 1862 with General McClellan in the Peninsular Campaign.

After she lost her lover in battle, Sarah wished to make a more impressive impact on the rebels and volunteered as a spy for McClellan's army. Using her ability to accurately imitate both black and white men and women, Sarah in the guise of "Old Ned" joined a black work detail in the Confederate stronghold at Yorktown and memorized the fortification's ground plan and the location of all the guns. She narrowly escaped death in a fight with Confederate pickets in returning to General McClellan with this vital intelligence.

In the spring of 1863, she was transferred with the 2nd Michigan Regiment to Kentucky to join the Army of the Ohio. She went AWOL (absent without leave) on April 22, 1863, and was listed as a deserter. After experiencing a relapse of a serious case of malaria she had contracted fighting in the Chickahominy Swamps of Virginia, Sarah feared that she would be forced to enter the hospital, where her true sex would discovered. After slipping away from her regiment, she traveled to Oberlin, Ohio, where she resumed wearing women's clothing.

Two decades later Sarah's unique contribution to the Union cause was recognized. On July 5, 1884, the Congress of the United States directed the secretary of the interior to "place on the pension roll the name of Sarah E. Seelye, alias Franklin Thompson," and to pay her the grand sum of twelve dollars a month.[58]

Anny Lillibridge, rather than be separated from her boyfriend, enlisted with him in the Union Army's 21st Regiment. Mary Hancock, a school teacher motivated by her hatred of slavery, joined the Illinois regiment. "La Belle" Morgan fought with the Michigan regiment, and Sarah Taylor, the eighteen-year-old "Tennessee Joan of Arc," fought in the Tennessee regiment.

The first and only woman to receive the Congressional Medal of Honor, the highest of all U.S. combat awards, was pioneer surgeon and later crusader for women's rights Mary Walker. She showed her bravery under fire at Gettysburg and a number of other battlefields by saving the lives of hundreds of Union soldiers.[59]

The decisive military event of the Civil War, the Union's Tennessee River Campaign, gave ultimate victory to the North. A member of Lincoln's "kitchen cabinet" and one of the formulators of the strategy was Anna Ella Carroll.[60]

Pauline Cushman, a gypsy and an actress, won the honorary rank of major in the Union Army for her intelligence gathering behind enemy lines in Tennessee and later in the West. After the Civil War, she ran a bar in an Arizona cow town and, with her service revolver always with her, helped the local sheriff maintain law and order. She was last heard from in San Francisco, where she publicly horsewhipped a man she had accused of spreading rumors damaging to her reputation.[61]

A great black woman warrior of the Civil War era, Harriet Tubman, was raised in slavery and later escaped to Philadelphia. As a soldier in the Union Army, she fought in several raids in Confederate territory. On June 2, 1863, Harriet, in command of three Union gunboats on a dangerous mission along the Tennessee River, destroyed a bridge and rescued over seven hundred slaves.

Her actions related to the "underground railroad," a secret route over which southern slaves escaped north to freedom, have earned her a singular place in American history. She wrote:

> For I had reasoned this out in my mind. There was one of two
> things I had a right to. Liberty or death. If I could not have one, I

would have the other, for no man should take me alive. I should fight for my liberty as long as my strength lasted.[62]

She made the perilous journey into the South to rescue slaves almost twenty times, and the Confederacy offered a $40,000 reward for her capture dead or alive. She lived nearly one hundred years.

Whereas Harriet Tubman's early life in slavery fueled her desire to fight against what she saw as injustice, Abigal Smith, wife of a captain of the Army of the Cumberland, abandoned a life of ease to join her husband on the battlefield. She proved to be an excellent scout and a courageous soldier, once capturing three Confederate soldiers, their horses, and weapons. On another occasion, on a long-range scouting mission, she discovered a large gathering of Rebel soldiers. Her desperate thirty-mile ride through a stormy night to warn her husband of a Confederate ambush saved the regiment.

A soldier with the 5th Rhode Island Regiment was referred to by the regiment commander as "one of the quickest and most accurate marksmen in the regiment."[63] The soldier's name—Kate Brownell. Kate first went to war with her husband, Orderly Sergeant R. S. Brownell, even reenlisting with him after fighting at Bull Run, Roanoke Island, and Newbern. During the Battle of Bull Run, she rescued the banner of her husband's company from the mortally wounded standard-bearer and carried it across the field of battle, receiving a bullet wound for her valor.

Civil War era women warriors also found action at sea. In 1863, the Confederate privateer *Retribution* captured the Federal brigantine *J. P. Ellicott*. The Union soldiers were transferred to the Confederate ship and placed in chains, while the captors secured their control of the Federal ship. The women on board were ignored by the Confederates; they were to cook and clean for their captors.

The wife of a warrant officer of the Federal ship seized the opportunity to ply the entire prize crew with spirits. When they were helplessly inebriated, she locked them below deck and single-handedly piloted the *J. P. Ellicott* into St. Thomas harbor, where she surrendered her prisoners to the Union garrison commander.[64] During the same period, pirate Mary Lovell captained her ship *Moonraker* in Asian and Pacific waters, and the wife of the captain of the *Frank N. Thayer*, with a pistol in each hand, assisted her husband to retake his ship after mutineers had killed five crew men and wounded six others.

In the years following the Civil War, a number of women outlaws populated the American scene. Their ability to successfully lead male comrades in raiding is noteworthy. Nancy Slaughter Walker rode with the notorious guerrilla leader William Clarke Quantrill and his "Quantrill's

Raiders." After the Civil War, she remained with the gang as they raided in Texas and the Indian Territories.

Like Nancy Slaughter Walker, the infamous outlaws Cole Younger and Frank and Jesse James also learned their methods riding with Quantrill's Raiders; so too did a young woman named Myra Belle Shirley. Born in Carthage, Missouri, on February 5, 1848, Myra became a fierce enemy of the Union Army after her brother Edward, a Confederate soldier fighting with Quantrill, was killed in action. She joined Quantrill's group, spurred by revenge.

When she learned after the war that raiders were not allowed to surrender as soldiers under the conventions of war, Myra turned her talents for violence into outlawry. She married a Cherokee Indian named Sam Starr and built a fortlike home in Cherokee territory that she named Younger's Bend. Raiding banks and trains up and down the Indian Territories, she became known as the "Queen of the Desperados." Jesse James often came to Younger's Bend when he needed a place to hide. Myra, now known as Belle Starr, always kept a few fast horses in the corral in case her friends needed to leave the area quickly. She was, in fact, a racing aficionada who was well-known for the horses she raced in the Dallas area.

Belle's husband, Sam, was killed in a gunfight in 1886, and she met her death on February 3, 1889, at the hands of a wanted murderer from Florida named Edgar Watson. He shot her in the back and in the face with a shotgun on a road a few miles from Younger's Bend.[65]

New York claimed barkeep Gallus Mag, a brawler and thief, who displayed neatly labeled jars of pickled human ears she had bitten off in her many fights. Sadie the Goat, another New Yorker, was famous for butting strangers in the stomach with such force that they were disabled while she robbed them.

One evening Sadie, despondent over losing an ear to Gallus Mag in a recent fight, walked along the New York waterfront. Hearing some shots, she discovered a robbery in progress and watched with fascination as a group of drunken men attempted to steal a small sailing sloop anchored midriver. A handful of crewmen easily drove the would-be pirates into the river.

Sadie assessed the soundness of the robbers' scheme as well as their ineptness in executing Hudson River piracy. Confident that she could captain the crew, she helped the floundering men out of the river and proposed her plans. Within days, she discovered a larger sloop, engineered its hijacking, and led her crew on a rampage of robbery, murder, arson, and kidnapping up and down the Hudson and Harlem Rivers. Sadie the Goat earned a fortune before the determined and organized farmers who lived along the Hudson River forced the end of her piracy career. She returned to the Fourth Ward, acclaimed as "Queen of the Waterfront." In a gesture of goodwill, Gallus Mag returned her ear, and a grateful Sadie mounted it in a locket, which she wore at all times.[66]

Like Gallus Mag, Etta Place also took an outlaw gang in tow. Etta met Harry Longabaugh, "the Sundance Kid," at a community gathering and joined him and his partner, Butch Cassidy. When their first raid, an attack on a Union Pacific train, earned them only fifty dollars, she took charge. In the next robbery, an ingenious bank holdup in which a skunk played a significant role, they absconded with $30,000.

In 1901 the trio traveled to South America and stole another $30,000 in a number of robberies. When Butch Cassidy was killed in Bolivia, Etta and Harry returned to the United States and parted company in 1907. The same year, a woman in male disguise, calling herself "John Wilkinson," served aboard the American battleship *Vermont*.

Women also functioned in command positions aboard a number of types of vessels. Mrs. S. E. Ballard captained the Mississippi steamboat *Lola*, and Mary Grenne, the steamboat *Greenland* from 1896 to 1949. Carrie B. Hunter was the licensed master of the steamer *Carrie* on the Chesapeake Bay, and Lillian McGowan, at the age of sixteen, commanded the six-hundred-ton schooner *Marengo*, which carried cargo on the Great Lakes. During the same period, Beebee Beam disguised herself as a man and fought for a year in the Spanish-American War in the Philippines.

In the early twentieth century, four brothers—Herman, Lloyd, Arthur, and Fred Barker—garnered, through their criminal endeavors in Missouri alone, at least three million dollars. The mastermind behind the series of payroll, post office, and bank robberies was their mother, "Ma" Barker.

As a child, Barker had seen Jesse James in action, and he became her hero. She grew up playing the fiddle, reading the Bible, and planning bank robberies. In the early 1930s, never having been arrested, Ma Barker and her son Fred were killed during an FBI (Federal Bureau of Investigation) raid at their hideout in Lake Weir, Florida.

As Ma Barker's boys raided midwestern banks, the Western democracies watched with growing concern the rise of totalitarian governments in Europe and Asia. Japan overran Manchuria in 1931 and invaded China in 1937. In 1935, Italy invaded Ethiopia. A year later Hitler sent his troops into the Rhineland and later signed a political and military pact with Mussolini called the Rome–Berlin Axis. When Axis ally Japan attacked the U.S. Navy at Pearl Harbor on December 7, 1941, President Roosevelt appeared before Congress and asked for a declaration of war against Japan.

In December 1942, U.S. Army General George Marshall ordered an experiment to determine what AAA (antiaircraft artillery) duties could be handled by women. This experiment remained secret because of the highly classified equipment that was used and because the army feared the negative publicity that might ensue when the nation discovered that the AAA crews included women.

The results of this experiment showed the superiority of women in all functions involving delicacy of manual dexterity, such as operation of the director, height finder, radar, and searchlight control systems. They performed routine repetitious tasks in a manner superior to that of men. Morale was also generally higher among the women. As a result, the AAA Command requested their retention and authorization of ten times more women. But, as Major General Holm in her *Women in the Military* notes:

> Over the years the experience would be forgotten, buried in Army files. Another thirty-five years would pass before the use of women in any form of combat in the U.S. armed forces would be seriously considered again.[67]

The navy too was experimenting with the martial potential of women. To discover if women could undergo the rigorous physical conditioning required for naval aviation assignments, a female public affairs officer at Naval Aviation Schools Command, Ensign B. A. Rodgers, was asked to assist the researchers. "She paved the way for the first women naval aviators by extracting herself from a cockpit turned upside down underwater, jumping from towers, being dragged through Pensacola Bay astern a navy landing craft and picked up by a helicopter, and surviving a prisoner-of-war training course."[68]

General Dwight D. Eisenhower, in his book *Crusade in Europe*, noted that his initial resistance to women in the military vanished after seeing British servicewomen firing antiaircraft artillery. He writes:

> From the day they (women soldiers) first reached us, their reputation as an efficient, effective corps continued to grow. Toward the end of the war the most stubborn die-hards had become convinced and demanded them in increasing numbers.[69]

Commanders in World War II reported few disciplinary problems with the female military: women's time lost from work was noticeably less than comparable groups of men (2.7 per hundred versus 3.6 per hundred); venereal disease rates for women were practically nonexistent, although the disease was endemic for men; fewer pregnancies existed than in the comparable çivilian population[70]; and the military women demonstrated a dramatically lower incidence of alcoholism and desertion than their male counterparts.

Hitler's weapons' production chief, Albert Speer, commented on American women's contribution to the war effort:

> How wise you were to bring your women into your military and into your labor force. Had we done that initially, as you did, it could well have affected the whole course of the war. We would have found out, as you did, that women are equally effective, and for some skills, superior to males.[71]

In September 1943 American secret agent Rolande Colas de La Nouye, trained by the British SOE (Special Operations Executive), parachuted from a Halifax bomber over German-occupied France. Standing slightly over five feet one inch and weighing at most one hundred pounds, she used the code name "Gerry." Several times she made the dangerous journey to gather intelligence needed in the preparations for D day. On her third jump, she was captured by Vichy policemen near Evron and taken to the infamous Avenue Foch headquarters of the Gestapo, where her fingernails were torn out to force her to reveal military secrets. She confessed nothing and was sent to the concentration camp at Mauthausen.

After liberation, Rolande returned to Paris and continued her work as an agent. She was assigned to bring the adviser of the former Czechoslovakian president and his family out of Czechoslovakia in the face of the Russian attempts to arrest them. She succeeded through a combination of luck, bluff, and courage.

In September 1976 at an air show in Paso Robles, California, Rolande commented during a parachuting demonstration that she had done that years earlier. A Special Forces officer overheard and asked where she had jumped. She briefly identified herself and, in so doing, solved a mystery. Special Forces historians had long been aware of the exploits of "Gerry," but they had not discovered her true identity. At the next Special Forces Association reunion, Rolande Colas de la Nouye was presented with an honorary green beret and named a lieutenant colonel of the regiment.[72]

In 1941 when Jacqueline Cochran first proposed that the Army Air Corps establish a unit of women pilots, commanding General Henry Harley "Hap" Arnold rebuffed her with the observation that there were already enough male pilots. In later years, he confessed the real reason: "Frankly, I didn't know in 1941 whether a slip of a young girl could fight the controls of a B-17 in the heavy weather they would naturally encounter in operational flying."[73]

General Arnold's mind was changed by the Women's Airforce Service Pilots (WASPs), who from 1942 to 1944 ferried bombers and fighter planes from the factories to the ports from which they would be sent into war. The WASP pilots were the first to handle the new military aircraft on long-distance flights—and sometimes the first to discover if they had flaws. Thirty-eight WASPs died in the line of duty.

The women flew B-17s, P-51s, P-38s, P-47s, P-39s, and B-29s. They logged over sixty million miles, ferried 12,650 military aircraft, and instructed hundreds of male pilots. They flew regularly and as long as male pilots in the same jobs and showed no difference in physical, mental, or psychological capabilities.[74] Averaging almost twelve hundred hours of flying experience, the Women's Air Force possessed some of America's most experienced young pilots, male or female, in 1942.

The granddaughters of World War II continue the woman warrior tradition. In 1983, during the Grenada operation, women air force pilots were landing cargo planes before the shooting had stopped. In 1985, women navy pilots flew supplies to the embattled Marines in Beirut, and in 1986 they performed carrier landings as part of the antiterrorism operation against Libya. Women air force pilots were members of flying tanker crews that provided combat support to the fighter planes that attacked Libya.

In 1989, eight hundred American women fighters were active in Panama in the action dubbed "Operation Just Cause." One hundred fifty women experienced enemy fire and in some cases were involved in a full-combat situation. In one case, because the Panamanian defense force had continued strong resistance against the invaders from their stronghold at Fort Amador, a full-scale assault was ordered.

Early on the morning of December 20, a flight of Blackhawk helicopters lifted off from Howard Air Force Base in Panama to ferry troops across the canal zone to Amador. Two of the pilots were women: First Lieutenant Lisa Kutschera and Warrant Officer Debra Mann. They delivered their charges while under antiaircraft and small-arms fire from the Panamanian Defense Forces below.

Army Specialist Sandy Hearn, a thirty-year-old military police officer (MP), saw combat in Panama and served as an M-60 gunner on escorts to protect military convoys. She also saw action in the Persian Gulf War.

Captain Linda Bray commanded the 988th Military Police Company. When Panamanian soldiers attempted to maintain control of an attack-dog compound that Bray had been ordered to take, the fight erupted. After a flurry of action, the MP's mission was accomplished, and Captain Bray became the first modern-day American military woman to engage hostile troops in face-to-face combat.[75]

A year later, on the other side of the world, the armies of Iraq invaded Kuwait and threatened Saudi Arabia. Within weeks the United Nations Security Council authorized a military mission composed of thirty-three nations headed by the United States to expel the Iraqis from Kuwait.

American military women helped from the beginning, building facilities that soldiers yet to arrive would require. The two "Seabee" (Navy construction) units that built the Naval Fleet Hospital at Al Jubayl included six women, two of them heavy-equipment operators.

Deborah Sheehan, a crane operator, described what it was like:

> We worked twelve hours on, twelve off. What we were offloading mostly was ammo, vehicles, tents, supplies for the fleet hospital at Al Jubayl. . . . While on the pier, we were under attack by Scuds (Iraqi missiles). One blew up over the warehouse while we were unloading some ammo. . . . Iraqi Death Squads had mapped our route to and from the piers, and there were a lot of drive-by shootings. . . . Women served as security, stood guard, manned machine guns. I drove a truck to and from the pier with another woman riding shotgun next to me. We had M-16s, M-60s, and small calibre hand guns.[76]

Female pilots of the 101st Airborne Division's Screaming Eagles flew Blackhawk and Chinook helicopters fifty miles into Iraq as part of the largest helicopter assault in military history. In fact, Major Marie Rossi, thirty-two, led a squadron of Chinooks during the first assault. Women piloted and crewed the jet tankers that refueled the fighter aircraft in midair. Captain Ann Weaver Worster flew her KC-135 tanker 250 miles into Iraq on one of several missions.

Sergeant Theresa Lynn Treloar, nicknamed "the Ice Lady" by virtue of her cool, detached professionalism, was stationed closer to the battlefront than any other woman in the Gulf War. Her army superiors refuse to discuss her top secret mission and do not allow photographs of her.

Captain Michael Mendell, the leader of the twenty-three-man, one-woman unit to which Treloar was assigned, had argued against the brass who felt that the location and nature of the assignment were too dangerous for a woman. Mendell said:

> She is the only woman I know who carries an M-16, a light anti-tank weapon, an AT-4 and grenades. I would trust her to cover my back in any situation.[77]

The range and power of the Iraqi Scud missiles used in the Gulf War made their destruction essential. Lieutenant Phoebe Jeter, a twenty-seven-year-old from Sharon, South Carolina, became the first female Scud buster in the Gulf War. She commanded the all-male Patriot Delta Battery, one of several established to protect Riyadh.

The first Scud attack on the capital came shortly after midnight, Monday, January 21. Lieutenant Jeter headed the engagement control center for Delta Battery and she analyzed information fed to her concerning the speed, location, possible target, and trajectory of the incoming Scuds. She issued the orders to her tactical control assistant to fire the Patriot missiles. Her first shot blew the Scud out of the sky. Soon, Jeter recalls that as she targeted and fired at the Scuds, she heard explosions directly above her as other Patriot batteries scored hits. Jeter's battery destroyed two Scuds, and Lieutenant Phoebe Jeter became the first woman in her battalion to win an Army Commendation Medal.

Captain Cynthia Mosley commanded Alpha Company of the 24th Support Battalion Forward, 24th Infantry Division (Mechanized). Her company supplied a mechanized brigade with fuel, water, ammunition, and necessities to operate in the field. During the ground assault, Captain Mosley's company followed closely behind the advancing forces on Highway 8 into Iraq. As the support unit closest to the front, Alpha Company refueled M1 tanks and Bradley fighting vehicles, enabling them to continue the attack. For a while, Mosley's command was supporting not only their assigned brigade, but all the brigades in that area of the front. The army awarded Captain Mosley the Bronze Star for meritorious combat service.

Lieutenant Kelly Franke was selected as the Naval Helicopter Association's "Pilot of the Year" in 1991 for her exploits during her 105 combat-support missions in the Gulf War. She flew numerous logistic flights before Iraqi gun positions had been cleared from sea-based oil platforms. Not only did she transport troops, prisoners of war, ammunition, and equipment in the war zone, she also accomplished a dramatic rescue. With nowhere to land, she hovered her craft seventy-five feet above the water in a twenty-knot tailwind while her crew hoisted an injured navy diver aboard.[78]

The women warriors of Desert Storm displayed many kinds of courage. Sergeant Laura Long, twenty-seven, of Sandusky, Ohio, served as a vehicle dispatcher with the 1st Tactical Fighter Wing. She took a personal interest in the drivers and worried as they drove under the threat of a Scud alert. Rather than following orders to enter a shelter at such times, Sergeant Long remained at her post in radio contact, keeping the drivers company through the night.

Lieutenant Colonel Roslyn Goff, forty-one, commanded eight hundred soldiers of a combat support battalion. Although her men initially doubted her ability to lead them through the minefields into Kuwait and Iraq, she proved herself. According to the army citation for the Bronze Star awarded Colonel Goff after the war, she "inspired her battalion to excellence under fire."[79]

Some women warriors in the Gulf War were taken prisoner by the enemy. Specialist Melissa Rathbun-Nealy and her partner, Specialist David Lockett, drove a twenty-five-wheeled truck used to transport tanks. On January 30, 1991, their stalled truck was an easy target for advancing Iraqi troops. Specialist Rathbun-Nealy was wounded by a bullet and shrapnel, and Specialist Lockett was hit in the chest by rifle fire. Her capture gave Specialist Rathbun-Nealy the distinction of being the first American woman prisoner of war since World War II.

A month later, Major Rhonda Cornum, an army surgeon and member of a Blackhawk helicopter crew, was sent to rescue a wounded airman down in Iraq. Small-arms and antiaircraft fire hit the Blackhawk only minutes after it had entered enemy territory, causing it to crash. Major Cornum broke both of her arms, and the survivors were captured by the Iraqi troops.

Desert Storm witnessed the greatest deployment of women warriors in modern times. The thirty-five thousand American women in the Gulf War did everything that men did, including taking part in combat. In addition to their service in communications, nursing, and various logistical operations, they piloted helicopters, tankers, and other types of aircraft over the war zone; directed the firing of Patriot missiles; manned .50-caliber machine guns; repaired M1 tanks and Bradley fighting vehicles; loaded laser-guided bombs on F-117s; guarded bases from terrorist attacks; commanded prisoner of war facilities; operated heavy equipment; and led platoons, brigades, companies, and battalions.

The world's modern armies have not always found it easy to integrate women into their forces, but the female martial history is much deeper and richer than is commonly understood. And women continue to make contributions to militaries of many countries. Here, a future woman warrior trains at the U.S. Military Academy at West Point.

U.S. Army Photo

CHAPTER 13

The Female Martial Heritage

This survey has documented that women's martial history is much richer and deeper by far than is commonly understood in the West. The historical record shows no martial domain exclusive to either males or females. Both attacked enemy strongholds, defended castles, laid sieges, and led expeditionary forces. Both built military empires, dueled for honor with sword and pistol, and designed military strategy. Spying, terrorism, banditry and piracy, assassination, demolitions, aerial combat, guerilla warfare, hand-to-hand combat—all boast expert women practitioners.

The cases in this book represent a bare tip of the iceberg. For every woman warrior that is known, thousands, perhaps millions, escaped detection. How many women who disguised themselves as men to enter war succeeded in their charade? The accounts of those women whose sexual identity was finally revealed showed them to be unusually courageous and intelligent, in some cases able to fool their male counterparts for many years. It seems evident that many more such women remained undiscovered.

And what do we know about the sexual composition of ancient armies? Roman sources told again and again of women warriors making up almost half of some European tribal armies. The Spanish accounts tell of women fighting along with men in Indian warfare in the New World. How many millions of women fought in such tribal armies all over the world over tens of thousands of years?

For all the accounts of women of nobility moving in the warrior's world, how many more untitled women, unheralded by court historians and scribes, took the field of battle? For that matter, because the scribe and historian have left the written pieces by which history is constructed, what of the thousands of societies, quite possibly heavily influenced by the woman warrior tradition, that existed in a nonliterate state or with no literary culture observing them?

In recent times "experts" have offered a variety of reasons why females should not enter the armed forces of modern nations. The various arguments generally hinge on three points: females do not have sufficient upper-body strength; females do not have the aggressive tendencies necessary for warfare; and female presence would disrupt the male bonding necessary to cement a fighting force.

As for upper-body strength, teachers of fighting arts will universally vouch that upper-body strength can be as much a hindrance in hand-to-hand combat as a help. Negatively, it calls up the image of the lumbering muscle-bound male whose center of gravity rests too high in his body for effective motion and balance. As a teacher of hand-to-hand combat, the author has observed this type of male for almost a quarter of a century as he struggles to grasp what is truly important to the fighter: footwork, balance, speed, experience, knowledge, mental equilibrium, and sensitivity to movement. Practically speaking, upper-body strength alone diminished as a crucial factor in warfare once projectile missiles and metal blades appeared on the scene. Further, the smallest fighter can level a giant with but a slight strike to the groin or eyes, two of the most vital striking targets on the body, areas that cannot be enhanced by muscular development. In practice, can some men defeat some women in combat? Yes. Can some women defeat some men in combat? Yes.

The author, like all teachers of fighting arts, routinely will match a skilled smaller person, often a woman, against a larger opponent, to pointedly demonstrate the error of thinking that large muscles mean strength in fighting. Once, while participating in an Aikido seminar with the Japanese martial arts master (*shihan*) Mitsugi Saotome, the author observed an interesting encounter during a break in the training sessions. Several of the American male students had removed the tops of their practice uniforms and were outside the facility enjoying the sunshine when Saotome Sensei appeared. Noting their massive arm and chest muscles obtained through weight training, the diminutive Japanese man poked them with his index finger and asked, "What are they for?" When the class resumed, he asked the two largest and most muscled of the students to grasp his arms and attempt to hold him. With an effortless flick of his wrist, he sent both goliaths flying, literally lifting them off their feet. He then turned to the class and said, "Man is not gorilla."

All who honor the warriors of world history pay special homage to the Spartans. In an address to the Spartan Assembly concerning an impending battle, the Spartan warrior king, Archidamus, said:

> The truth is that the intrinsic differences between individuals are negligible, and that the victory is to those who are trained in the strictest essentials. This is the tradition which we have inherited from our fathers, and which we have never had reason to regret.[1]

In the same era, Plato's *Republic* depicted the ideal state, defended by "Guardians," a warrior clan whose numbers were defined by "spiritedness" (Greek: *thymos*), a trait found in individuals of both sexes. Plato concluded: "What has to do with war, must be assigned to women also, and they must be used in the same ways."[2]

As for the putative aggressiveness of males vis-à-vis females, the issue is the precise meaning and intent of the word *aggression*. Dictionary definitions suggest that the word has to do with "combative readiness," "driving forceful energy or initiative," "self-assertive and enterprising behavior," and that synonyms include "militant, assertive, disposition to dominate, bold self-confidence in expression of opinion, militant devotion to a cause, a fighting disposition," and the like. Can the reader find any instance of aggressive behavior, however defined, that the preceding survey has not shown to be found in the countless women warriors who have marched through world history?

As for the notion that the presence of females will disrupt "male bonding" in warfare, history indicates that the direct opposite is often the case. The effect of the Arabian battle queens on bedouin warriors presents one of thousands of examples of women actually spurring males to heightened war effort. Further, the testament of time demonstrates myriad instances, from the time of the ancients to the Persian Gulf War, of females successfully leading males in battle.

Women have always possessed the capability to acquire and to lose through the application of martial force. From the earliest times, women warriors have taken the field and have wielded the weapons of their day. They have served as captains, generals, and commanders in chief, and they have fought in the front lines with the shock troops of the infantry and charged with the cavalry. They have fought for what men have fought for, what humans fight for—defense of home and country, protection of family, righting of wrongs, adventure, and lust for power. Women can share equally with men in the title of "warrior."

In 1911, author Olive Schreiner spoke for women warriors everywhere when she wrote:

> We are women of a breed whose racial ideal was no Helen of Troy, passed passively from male hand to male hand. . . . We are of a race of women that of old knew no fear, and feared no death, and lived great lives and hoped great hopes; and if today some of us have fallen on evil and degenerate times, there moves in us yet the throb of the old blood.[3]

Notes

CHAPTER 1

Sugar and Spice and Everything Nice?

1. James Axtell, "The Vengeful Women of Marblehead: Robert Roules' Deposition of 1677," *William and Mary Quarterly* 31 (1974): 647–652.
2. Ibid., p. 652.
3. Vitus B. Droscher, *The Friendly Beast* (New York: Harper & Row, 1971), pp. 2–3.
4. E. A. Blacksmith (ed.), *Women in the Military* (New York: H. W. Wilson Company, 1992), p. 26.
5. Helen Diner, *Mothers and Amazons* (New York: Anchor Press, 1954), p. 102.
6. Abby Wettan Kleinbaum, *The War against the Amazons* (New York: McGraw-Hill, 1983), p. 9.
7. Sharon Macdonald, Pat Holden, and Shirley Ardener, *Images of Women in Peace and War* (Madison: University of Wisconsin Press, 1987), pp. 29–30.
8. Kleinbaum, *War against the Amazons*, p. 9.

CHAPTER 2

Arabia: Land of the Battle Queens

1. E. Leigh, *Sir Richard Burton: The Erotic Traveler* (New York: Barnes & Noble Books, 1966), p. 151.
2. The accounts of early Arab battle queens are derived from Elise Boulding, *The Underside of History* (Boulder, Colorado: Westview Press, 1976); Antonia Fraser, *The Warrior Queens* (New York: Alfred E. Knopf, 1989); Jessica Amanda Salmonson, *The Encyclopedia of Amazons* (New York: Paragon House, 1991); and Rosalind Miles, *The Women's History of the World* (London: Michael Joseph, 1988).
3. Bat Zabbai's story is told in detail by Kenneth P. Czech, "Queen of the East," *Military History* April (1991): 8ff; and Fraser, *Warrior Queens*. (The quoted materials concerning Bat Zabbai's correspondence to Aurelian are after Fraser.) Discussions of the famous queen of Palmyra are also found in Salmonson, *Encyclopedia*, and Sarah Joseph Hale, *Woman's Record* (New York: Source Book Press, 1855).
4. Accounts of Ayesha, Khawlah Bint al-Kindiyyah, Alfra'Bint Ghifar al-Humayriah, Oserrah, and Wafeira can be found in Wiebke Walther, *Women in Islam* (New York: Abner Schram, 1981).
5. Hale, *Woman's Record*, p. 43.
6. Guy Cadogan Rothery, *The Amazons in History and Modern Times* (London, 1910), p. 91.
7. Czech, "Queen of the East," p. 9.

CHAPTER 3
Asia: The Sword Is My Child

1. Discussions of the Chinese women warriors of the Shang, Tang, Sung, and Ming Dynasties can be found in Elise Boulding, *Underside of History*; Susan Raven and Allison Weir, *Women of Achievement* (New York: Harmony Books, 1981); Salmonson, *Encyclopedia*; Florence Ayscough, *Chinese Women* (New York: Decapo Press, 1975); Margery Wolf and Roxanne Witkes, *Women in Chinese Culture* (Stanford: Stanford University Press, 1975); and James Preseton, *Mother Worship: Theme and Variation* (Chapel Hill: University of North Carolina Press, 1982).

2. Materials related to the career of Hsi Kai Ching are from Robert De La Croix, *A History of Piracy* (New York: Manor Books, 1978); Macdonald, Holden, and Ardener, *Images of Women*, from which Hsi Kai Ching's short speech is quoted (p. 506); and Linda Grant DePauw, *Seafaring Women* (Boston: Houghton Mifflin Company, 1982).

3. Leigh, *Sir Richard Burton*, p. 152.

4. Ch'iu Chin's career is recounted in Margot Duley and Mary Edwards, *The Cross-Cultural Study of Women* (New York: CUNY Press, 1986), pp. 249–250.

5. The Chinese pirates Lai Cho San and Huang Pemei are described in de La Croix, *History of Piracy*, and Edward Rowe Snow, *Women of the Seas* (London: Alvin Redman, 1962).

6. Accounts of the various Khatun of Mongolia are after Ayscough, *Chinese Women*, 226ff.

7. The report of the French journalist on the Siamese women's elite military corps is found in John Laffin, *Women in Battle* (London: Abelard-Schuman, 1967), pp. 46–47.

8. The general recounting of the story of Vietnamese women warriors comes largely from Arlene Bergman, *Women of Viet Nam* (San Francisco: Peoples Press, 1974), from which Madame Dinh's speech is taken (p. 175); as well as Fraser, *Warrior Queens*; Salmonson, *Encyclopedia*; and Laffin, *Women in Battle*.

9. Bergman, *Women of Viet Nam*, p. 54.

10. Laffin, *Women in Battle*, p. 139.

11. Salmonson, *Encyclopedia*, p. 115.

12. The Japanese women warriors' account owes much to Inazo Nitobe, *Bushido: The Warrior Code* (Burbank, California: Ohara Publications, 1979), from which the initial long quotation is derived (p. 87); Salmonson, *Encyclopedia*; Mary R. Beard, *The Force of Women in Japanese History* (Washington, D.C.: Public Affairs Press, 1953); Sally Hayton-Keeva, *Valiant Women* (San Francisco: City Lights Books, 1987); and Oscar Ratti and Adele Westbrook, *Secrets of the Samurai* (New York: Charles E. Tuttle Company, 1973).

CHAPTER 4
India: Kali's Daughters

1. The information on Indian women warriors prior to the thirteenth century is indebted to Boulding, *Underside of History*; Diner, *Mothers and Amazons*; Leigh, *Sir Richard Burton*; and Salmonson, *Encyclopedia*.

2. Sultana Raziyya's story is told by Walther, *Women of Islam*, and John J. Pool, *Famous Women in India* (Calcutta: Susil-Gupta, 1954), 83ff.

3. The history of the Indian Queens Padmini, Karnavatti, and Durgautti is found in Pool, *Famous Women of India*, and Masud-Ul-Hasan, *Unique Women of the World* (Baghdad: Unique Publications, 1954).

4. Queen Nur Jehan's encounter with the Mogul General Mohabat Khan is described in Starling, *Noble Deeds*.

5. Salmonson, *Encyclopedia*, p. 198, was the source for the story of Juliana D'Acosta.

6. The profiles of the Marathan women warriors were derived from Hale, *Woman's Record*, 370ff.

7. Pool, *Famous Women of India*, p. 146.

8. Philip W. Sergeant, *Dominant Women* (New York: Books for the Libraries, 1929), p. 112.

9. Fraser, *Warrior Queens*, p. 227.

10. The life of Farzana Somru is told by Masud-Ul-Hasan, *Unique Women*, pp. 23–30.

11. The quotation by W. H. Russel concerning Hazrat Mahal is found in Salmonson, *Encyclopedia*, p. 212.

12. Ibid., p. 5.

13. Ibid., p. 243. Additional information on the rani's career is found in Fraser, *Battle Queens*.

14. Raven and Weir, *Women of Achievement*, pp. 15–16.

15. Rothery, *Amazons in History and Modern Times*, pp. 74–75.

16. Observations of Indian women warriors of the twentieth century are derived from Fraser, *Warrior Queens*; Rothery, *Amazons in History and Modern Times*; Duley and Edwards, *Cross-Cultural Study of Women*; Salmonson, *Encyclopedia*; and Eva Isaksson, *Women in the Military System* (New York: St. Martin's Press, 1988).

17. Fraser, *Warrior Queens*, p. 139.

CHAPTER 5
British Isles: Queen by the Wrath of God

1. Jean Markale, *Women of the Celts* (London: Gordon Cremnes, 1972), p. 38.

2. Ibid.

3. Macdonald, Holden, and Ardener, *Images of Women*, p. 43.

4. Boulding, *Underside of History*, p. 319.

5. Fraser, *Warrior Queens*, 15ff.

6. Boulding, *Underside of History*, p. 319.

7. Nora Chadwick, *The Celts* (New York: Pelican Books, 1970), p. 5.

8. Ibid.

9. The citations concerning the early accounts of warrior women of the Welsh, Irish, and Picts are derived from Markale, *Women of the Celts*; Peter Beresford Ellis, *A Dictionary of Irish Mythology* (London: Constable, 1987); and Helen Damico, *Beowulf's Wealhtheow and the Valkyrie Tradition* (Madison: University of Wisconsin Press, 1984).

10. Fraser, *Warrior Queens*, p. 83.

11. Markale, *Women of the Celts*, p. 119.

12. Fraser, *Warrior Queens*, p. 95.

13. Doris M. Stenton, *The English Woman in History* (New York: Schocken, 1977), pp. 1–4.
14. The information concerning Aethelburg and Cynethryth comes from Stenton, *English Woman in History*; and Anne Crawford, *The Europa Biographical Dictionary of English Women* (Detroit: Gale Research, 1983).
15. Damico, *Beowulf's Wealththeow*, p. 45.
16. Salmonson, *Encyclopedia*, p. 3.
17. Frances and Joseph Gies, *Women in the Middle Ages* (New York: Thomas Y. Crowell Company, 1978).
18. The stories of Lady Gwenllian of Wales and Nicola de La Haye, castellan of Lincoln, are found in Salmonson, *Encyclopedia*.
19. The accounts of Lady Christian Bruce, Marjory Bruce, and Christian's sister, Isobel, countess of Buchan, can be found in Rosalind K. Marshall, *Virgins and Viragos: A History of Scotland from 1080–1980* (Chicago: Academy Chicago, 1980).
20. Hale, *Woman's Record*, p. 120.
21. Edith Rickert, *Chaucer's World* (New York: Columbia University Press, 1948), p. 217.
22. Robert Scot Fittis, *Heroines of Scotland* (London: Alexander Gardener, 1889). The account of Lady Agnes Dunbar is from Fittis.
23. Henry C. Watson, *Heroic Women of History* (Philadelphia: John Potter and Company, 1931), p. 29.
24. Kathryn Taylor, *Generations of Denial* (New York: Times Change Press, 1971), p. 19.
25. Francis Gribble, *Women in War* (New York: E. P. Dutton, 1917).
26. Simon Shepherd, *Amazons and Warrior Women: Varieties of Feminism in Seventeenth-Century Drama* (New York: St. Martin's Press, 1981), p. 22.
27. The tragedy of Lady Towie at Castle Corgarff is told in Fittis, *Heroines of Scotland*, pp. 167–182.
28. DePauw, *Seafaring Women*, p. 84.
29. A. G. Course, *Pirates of the Western Seas* (London: Frederick Muller, 1969), p. 38.
30. DePauw, *Seafaring Women*, pp. 84–85.
31. Ibid., pp. 44–46.
32. Fittis, *Heroines of Scotland*, p. 166.
33. Shepherd, *Amazons and Warrior Women*, p. 16.
34. Salmonson, *Encyclopedia*, p. 116.
35. The descriptions of Mary Firth and the "Roaring Girls" are after Shepherd, *Amazons and Warrior Women*, pp. 67–68.
36. Lady Cunningham's account is from Salmonson, *Encyclopedia*, and Antonia Fraser, *The Weaker Vessel* (New York: Alfred A. Knopf, 1984). The references to Anne Dymoke and Mary, countess of Falconburg, are also from Fraser.
37. Boulding, *Underside of History*, p. 558.
38. The accounts of the gallant Lady Derby's defense of Lathom House, Honora of Wincester's defense of Basing House, and Lady Harley's defense of Brampton Bryan Castle are found in Fraser, *Weaker Vessel*, pp. 164–189.
39. Starling, *Noble Deeds*, p. 91.
40. The defense of Lyme is recounted in Fraser, *Weaker Vessel*, pp. 198–199.

41. Fittis, *Heroines of Scotland*, pp. 278–289.
42. Gribble, *Women in War*, p. 27.
43. Laffin, *Women in Battle*, p. 29.
44. The tale of Hannah Snell is told by both DePauw, *Seafaring Women*, and Salmonson, *Encyclopedia*.
45. Rothery, *Amazons in History and Modern Times*, p. 99.
46. Charles Gaines, *Pumping Iron II: The Unprecedented Women* (New York: Simon and Schuster, 1984), pp. 24–25.
47. The life of Countess Markievicz is told in Laffin, *Women in Battle*, pp. 58–61.
48. Magnus Hirschfeld, *The Sexual History of the World War* (New York: The Panurge Press, 1934), pp. 166–177.
49. Russel Miller, *The Resistance* (Alexandria, Virginia: Time-Life Books, 1979), p. 105.
50. Joan and Kenneth Macksey, *Book of Women's Achievements* (New York: Stein & Day, 1975), p. 273.
51. H. R. Ellis Davidson, *Gods and Myths of Northern Europe* (Baltimore, Maryland: Penguin Books, 1964), pp. 64–65.

CHAPTER 6
Africa: Mother of Nations

1. Diner, *Mothers and Amazons*, p. 104.
2. Heinrich Loth, *Women in Ancient Africa* (Westport, Connecticut: Lawrence Hill, 1987), p. 62.
3. The *Kentakes* are discussed by Christine N. Qunta, *Women in Southern Africa* (London: Allison & Busby Limited, 1987), 46ff; William Chancellor, *The Destruction of the Black Civilization* (Chicago: Third World Press, 1976), pp. 397–398; and Larry Williams and Charles S. Finch, "The Great Queens of Ethiopia," in Ivan Van Sertima (ed.), *Black Women of Antiquity* (New Brunswick: Transaction Publishers, 1992), p. 28.
4. Salmonson, *Encyclopedia*, 257ff.
5. Kleinbaum, *War against the Amazons*, 131ff.
6. Duley and Edwards, *Cross-Cultural Study of Women*, p. 320.
7. Leigh, *Sir Richard Burton*, p. 179.
8. Oliva Vlahos, *African Beginnings* (New York: The Viking Press, 1967), pp. 130–135.
9. John Henrik Clarke, "African Warrior Queens," in Sertima, *Black Women in Antiquity*, pp. 128–129.
10. Loth, *Women in Ancient Africa*, p. 59.
11. Ibid., p. 60.
12. Qunta, *Women in Southern Africa*, p. 36.
13. Donald R. Morris, *The Washing of the Spears: A History of the Rise of the Zulu Nation under Shaka and Its Fall in the Zulu War of 1879* (New York: Simon and Schuster, 1965), 157ff.
14. Melville Herskovits, *Dahomey* (Evanston: Northwestern University Press, 1967), p. 98.
15. Fraser, *Warrior Queens*, p. 97.
16. Loth, *Women in Ancient Africa*, p. 63.

17. Michael Rustand, *Women in Khaki* (New York: Praeger, 1982), p. 10.
18. Qunta, *Women in Southern Africa*, pp. 57–58.
19. Clarke, "African Warrior Queens," p. 133.
20. Sertima, *Black Women in Antiquity*, p. 39.

CHAPTER 7
Latin America: Las Guerreras

1. Kleinbaum, *War against the Amazons*, p. 104.
2. Macdonald, Holden, and Ardener, *Images of Women*, 62ff.
3. Ibid., p. 64.
4. Kleinbaum, *War against the Amazons*, 126ff.
5. Ibid., p. 123.
6. Salmonson, *Encyclopedia*, 237ff.
7. Don Shepherd, *Women in History* (Los Angeles: Mankind Publishing Company, 1973), p. 103.
8. Bryan Hodgson, "El Libertador: Simon Bolivar." In *National Geographic* 185 (1994): 56ff.
9. Starling, *Noble Deeds*, p. 330.
10. William E. Barrett, *Woman on Horseback: The Biography of Francisco Lopez and Eliza Lynch* (New York: Frederick A. Stokes Company, 1938), 263ff.
11. Shirlene A. Soto, *The Mexican Women: A Study of Her Participation in the Revolution, 1910–1940* (Palo Alto, California: R & E Research Associates, 1979), pp. 22–32.
12. Hayton-Keeva, *Valiant Women*, p. 1.
13. Isaksson, *Women in the Military System*, 190ff.
14. Elizabeth Stone, *Women of the Cuban Revolution* (New York: Pathfinder Press, 1981), p. 7.
15. Stone, *Women of Cuban Revolution*, p. 91.

CHAPTER 8
Egypt: The Commander of Storms

1. Diedre Wimby, "The Female Horuses and Great Wives of Kemet." In Sertima, *Black Women in Antiquity*, 38ff.
2. Danita Reed, "Hatshepsut." In Sertima, *Black Women in Antiquity*, p. 190.
3. Wimby, "Female Horuses," p. 42.
4. Redd, "Hatshepsut," p. 210.
5. Wimby, "Female Horuses," p. 47.
6. Sarah Pomeroy, *Goddesses, Whores, Wives, and Slaves: Women in Classical Antiquity* (New York: Schocken Books, 1975), p. 124.
7. Sidney Dark, *Twelve More Ladies* (New York: Books for Libraries Press, 1969), 31ff.
8. Henry Thomas and Dana Lee Thomas, *Living Biographies of Famous Women* (New York: Garden City Publishing Company, 1942), p. 5.
9. Ibid., p. 6.

CHAPTER 9
Middle East: More Blood Than You Can Drink

1. Diner, *Mothers and Amazons*, p. 189.

2. Salmonson, *Encyclopedia*, p. 232.
3. William C. King, *Woman: Her Position, Influence, and Achievement throughout the Civilized World* (Springfield, Massachusetts: King-Richardson, 1902), p. 53.
4. Salmonson, *Encyclopedia*, p. 11.
5. Fraser, *Warrior Queens*, p. 30.
6. Ibid., p. 31.
7. Norma Goodrich, *Medieval Myths* (New York: Signet, 1977), p. 71.
8. Fraser, *Warrior Queens*, p. 32.
9. Salmonson, *Encyclopedia*, p. 22.
10. References to Artabazus, Aba, Rhodogune, Pythodoris, Hypsicratea, and Adelaide are found in Salmonson, *Encyclopedia*.
11. Walther, *Women in Islam*, pp. 82–84.
12. Bernard Hamilton, "Women in the Crusader States: The Queens of Jerusalem." In Derek Baker (ed.), *Medieval Woman* (Oxford: Blackwell, 1978), 154ff.
13. Joseph Adelman, *Famous Women* (New York: Ellis M. Lonow, 1926), pp. 108–109.
14. Nancy Goldman, *Female Soldiers: Combatants or Noncombatants?* (Westport, Connecticut, 1982), p. 150.
15. Ibid., p. 10.

CHAPTER 10

Eastern Europe: Battalions of Death

1. Diner, *Mothers and Amazons*, p. 115.
2. Herman Schoenfeld, *Women in the Teutonic Nations* (Philadelphia: The Rittenhouse Press, 1907), p. 181.
3. R. Shepherd (trans.), *Polyaenus's Stratagems of War* (Chicago: Ares Publishers, Inc., 1974), p. 339.
4. Mary R. Beard, *Woman as Force in History* (New York: Octagon Books, 1967), p. 291. Further discussion of Macedonian women warriors is found in Grace Harriet Macurdy, *Hellenistic Queens: A Study of Woman-Power in Macedonia, Seleucia, Syria, and Ptolemaic Egypt* (Baltimore: Johns Hopkins University Press, 1932).
5. Pomeroy, *Women in Classical Antiquity*, p. 297.
6. Hale, *Woman's Record*, p. 210. Shepherd, *Polyaenus*, and Macurdy, *Hellenistic Queens* also contain relevant information.
7. H. A. Omerod, *Piracy in the Ancient World* (New York: Dorset Press, 1987), 71ff.
8. Fraser, *Warrior Queens*, p. 18.
9. Charles Morris, *Historical Tales: The Romance of Reality* (Los Angeles: Angelus Press, 1908), p. 90.
10. Jerome Blum, *Lord and Peasant in Russia* (New York: Atheneum, 1966), pp. 33–35. Also see Mary Lou Colbert Neale, "Russia's Women of War." In *Military History*, December 1993, and Beard, *Woman as Force*, for additional information on Olga's career.
11. Starling, *Noble Deeds*, p. 470.
12. Hale, *Woman's Record*, p. 150.
13. Rothery, *The Amazons*, p. 89.

14. Sula Benet, *Abkhasians: The Long-Living People of the Caucasus* (New York: Holt, Rinehart & Winston, 1974), p. 79.
15. Salmonson, *Encyclopedia*, p. 166.
16. Morris, *Historical Tales*, p. 74.
17. John Willis Abbot, *Notable Women in History* (Philadelphia, 1913), p. 137.
18. Ibid., p. 116.
19. Gribble, *Women in War*, p. 74.
20. Truman R. Strobridge, "White Rose of the Skies," *Military History*, December 1986, pp. 14–61.
21. Jeanne Holm, *Women in the Military* (Novato, California: Presidio, 1982), p. 316.
22. Hirschfeld, *Sexual History*, p. 113.
23. Macksey, *Women's Achievements*, p. 181.
24. Ibid., p. 182.
25. Hirschfeld, *Sexual History*, p. 114.
26. Laffin, *Women in Battle*, pp. 151ff.
27. Neale, "Russia's Women of War," pp. 36–39.
28. Hirschfeld, *Sexual History*, p. 78.
29. Mackscy, *Women's Achievements*, p. 211.
30. Hirshfeld, *Sexual History*, p. 120.
31. Ibid., p. 122–123.
32. Jean Elshtain, *Women and War* (New York: Basic Books, 1987), p. 178.
33. Michael Rustad, *Women in Khaki* (New York: Praeger, 1983), p. 37.
34. Laffin, *Women in Battle*, pp. 163–168.
35. Ibid., p. 171.
36. Ibid., p. 173.
37. Neale, "Russia's Women of War," p. 72.
38. Ibid., p. 73.
39. Salmonson, *Encyclopedia*, p. 27.
40. Neale, "Russia's Women of War," p. 40.
41. Laffin, *Women in Battle*, p. 71.

CHAPTER 11
Western Europe: For Duty, All

1. R. Shepherd, *Polyaenus*, p. 302.
2. Boulding, *Underside of History*, p. 353.
3. Goodrich, *Medieval Myths*, p. 57.
4. Salmonson, *Encyclopedia*, pp. 58–59.
5. Schoenfeld, *Women of the Teutonic Nations*, p. 28.
6. Kleinbaum, *War against the Amazons*, p. 157.
7. L. Collison-Morley, *The Story of the Sforzas* (New York: E. P. Dutton, Inc., 1934), p. 224.
8. Salmonson, *Encyclopedia*, pp. 100–102.
9. Christine de Pisan, *The Book of the City of Ladies* (New York: Persea Books, 1982), p. 205.
10. Hale, *Woman's Record*, pp. 87–88.
11. Ibid., p. 88. Brunehaut is also discussed in Boulding, *Underside of History*; De Pisan, *Book of the City of Ladies*; and Francis Gies, *Women in the Middle Ages* (New York: Thomas Y. Crowell, 1978).

12. Gies, *Women in the Middle Ages*, pp. 90–91.
13. Bebel Gerritsen, *Women in the Past, Present and Future* (San Francisco, 1897), p. 22.
14. Salmonson, *Encyclopedia*, p. 172.
15. Joan Morris, *The Lady Was a Bishop: The Hidden History of Women* (New York: Macmillan, 1973), pp. 1–2.
16. Ibid., p. 2.
17. Beard, *Women as Force*, p. 311.
18. Starling, *Noble Deeds*, p. 300.
19. Salmonson, *Encyclopedia*, p. 173.
20. Ibid., p. 192.
21. Davidson, *Gods and Myths*, pp. 235ff.
22. Hale, *Woman's Record*, pp. 297–298.
23. Salmonson, *Encyclopedia*, p. 133.
24. Fraser, *Warrior Queens*, p. 134.
25. Jon Guttman, "Matilda of Canossa," *Military History*, October (1993): 80–85.
26. Geis, *Women in the Middle Ages*, pp. 117–119.
27. Bernard Reilly, *The Kingdom of Leon-Castille under Queen Urraca: 1109–1126* (Princeton: Princeton University Press, 1982).
28. Amy Kelly, *Eleanor of Aquitaine and the Four Kings* (Cambridge: Harvard University Press, 1950), pp. 85ff.
29. Fraser, *Warrior Queens*, p. 43.
30. Hale, *Woman's Record*, p. 69.
31. DePauw, *Seafaring Women*, p. 20.
32. Paul Bohannan (ed.), *Law and Warfare* (Austin: University of Texas Press, 1967), p. 244.
33. Salmonson, *Encyclopedia*, p. 167.
34. Boulding, *Underside of History*, p. 444.
35. Edouard de Beaumont, *The Sword and Womankind* (New York: Panurge Press, 1929), pp. 377–378.
36. Salmonson, *Encyclopedia*, pp. 170–172.
37. Gerritsen, *Women in the Past, Present and Future*, p. 23.
38. Ibid., p. 23.
39. Boulding, *Underside of History*, p. 113.
40. Starling, *Noble Deeds*, p. 304.
41. Thomas and Thomas, *Living Biographies*, p. 74.
42. Fittis, *Heroines of Scotland*, pp. 38–39.
43. Ibid., p. 39.
44. De La Croix, *History of Piracy*, pp. 165–166.
45. Hale, *Woman's Record*, p. 298.
46. Ibid., p. 81.
47. E. S. Brooks, *Historic Girls* (New York: Putnam, 1887), pp. 114–133.
48. Dark, *Twelve More Ladies*, pp. 59ff; also Thomas and Thomas, *Living Biographies*, and Henry C. Watson, *Heroic Women of History* (Philadelphia: John Potter, 1931).
49. Thomas and Thomas, *Living Biographies*, p. 36.
50. Salmonson, *Encyclopedia*, p. 130.
51. Dark, *Twelve More Ladies*, p. 59.

52. Ibid., p. 96.
53. R. de Maulde la Claviere, *The Women of the Renaissance* (New York: Putnam, 1905), p. 322.
54. Hale, *Woman's Record*, p. 21.
55. Boulding, *Underside of History*, pp. 443–444.
56. Fraser, *Warrior Queens*, p. 182.
57. Salmonson, *Encyclopedia*, p. 132.
58. Raven and Weir, *Women of Achievement*, pp. 32–33.
59. De Maulde La Claviere, *Women of the Renaissance*, p. 323.
60. Hale, *Woman's Record*, p. 74.
61. De Maulde La Claviere, *Women of the Renaissance*, p. 313.
62. Karen Petersen and J. J. Wilson, *Women Artists* (New York: Harper & Row, 1976), p. 22.
63. Gribble, *Women in War*, p. 122.
64. Salmonson, *Encyclopedia*, p. 55.
65. Collison-Morley, *Story of the Sforzas*, pp. 265–283.
66. De Maulde La Claviere, *Women of the Renaissance*, p. 320.
67. Fraser, *Warrior Queens*, p. 196.
68. George R. Marek, *The Bed and the Throne: The Life of Isabella d'Estes* (New York: Harper & Row, 1976), p. 9.
69. Ibid., p. 11.
70. Boulding, *Underside of History*, p. 98.
71. Goldman, *Female Soldiers*, p. 203.
72. Gribble, *Women in War*, p. 139.
73. Hale, *Woman's Record*, pp. 298–299.
74. Ibid., pp. 417–418.
75. Ibid., p. 423.
76. Gribble, *Women in War*, p. 267.
77. Salmonson, *Encyclopedia*, p. 267.
78. Ibid., p. 10.
79. Ibid., p. 160.
80. Nancy Myron and Charlotte Bunch, *Women Remembered* (Baltimore: Diana Press, 1974), p. 132.
81. R. Shepherd, *Polyaenus*, p. 102.
82. Hale, *Woman's Record*, p. 54.
83. Salmonson, *Encyclopedia*, p. 167.
84. Starling, *Noble Deeds*, p. 304.
85. John Willis Abbot, *Notable Women in History* (Philadelphia: 1913), p. 148.
86. Salmonson, *Encyclopedia*, p. 168.
87. Starling, *Noble Deeds*, pp. 478–479.
88. Laffin, *Women in Battle*, p. 28.
89. De La Croix, *History of Piracy*, p. 43.
90. Macdonald, Holden, and Ardener, *Images of Women*, pp. 207ff.
91. Hale, *Woman's Record*, p. 530.
92. Boulding, *Underside of History*, p. 591.
93. Julia Kavanagh, *Women in France during the Eighteenth Century* (New York: Putnam, 1993), p. 97.
94. Adelman, *Famous Women*, p. 93.
95. Gribble, *Women in War*, p. 19.

96. Ibid., p. 21.
97. Starling, *Noble Deeds*, p. 334.
98. Laffin, *Women in Battle*, p. 36.
99. Ibid.
100. Ibid., p. 37.
101. C. Morris, *Historical Tales*, p. 89.
102. Ibid., p. 35.
103. Ibid., p. 36.
104. Hale, *Woman's Record*, p. 160.
105. C. Morris, *Historical Tales*, p. 42.
106. Ibid., p. 43.
107. DePauw, *Seafaring Women*, p. 86.
108. Laffin, *Women in Battle*, p. 45.
109. Taylor, *Generations of Denial*, p. 33.
110. Hale, *Woman's Record*, p. 578.
111. Laffin, *Women in Battle*, p. 36.
112. Rosalind Miles, *The Women's History of the World* (London: Michael Joseph, 1988), p. 164.
113. Raven and Weir, *Women of Achievement*, p. 32.
114. Laffin, *Women in Battle*, p. 56.
115. Earl F. Ziemke, *The Soviet Juggernaut* (Alexandria, Virginia: Time-Life Books, 1980), p. 176.
116. Miller, *The Resistance*, p. 183.
117. Elshtain, *Women in War*, p. 177.
118. Ronald H. Bailey, *Prisoners of War* (Alexandria, Virginia: Time-Life Books, 1981), p. 19.
119. Miller, *The Resistance*, p. 183.
120. Laffin, *Women in Battle*, p. 75.
121. Miller, *The Resistance*, p. 183.
122. Ibid., p. 184.
123. Laffin, *Women in Battle*, p. 182.
124. Ibid., p. 180.
125. Ibid., p. 182.

CHAPTER 12
North America: New World Warriors

1. Kleinbaum, *War against the Amazons*, p. 126.
2. Editors, *The Way of the Warrior* (Alexandria, Virginia: Time-Life Books, 1993), p. 53.
3. Ibid., p. 95.
4. Marion Gridley, *American Indian Women* (New York: Hawthorne Books, 1974), pp. 54ff.
5. Salmonson, *Encyclopedia*, p. 270.
6. Carolyn Niethammer, *Daughters of the Earth* (New York: Macmillan, 1977), pp. 167–168.
7. Merwyn Garbarino, *Native American Heritage* (Prospect Heights, Illinois: Waveland Press, 1988), pp. 265–266.
8. C. J. Brafford and Laine Thom, *Dancing Colors* (San Francisco: Chronicle Books, 1989), pp. 106–111.

9. Editors, *Way of the Warrior*, p. 155.
10. Salmonson, *Encyclopedia*, p. 32.
11. Niethammer, *Daughters*, pp. 171–172.
12. Ibid., pp. 169–170.
13. Carolyn Foreman, *Indian Women Chiefs* (Washington, D.C.: Zenger Press, 1954), pp. 23–24.
14. Ibid., pp. 31–32.
15. Gridley, *American Indian Women*, 13ff.
16. Niethammer, *Daughters*, p. 141.
17. Foreman, *Indian Women Chiefs*, pp. 26–27.
18. Jesse Clement, *Noble Deeds of Women* (Buffalo: Derby and Company, 1851), p. 244.
19. Gridley, *American Indian Women*, p. 36.
20. Virginia B. Peters, *The Florida Wars* (Hamden, Connecticut: Archon Books, 1979), p. 174.
21. Clement, *Noble Deeds of Women*, p. 465.
22. Ibid., pp. 346–347.
23. Salmonson, *Encyclopedia*, p. 262.
24. Ibid., p. 91.
25. Ibid., p. 36; see also Clement, *Noble Deeds of Women*, p. 433.
26. Boulding, *Underside of History*, p. 597.
27. Clement, *Noble Deeds of Women*, p. 5.
28. Ellis, *Irish Mythology*, pp. 444ff.
29. Edith P. Meyer, *Petticoat Patriots of the American Revolution* (New York: Vanguard Press, 1976), p. 129. Additional information in Clement, *Noble Deeds of Women*, pp. 237–238.
30. Meyer, *Petticoat Patriots*, p. 109, and J. A. Logan, *The Part Taken by Women in American History* (Wilmington, Delaware: The Perry-Nalle Publishing Company, 1912), pp. 162–163.
31. Clement, *Noble Deeds of Women*, pp. 221–222.
32. Meyer, *Petticoat Patriots*, p. 61.
33. Ibid., pp. 206–211.
34. Logan, *Women in American History*, p. 210.
35. Meyer, *Petticoat Patriots*, pp. 99–101.
36. Holm, *Women in the Military*, p. 435.
37. Logan, *Women in American History*, pp. 65–66.
38. Herman Mann, *The Life of Deborah Sampson* (New York: Arno Press, 1972), p. 187.
39. Ibid., p. 190.
40. DePauw, *Seafaring Women*, p. 59.
41. Ibid., p. 160.
42. Ibid., pp. 199–203.
43. Ibid., p. 199.
44. Francis Simkins and James Welch Patton, *The Women of the Confederacy* (New York: Garrett and Massie, 1936), pp. 71–72.
45. Ibid.
46. Burke Davis, *The Civil War: Strange and Fascinating Facts* (New York: Wings Books, 1978), p. 66.
47. Simkins and Patton, *Women of the Confederacy*, pp. 78–80.

48. Simkins and Patton, *Women of the Confederacy*, p. 79.
49. C. J. Worthington, *The Woman in Battle* (New York: Arno Press, 1972), p. 51.
50. Ibid., p. 42.
51. Ibid., p. 97.
52. Ibid., p. 100.
53. Ibid., pp. 124–125.
54. Ibid., pp. 167–168.
55. Jones, *Heroines*, pp. 290–291.
56. Simkins and Patton, *Women of the Confederacy*, p. 81.
57. Lucy W. Anderson, *North Carolina Women of the Confederacy* (Fayetteville: 1926), p. 15.
58. Patricia Lee Holt, "Female Spy, Male Nurse," *Military History* (November 1987): 9.
59. Carl Sifakis, *American Eccentrics* (New York: Galahad Books, 1984), p. 230.
60. Katharine Jones, *Heroines of Dixie* (Westport, Connecticut: Greenwood Press, 1955), p. xxxi.
61. Macdonald, Holden, and Ardener, *Images of Women*, p. 454.
62. Ibid.
63. Jones, *Heroines*, p. xxxi.
64. DePauw, *Seafaring Women*, pp. 100–101.
65. Cameron Rogers, *Gallant Ladies* (New York: Harcourt, Brace, 1928), pp. 118ff.
66. Salmonson, *Encyclopedia*, p. 371, and Herbert Asbury, *The Gangs of New York* (New York: Garden City Publishers, 1928), pp. 239–240.
67. Holm, *Women in the Military*, p. 67.
68. Jean Ebbert and Marie-Beth Hall, *Crossed Currents* (McLean, Virginia: Brassey's, 1993), p. 243.
69. Holm, *Women in the Military*, p. 82.
70. Ebbert and Hall, *Crossed Currents*, p. 83.
71. Ibid., p. 100.
72. John F. Mullins, "Code Name Gerry," *The Retired Officer* (October 1994): 26.
73. Holm, *Women in the Military*, p. 314.
74. Ibid., pp. 314–315.
75. E. A. Blacksmith, *Women in the Military* (New York: H. H. Wilson, 1992), p. 17.
76. Ebbert and Hall, *Crossed Currents*, p. 264.
77. Blacksmith, *Women in the Military*, p. 64.
78. Ebbert and Hall, *Crossed Currents*, p. 264–265.
79. Ibid., p. 73.

CHAPTER 13
The Female Martial Heritage

1. Arnold J. Toynbee, *Greek Civilization and Character* (New York: Mentor Books, 1961), p. 132.
2. Rosemary Mariner, "Women Enhance Military's Power," *The Orlando Sentinel* (June 1996): p. G1.
3. Olive Schreiner, "Women and Labour," in S. Shepherd, *Amazons and Warrior Women*, p. 219.

Index

About the Author

DAVID E. JONES received his Bachelor of Arts degree in anthropology from the University of North Carolina at Chapel Hill and his doctorate in anthropology from the University of Oklahoma. While in Oklahoma, Dr. Jones wrote his first book, *Sanapia: Comanche Medicine Woman* (Holt, Rinehart & Winston, 1972) and also became interested in the warrior societies of the Plains Indians. He extended his comparative study of military organizations by focusing on the Japanese samurai. This work led to a tenure as a Fulbright Scholar in Japan from 1988 to 1989. At present Dr. Jones resides in Winter Springs, Florida, with his wife and two sons and teaches cultural anthropology at the University of Central Florida in Orlando.